Psychological Approaches to the Care of the Elderly

Edited by Ian Hanley
and John Hodge

CROOM HELM
London & Sydney

METHUEN
New York

© 1984 Ian Hanley and John Hodge
Croom Helm Ltd, Provident House,
Burrell Row, Beckenham,
Kent BR3 1AT

Croom Helm Australia Pty Ltd,
G.P.O.Box 5097, Sydney,
NSW 2001, Australia

British Library Cataloguing in Publication Data

Hanley, Ian
    Psychological approaches to the care of the elderly.
    1. Aged—Care and hygiene
    I. Title   II. Hodge, John
    362.6   HV1451

    ISBN 0-7099-1279-X

Published in the United States of America by
Methuen, Inc., 733 Third Avenue,
New York, N.Y. 10017

Library of Congress Cataloging in Publication Data
Main entry under title:

Psychological approaches to the care of the elderly.

    Bibliography: p.
    Includes index.
    1. Aged—Mental health services. I. Hanley, Ian.
II. Hodge, John.
RC451.4.A5P777 1984   618.97'891   83-26433
ISBN 0-416-00941-7

Printed and bound in Great Britain

PSYCHOLOGICAL APPROACHES TO THE CARE OF THE ELDERLY

CONTENTS

Contributors
Preface

CONTRIBUTORS

Elizabeth M. Baikie, Senior Psychologist, Bangour Village Hospital, Broxburn, West Lothian, Scotland.

Mary L.M. Gilhooly, MRC Medical Sociology Unit, Institute of Medical Sociology, Westburn Road, Aberdeen AB9 2ZE, Scotland.

Chris J. Gilleard, Lecturer in Clinical Psychology, University Department of Psychiatry, Royal Edinburgh Hospital, Morningside Park, Edinburgh EH10 5HF, Scotland.

John Gerald Greene, Principal Psychologist, Gartnavel Royal Hospital, 3 Whittingham Gardens, Glasgow G12 0AA, Scotland.

Ian Hanley, Principal Psychologist, Department of Psychological Services and Research, Crichton Royal Hospital, Dumfries DG1 4TG, Scotland.

John Hodge, Principal Psychologist, Argyll and Bute Hospital, Lochgilphead, Argyll PA31 8LD, Scotland.

David Jeffery, Senior Psychologist, Torbay Health Authority, Devon, England.

Ron Lyle, Principal Psychologist, Stobhill General Hospital, 133 Balornock Road, Springburn, Glasgow G21 3UW, Scotland.

Malcolm McFadyen, Principal Psychologist, Royal Cornhill Hospital, Cornhill Road, Aberdeen AB9 2ZH, Scotland.

Peter Saxby, District Psychologist, Plymouth Health Authority, Moorhaven Hospital, Bittadon, near Ivybridge, Devon PL21 0EX, England.

PREFACE

In recent years the number of clinical psychologists who have developed a primary interest in working with the elderly has risen dramatically. Less than six years ago, in 1977, when the Scottish Special Interests Group in the Elderly, PACE, (Psychology Applied to the Care of the Elderly) was first formed, it had a nucleus of four members all with a special interest in the elderly. Now, in 1983, it and its English equivalent PSIGE (Psychologists' Special Interest Group in the Elderly) are both well endowed with members actively involved in the assessment, care and treatment of the elderly within the British National Health Service. This book is primarily a statement of the kinds of interests held and of work which has been done by the members of the Scottish Special Interest Group, PACE, since its conception. All but one chapter (that by Jeffery and Saxby) have been written by members of PACE.

The overall purpose of this book is to provide ideas and suggestions about the usefulness of applied psychology in dealing with some of the problems of the elderly. We do not make any claim to have written a comprehensive textbook. Many problems of the elderly are omitted or barely mentioned in our text. What we do want to do is put forward ideas which we, both individually and collectively, have found to be of practical value in dealing with the kinds of problem we have found to be most urgent. Despite the recent increase of interest by psychologists in this field, many professional and non-professional workers will not have had any experience in working alongside a psychologist. In addition, there are many professional psychologists who have had little to do with this specialist field. These are the two groups at whom this book is aimed.

Despite the overall diversity of themes, some

general statements can be made which all have in common. One such statement is that we do not believe that chronological age in itself should be used as an explanation for either abnormalities or deficits in behaviour. The variability of behaviour increases with age, which means that there are probably as many highly competent, aged individuals as there are old people who require some form of professional help. Despite this, the overall general attitude of British society towards ageing is a highly negative one, unlike that in other cultures such as in the Far East. It is our contention that society's attitudes to the aged lie at the root of many of society's problems with the aged. Since the elderly are part of society, they tend to share these attitudes and often have a low opinion of their own age group. This provides fertile ground for dependency, depression and apathy, which are probably the three most serious and prevalent problems suffered by the elderly in society today.

A second general statement is that the aged cannot be seen as a separate group, but rather as a generational network. Problems with the elderly inevitably involve problems for their whole social milieu, their caretakers, their family and their neighbourhood. Discrimination of the elderly as a group is a meaningless and highly destructive way of attempting to separate the generational matrix, which is unlikely to have any beneficial effect for any of the parties concerned.

A third general statement is that improvement in the quality of life for the elderly (which is the goal of applied psychology in this field) cannot be achieved simply by trying to fill in their time with diversional tactics. In order to have a good quality of life, there must be positive self-regard. This can only be achieved by feelings of usefulness and purposefulness. Many elderly people no longer have these attitudes. If we are to achieve the goal of improving their quality of life, we must find ways of letting them perceive themselves as useful and of providing them with a purpose.

The chapters of this book range from the more traditional psychological topic of assessment through to psychological treatment and management approaches for various problems. For many years, the traditional role of the clinical psychologist with the elderly has been one of assessment. The forms of assessment used were often barren of ideas or implications for treatment and therapy and were rejected by many clinical psychologists. However, therapy cannot proceed without a proper data base and a number of the chapters look at assessment in terms of providing suitable data for different practical applications. Our contention is that assessment per se is useless unless specifically linked to some therapeutic regime.

In Chapter 1, Chris Gilleard examines the usefulness of traditional intellectual assessment and repudiates this in favour of briefer and more practical assessment procedures. In Chapter 2, Ron Lyle demonstrates the usefulness of psychometric techniques for practical clinical assessment procedures with the physically-handicapped elderly. Chapter 3, also by Chris Gilleard, looks at behavioural assessment of the elderly and demonstrates the necessity for environmental assessment to be done hand-in-hand with the assessment of behaviour. In Chapter 4, John Hodge examines the present evidence on the usefulness of behaviour modification with dementing elderly groups, and recommends an integration of traditional analysis with psychobiological factors to overcome the difficulties inherent in using this powerful therapeutic approach with this difficult population.

Mary Gilhooly (Chapter 5) examines the relatively neglected area of the effects of the demented elderly living at home on their caregiver, and examines the problems that this leads to and some of the ways in which relatives cope. The effects of institutional care are discussed by Malcolm McFadyen in Chapter 6, where he argues that quality of life can best be measured at present in terms of engagement, and provides a generally applicable and practical measure of engagement for use within the institutional setting. In Chapter 7, Ian Hanley examines the usefulness of 24-hour reality orientation as a therapeutic strategy for maximising individual competence of demented in-patients. In Chapter 8, Jerry Greene evaluates the evidence for the effectiveness of 'classroom' reality orientation at the present time. In Chapter 9, Ian Hanley and Elizabeth Baikie look at what is possibly the main problem area with old people, other than dementia, that of depression. They discuss the usefulness of behavioural and cognitive models for depression in the elderly in terms of their therapeutic usefulness. Liz Baikie, in Chapter 10, considers sexual problems in the elderly, which serves as an illustration that the elderly do not require to be treated differently from any other age group, and that changes in sexual function do not necessarily mean a deterioration in sexual functioning. Finally, Jeffery and Saxby take a slightly speculative look at alternative strategies for providing an effective psychological service to the elderly as a population. They make the point that psychologists are too often on the peripheries of care provision and that a major challenge is to influence the way care systems work.

While this book necessarily concentrates predominantly on the problems of the elderly, we would not wish the reader to believe that the contributors conceive of old people as a problem. Most textbooks of this kind typically ignore the many examples of positive ageing which can be seen if we simply look around us: many eminent politicians, scientists and industrialists are, in age, elderly but are not treated that way, possibly because they do not behave in an 'elderly' fashion. Perhaps our role as applied psychologists working with the elderly is to show them and those who provide for their 'care' how best to achieve an optimal return from the later years of life.

I.H. and J.H.

Chapter One

ASSESSMENT OF COGNITIVE IMPAIRMENT IN THE ELDERLY: A REVIEW

Chris Gilleard

Introduction

After the age of 60, if not before, there is an associated decline in many areas of cognitive performance, particularly those involving speed on information processing, transmission and retrieval. Whether this is a pure ageing effect, or the effect of historical and pathological forces exogenous to the ageing process, is of considerable theoretical importance, but in clincial settings it is perhaps a tangential issue. The clinical evaluation of cognitive impairment is primarily related to the consequences varying degrees of cognitive deficit have on the adaptability of the individual patient. Thus assessment of cognitive impairment is an assessment of: (1) the likelihood that overt maladjustment of the older patient is attributable to an impaired ability to make judgements, learn and recall information, and intend their own actions; and (2) the likelihood that such deficits will prove stable predictors of continuing or progressive maladjustment in the patient's current environment. Within this framework, tests of mental functioning need to have both concurrent and predictive validity, that is, they need to reflect individual differences in adjustment/coping with everyday tasks of self-help and instrumental activities of daily living, and they need to predict, within limits, the stability of such differences.

Within this framework one might argue that a reliable knowledge of the person's clinical state and behavioural competence renders the need for cognitive assessment redundant. If the person is manifestly unable to cope with self-help and instrumental activities, then cognitive tests are superfluous measures of intervening constructs,

1

located in a hypothetical space between overt behavioural deficits and structural pathology or pathophysiology within the central nervous system. Some support for this position may be gleaned from the work of Blessed et al. (1968) who found a closer relationship between a clinical/behavioural rating of dementia and senile plaque counts (indices of degenerating neuronal processes) compared to the association between such plaque counts and cognitive test scores (Blessed et al., 1968; Roth, 1972).

However, there are a number of counter-arguments to such a position. First is the extent to which reliable clinical information can be obtained from elderly patients, especially those living on their own, or with an elderly, possibly equally impaired spouse. Kellett et al. (1975) have shown that over 60 per cent of the changes in psychiatric diagnoses made on the basis of a clinical interview with elderly patients came from information provided by relatives. Adequate clinical information, of course, involves assessment of the mental state such that when the criterion of diagnosis is used as a marker for 'unable to cope due to cognitive impairment', it is difficult to judge the significance of other contributing information regarding behavioural deficits. In the absence of reliable historical and current information regarding disabilities and incompetences, the study by Kuriansky et al. (1976) suggests this is often considerably unreliable when coming from either the patient or relatives. The examination of cognitive state could therefore be a potentially useful marker for such disabilities.

The second counter-argument to the non-utility of cognitive assessment is that it is currently far beyond existing knowledge to assume that measures of brain function or brain pathology have clear-cut correlations with present and future incompetence. There is a lack of concurrent validity between measures of CNS dysfunction and CNS atrophy (Stefoski et al., 1976), as well as between measures of CNS atrophy and behavioural impairment, both current (Roberts and Caird, 1976) and predictively (Nott and Fleminger, 1975).

The third principal counter-argument relates to the lack of construct validity of purely clinical-behavioural information. Global judgements of disability are unreliable (Robertson and Malchik, 1968), and, as Platt (1980) has pointed out, when the investigator is not in a position to observe behaviour 'he cannot rely on the reports of others as corroboration of an informant's account.' This problem applies even to nurses' accounts of disability. In an unpublished study, Gilleard and Rizvi (1) examined the inter-rater reliability of judgements of 'degree of dementia' amongst nurses from four psychogeriatric wards, with rating points ranging from zero (no dementia) to 5 (severe dementia). The values of weighted kappa (Cohen, 1968) for the degree of agreement taking account of chance ranged from minus 0.05 to +0.19, the latter only reaching statistical significance. Examining the choice of behaviours employed by the nurses in reaching their judgement, it was apparent that nurses varied on how many criteria they used (ranging from one or two, such as 'dependency', 'disorientation', to five or six, including 'management problem', 'psychiatric state', etc.). Moreover, the same nurse would vary the criteria used from patient to patient. It was apparent from this small study that global judgements of incapacity by clinicians reflect unpredictable and inconsistent referents, with potentially misleading results. The reliability and construct validity of cognitive tests are likely to be superior, therefore, to historical and current behavioural accounts from informants.

It seems to the present writer that there is thus a case for cognitive assessment. The main issue is the form such assessment should take. There are three principal approaches to cognitive assessment of the elderly: the particular measure – such as a verbal learning test – which may be developed as a screening test for brain damage; the psychometric test battery, such as a neuropsychological test battery; and cognitive screening instruments, such as the mental status questionnaire. Each of these will be examined in turn.

Specific Measures of Brain Damage

Some of the earliest approaches towards specifying what to assess as a 'core' index were developed and reported on in the 1950s by the Maudsley group of clinical psychologists, largely under the influence of M.B. Shapiro. Shapiro provided both a theoretical critique of earlier measures of mental deterioration, namely the Babcock tests (Shapiro and Nelson, 1955), an empirical demonstration of the invalidity of much of the clinical mental status examination (Shapiro et al., 1956) and suggested a more theoretical approach based on the hypothesis of an intensification of cortical inhibitory processes in organic brain disease. This led to the use of spiral after-effect measures as a more appropriate means of detecting brain damage (Shapiro, 1953; Holland and Beech, 1958). At the same time, Inglis began to examine the potential of 'new learning' tests as a means of investigating memory disorder in elderly psychiatric patients (Inglis et al., 1956; Inglis, 1957). Shapiro's reluctance to see much validity in tests of memory function was strongly influenced by the earlier work of Eysenck and Halstead (1947) who had demonstrated that the principal source of covariation amongst measures of 'memory' appeared to be differences in intellectual ability. Inglis, however, failed to find support for these findings, and suggested that 'memory impairment' was indeed a source of variation in the performance of elderly psychiatric patients, though initially not one which corresponded to the functional-organic dichotomy (Inglis et al., 1956). However his later work suggested that measures of auditory paired associate learning could be useful indicators of both diagnosis and prognosis (Inglis, 1957, 1959), and he went on to propose a model of impaired fluid ability which resulted in difficulties with any 'new' learning, be it problem-solving, paired associate learning or abstract reasoning.

Thus from a critique of assessing memory functioning there developed a theoretical model of 'new learning impairment' from which a number of clinical tests originated - notably the Inglis Paired Associate Learning Test, IPALT, (Inglis, 1959) the Modified New Word Learning Test, MNWLT, (Walton, 1958b), Kendrick's Synonym Learning Test, SLT, (Kendrick, 1965) and Hetherington's Word Learning Test (Hetherington, 1965).

This tradition of using verbal learning tests has also provided a further basis for experimentation, illustrated by Miller's work on the nature of the memory disorder in Alzheimer's disease (Miller, 1977) besides proposals for new clinical tests such as Alexander's Nonsense Syllable Learning Test (Alexander, 1973) and Larner's False Recognition Test (Larner, 1977). Developments in the experimental study of verbal memory have in turn provided the basis for further studies of verbal memory failure in dementing patients (e.g. Weingartner et al. 1981). There seems now to be a steady stream of investigations into the nature of the mechanisms of the memory impairment in dementia, which have established the central position of memory failure in characterising the deficits of elderly organic patients.

Other specific tests have a less obvious pattern of clear-cut historical and theoretical development. The use of general tests of brain damage, such as the Memory for Designs Test, Benton Visual Retention Test and Bender-Gestalt, have all been employed in the detection of dementia, but rarely have they been used outside of this framework of concurrent validation with clinical assignment to a demented vs. functional category. Other more specialised tests have been employed by particular groups of researchers, such as Corsi's block tapping test, which has been investigated by Grossi and co-workers in a recent series of studies (Grossi et al., 1977; Cantone et al., 1978). The results of such investigations have not, however, supplanted the place of verbal learning tests in this approach to measuring organically-based impairment in the elderly.

Perhaps the most important exception has been the use of the Digit Copying Test (DCT), first employed by Kendrick in his studies of elderly psychiatric patients (Kendrick, 1965). This test was conceived of as a measure of sensory-motor performance which was predicted to be related to diffuse brain damage, but not the 'pseudo-dementia' characterising certain depressive elderly patients (Kendrick, 1972). Kendrick has since developed a successor to the Synonym Learning Test (linked historically to the 'new learning' approach developed by Inglis) based on the recall of objects, rather than the meaning of words (Gibson and Kendrick, 1980), but has maintained the utility of the DCT as an accompanying test.

Several independent studies have demonstrated that the DCT does yield significantly lower scores in dementing patients compared to other elderly psychiatric patient groups (Hemsi et al., 1968; Alexander, 1971; Cowan et al., 1975; Davies et al., 1978), but the range of mean scores for the two groups varies considerably across studies (see Table 1.1).

An important problem with Kendrick's (1972) theoretical model is that it assumes the absence of a 'pseudo-dementing' effect on the DCT. Follow-up studies (Hemsi et al., 1968; Cowan et al., 1975; Davies et al., 1978) have all, however, demonstrated a significant improvement on DCT performance in depressives following treatment. This would seem to suggest that the test, like many verbal learning measures, is sensitive to the effects of depression, as well as those of dementia. Moreover, Whitehead (1976) failed to find any significant prediction of two-year outcome from the DCT, suggesting that a satisfactory diagnostic test does not necessarily validly predict outcome.

Test Battery Approaches

The employment of test batteries to identify dementia is probably a very individualistic matter. Some procedures have an inherent 'differential' ability pattern (e.g. WAIS), while others have been put together for a specific research purpose (Irving et al., 1970; Cowan et al., 1975; Whitehead, 1976). Screening batteries based upon examining mental status such as the Kew Tests (McDonald, 1969), the Mental Status Questionnaire and Face-Hand test (Kahn et al., 1960b), the Mini-Mental State Examination (Folstein et al., 1975) and the Clifton Assessment Schedule (Pattie and Gilleard, 1976) will be considered in the next section. Here the concern is the validity of formal psychological tests based upon assumptions of a normal distribution in the cognitive functions being measured.

The most widely employed tests are the WAIS (Wechsler, 1958), the Coloured Progressive Matrices/Mill Hill Vocabulary Scale combination (Raven, 1956) and the Wechsler Memory Scale (Wechsler, 1945), including Russell's (1975) modification of this latter scale. As with the more specific tests, almost all the research investigating measurement of cognitive impairment with these scales has concentrated on concurrent validation of scores with the diagnostic dichotomy of organic vs. functional.

The work of Savage and his colleagues in the 1960s involved a fairly exhaustive investigation of the WAIS (in shortened form) and its value in discriminating organic from non-organic patients (Bolton et al., 1966). They found that none of six indicators of organicity was able to predict a diagnosis of dementia with any degree of clinical validity, and concluded 'the practice of using the WAIS diagnostic indicators to classify people into psychiatric groups appears to be invalid.' Further, there seems little evidence that WAIS scores can predict outcome with any validity (Pattie and Gilleard, 1979).

Orme (1957), Kendrick and Post (1967) and Irving et al. (1970) all found the Coloured Progressive

Matrices (CPM) to differentiate between organic and non-organic elderly psychiatric patients, while Kendrick (1964) has suggested that the synonym section of the Mill Hill Vocabularly Scale (MHVS) is a useful index of pre-morbid intellectual level. Again, however, the demonstration of group differences does not guarantee valid information in the individual case, and studies have been reported which have failed to show even group differences on the CPM (Alexander, 1973).

The Wechsler Memory Scale (WMS) is in many ways an unsatisfactory psychometric test (see Erikson and Scott, 1977, for a detailed critique). Nevertheless, one of the first studies to employ the scale with elderly psychiatric patients found it useful both in terms of concurrent and predictive validity (Walton, 1958a). Since Walton's study there have been few reports of its use with this population until quite recently. Weingartner et al. (1981) found a mean 30 point difference in Memory Quotients (MQs) between normal elderly subjects and patients with progressive idiopathic dementia 'in the earliest stage', although both groups were matched for verbal IQ. Gilleard (1980) reported a mean 28 point difference in MQs between elderly functional and organic patients; while Klinger et al. (1976) also reported useful discrimination between these groups using the WMS. Concurrent validity for the WMS has been provided against disability ratings made on elderly residents of a nursing home (Cyr and Stones, 1977) and Russell's (1975) modification of the WMS using only the Logical Memory Passages and Visual Reproduction sub-tests, with 30-minute delayed recall for both, has proved effective in discriminating the dementing from normal aged subjects (Logue and Wyrick, 1979). The potential value of the WMS no doubt reflects its relationship to both 'verbal learning' tests, such as the IPALT and MNWLT, but also perhaps because of the orientation and current information items which have frequently proved of value in examination of the mental state in the elderly.

Mental State Screening Instruments

The formal scoring of procedures typically employed in the examination of the mental state in psychiatry has provided the basis of a third approach to cognitive assessment in the elderly. Some of the earlier work of Maudsley psychologists and

7

psychiatrists described in the preceding sections illustrates the quantification of 'tests of the clinical sensorium' (Shapiro et al., 1956). One of the more recent investigations of the value of such mental state examinations was carried out by Hinton and Withers (1971), which confirmed many earlier findings (e.g. Roth and Hopkins, 1953; Shapiro et al., 1956; Kahn et al., 1960a; Irving et al., 1970) that tests of orientation in time and place, and general information are useful tests for organic brain disease. All other tests (e.g. recall of stories, serial subtraction of 7s, repeating days of the week backwards, backward and forward digit span, recall of name, address and telephone number) were found wanting in one way or another. Depression particularly affected verbal learning (stories, immediate and delayed recall) and tests of concentration (serial 7s). These authors' recommend-ations, namely that 'tests of Orientation and General Information are clincially useful' (op cit.) are reflected in the increasingly widespread use of such questions in geriatric and psychogeriatric settings. Gurland (1980) has recently reviewed the content of some half dozen mental status screening instruments; Table 1.2 records the principal screening instruments of this nature currently in use. All these measures either (a) consist only of orientation and information questions, or (b) include as a principal feature orientation/information questions.

The 10- or 12-item mental status questionnaires appear to be at least as adequate as the longer versions (Qureshi and Hodkinson, 1974), and are particularly useful as a brief measure that can be easily repeated - a procedure which enhances their effectiveness in clarifying diagnostic status (Storier, 1974). They have shown adequate short-term stability, for example, Meer and Baker (1965) found test-retest correlations ranging from 0.84 to 0.94 for the Information and Orientation sub-tests of the Wechsler Memory Scale, the content of which is very similar to the MSQ-type of test. They have shown a close relationship with measures of functional status (Kahn et al., 1960b) and have been found highly predictive of outcome of psychiatric hospitalisation (Pattie and Gilleard, 1979), mortality within the institutionalised elderly (Goldfarb et al., 1966), as well as mortality in more specificially demented samples (Naguib and Levy, 1982). In this respect they have proved superior to standard intellectual and verbal learning tests (Whitehead, 1976; Whitehead and Hunt, 1982). The value of associated tests, linked to MSQ items is less clear. The modified paired associate learning test of Isaacs and Walkey's test battery has, for example, not been found to show much concurrent validation against diagnostic status (Priest <u>et al.</u>, 1969), and the mental ability sub-scale of the CAS has proved of little diagnostic value (Pattie and Gilleard, 1976). In contrast, some of McDonald's brief tests, notably the parietal scale, have provided both useful clinical information (Hare, 1978) and increased the validity of attempts to effect relevant differentiation within a dementing population, differentiation that has prognostic value (McDonald, 1969; Naguib and Levy, 1982).

It seems likely that mental status screening instruments have an evident, though coarse, value in assessing mental competence in the elderly. Further refinement of contents will no doubt continue to be made in order to meet specific needs. Examples include the OSGP (Berg and Svensson, 1980) as a measure particularly relevant to the current environment of the institutionalised elderly patient, when used to evaluate the impact of psychosocial treatment packages in hospital settings. Direct behaviour performance testing of ward orientation has also been employed in studies of rehabilitation (Hanley, 1981).

Perhaps the greatest deficit in mental status screening instruments is their continued reliance on diagnostic status as the principal source of concurrent validation. As was pointed out at the beginning of this section, an important element in any cognitive assessment is its predictive validity and, related to this, the stability of any measured impairment. Obviously one distinction between the clinical interview and a mental status test is the lack of historical and developmental content in the latter. Short-term stability of orientation and current information measures over a matter of days have been established (Meer and Baker, 1965, Pattie and Gilleard, 1979). However, little is known concerning the stability of performance deficits over differing lengths of time, and in different settings, with different groups of patients. A valid relationship between coping and cognitive competence, as measured by mental status screening instruments seems evident. It seems equally evident that only minimal changes are effected, even by strenuous training efforts in cognitive and behavioural competence, in populations of institutionalised dementing patients (see Chapters 7 and 8 in this volume; Powell-Proctor and Miller, 1982; and Woods and Holden, 1982 for recent reviews of reality-orientation treatment effects). Pattie et al., (2) (1979) carried out mental status assessments and obtained behavioural disability ratings on a sample of 400 elderly subjects, using the CAPE scales. Taking only the categories of impairment from the CAPE survey version (Pattie, 1981) which is made up from the CAS Information/Orientation test, and the Physical Disability section of the BRS, they followed up their sample over a two-year period. The 400 people were made up from (a) 100 elderly living in the community, (b) 100 elderly living in social services institutions, (c) 100 elderly admitted to geriatric or general medical wards, and (d) 100 elderly admitted to psychogeriatric wards. Table 1.3 indicates the relationship between initial and final score grade. The system of grading ranged from A, no impairment; B, mild impairment; C, moderate impairment; D, marked impairment; and E, maximum impairment.

Over the two-year period 55 per cent remained at the same level of disability, 31 per cent deteriorated, and 14 per cent, improved by at least one grade. If the criterion is shifted to a change of two grade points, which would be clinically a quite noticeable difference in functional level, almost 90 per cent would be unchanged, just less than 4 per cent improved, and just over 6 per cent deteriorated. When the four sub-populations were examined in greater detail, it was apparent that the greatest change occurred in the psychogeriatric sample, where half of the improvers could be located.

These findings are relatively isolated, and yet are the necessary forms of evaluation of mental status tests if they are to have practical utility. Without such reference to variability, any cross-sectional estimate is of limited practical value. Of course, identification of confusion in the elderly is of inherent importance in determining how any interview should proceed, indicating the need to check external informants, the risk of accidents or wandering, identifying likely limitations in adequate self-care, the need for medical investigations, and the demands that will be imposed on supporting relatives. The mental status test, too, provides an easily employed device which can be used by a variety of health and social service professionals. However, at present it is uncertain as to whether such evaluations may lead to professional 'giving up' on a patient, or to missing opportunities for intervention that would lead to recovery of function. The problem of severe depressive pseudo-dementia is an extremely important example, and reflects the problems that generally exist in the use of cognitive tests for behaviourally disabled or disturbed elderly people.

The problem of pseudo-dementia is that elderly people, usually demonstrating a history of increasing incompetence and apathy of less than six months' duration, present in health-care settings with clinically evident impaired mental function. They may be described as forgetful, disoriented and sometimes seemingly reluctant even to speak. They may show deteriorated self-care, and even incontinence. Performance on cognitive tests is invariably poor, and often it is the discovery of a history of depressive illness that leads to vigorous anti-depressant treatment and subsequent recovery of cognitive and behavioural competence. In contrast to many so-called 'potentially reversible' dementias associated with metabolic or nutritional disorders who often fail to demonstrate any significant recovery of cognitive competence despite appropriate treatment (cf. Kral <u>et al</u>., 1970; Henschke and Pain, 1977), it is rare for anyone working in clinical psychogeriatric settings not to find himself totally surprised by both the pervasive nature of cognitive deficit, and its remarkable subsequent recovery in such conditions. Because of the retrospective nature of the diagnostic or clinical description, it is extremely difficult to carry out adequate investigations of cognitive functions in such a group. Perhaps as a result of the sometimes over-enthusiastic use of this diagnostic term, some workers, (e.g. Shraberg, 1978) have questioned its separate existence, arguing either that both dementia and depression co-exist in such patients, or that adequate cognitive testing would not demonstrate such an evident deterioration as appears from the clinical picture. More recently, some workers have turned to alternative diagnostic aids to help identify the 'hidden' depression in pseudo-dementia. One of the more interesting approaches has been a neuroendocrine measure, the dexamethasom suppression test (Carroll <u>et al</u>., 1981), which in some clinical cases has proved useful (McAllister <u>et al</u>., 1982), though false positives may prove such promises largely illusory (Spar and Gurney, 1982). The potential of serial mental status examination in such patients has already been referred to (Storier, 1974) and it would be unfortunate if diagnostic inaccuracy was accepted by reliance upon single cross-sectional test performance.

It seems to the present writer that more interest could be focused on the novel use of existing tests, rather than continuing the development of still more one-off performance measures. By more thorough investigation of the parameters underlying an impairment score, it may well be possible to increase the level of useful predictive judgements about an older person's cognitive state. Whitehead (1973) suggested one interesting way of increasing the information yield from paired associate learning tests by examining the types of error made by depressives and dementing patients. Miller and Lewis (1977) provide another example, examining errors made by means of a signal detection model. Other alternatives might be to examine the relationship between measured cognitive competence and behavioural competence, and to judge the significance of patterns of deficit which are out of phase with each other. Williams (1968) made use of structured cueing in her test of delayed recall, and it should be possible to examine the differential responsiveness of patients to cues in examining mental status. Other possibilities include measuring the latency of responses, the willingness or otherwise to respond when urged to guess, and the extent of incidental learning. It is often considered clinically useful to contrast level of aspiration with level of performance; depressed patients are thought to underestimate their ability to remember, while patients with dementia are considered to overestimate their abilities in this direction. While many experienced clinicians no doubt have developed such additional strategies going beyond the test score to interpret performance, there is a need to demonstrate empirically the incremental validity of such methods, if for no other reason than that it increases the 'teachability' of such skills to the less experienced.

Summary

The use of both specific tests of organic impairment, whether linked to verbal learning, or visuomotor function, has increasingly been replaced by more theoretically limited tests of mental status. This reflects empirical and clinical practice, and more particularly the evidence from concurrent and predictive validity studies. Outside of treatment research, the test battery approach has also seen a decline in utility. The emerging possibility of ecologically-adapted tests of orientation and the elderly person's efficiency in updating current intelligence/information is one promising avenue for directing clinical interest in both identifying cognitively-based behavioural deficits, and in possibly alleviating them, or at least reducing their impact. There remains, however, a need to examine patterns of stability and change in simple tests of mental status over both long-and short-term periods, in differing clinical settings, and with different 'helping' strategies employed by the examiner. Additionally, the prospect of simplified neuro-psychological examinations, such as McDonald's Kew Test, provides hope for usefully discriminating clinically important sub-populations within the elderly mentally-impaired population. The prospect of achieving absolute diagnostic accuracy is increasingly being recognised as the myth that it almost has to be. Also, the search for an equivalent predictive accuracy should be laid to rest. In its place must come the realisation that outcome variance is determined by both organismic and environmental influences. While organismic influences increase as one moves down the scale of cognitive competence, adaptive existence at all levels of cognitive competence is as dependent on the ability of the environment to change as it is on the ability of the organism to do so. When the potential for improved organismic function is limited, the need to focus upon implementing environmental change is consider-ably greater.

TABLE 1.1: DCT Scores in Dementing Patients Compared to Others

	Kendrick et al.	Hemsi et al.	Alexander	Cowan et al.*		Davies et al.
Normal elderly	-	-	89.1	-	-	109.2
Depressives/ Functional	81.1	62.1	86.1	62.5	42.0	68.4
Dements	49.3	41.3	53.1	17.5	9.0	39.2

Note: * Median not mean values.

TABLE 1.2: Mental Status Screening Tests

Authors	Name	Operative abbreviation
Roth and Hopkins (1953)	Roth and Hopkins	(RH)
Kahn et al. (1960a)	Mental status questionnaire	(MSQ)
Isaacs and Walkey (1964)	Tests of mental impairment	(TMI)
Robinson (1965)	Crichton memory and intelligence test	(CMIT)
McDonald (1969)	Kew Test	(KT)
Irving et al., (1970)	Orientation Test	(OT)
Hodkinson (1972)	Abbreviated Mental Test	(AMT)
Pfeiffer (1975)	Short Portable Mental Status Questionnaire	(SPMSQ)
Pattie and Gilleard (1976)	Clifton Assessment Schedule	(CAS)
Folstein et al. (1975)	Mini-Mental State Examination	(MMSE)
Berg and Svensson (1980)	Orientation Scale for Geriatric Patients	(OSGP)

<u>TABLE 1.3:</u> Relationship between Initial and Final Cognitive/Behavioural Disability Level in the Total Sample of 400

Initial CAPE Survey Grade		Final CAPE Survey Grade					Died
	n	A	B	C	D	E	
A	64	41	11	4	0	0	9
B	84	11	29	9	1	2	32
C	72	4	7	12	12	6	31
D	71	0	1	3	13	19	35
E	77	0	1	2	0	19	55

Notes

1. Gilleard, C.J. and Rizvi, S., (1980) 'Global Ratings of Severity of Dementia in a Psychogeriatric Hospitalised Population: Factors Associated with Inter-judge Unreliability', unpublished report, Dept of Psychiatry, University of Edinburgh.
2. Pattie, A.H., Gilleard, C.J. and Bell, J. (1979) 'The Relationship of the Intellectual and Behavioural Competence of the Elderly to their Present and Future Needs from Community, Residential and Hospital Services'. Report to the Yorkshire Regional Health Authority.

References

Alexander, D.A. (1971) 'Two Tests of Psychomotor Function in Detection of Organic Brain Disease in Elderly Psychiatric Patients', Perceptual and Motor Skills, 33, 1291-7.

Alexander, D.A. (1973) 'Some Tests of Intelligence and Learning for Elderly Psychiatric Patients: A Validation Study', British Journal of Social and Clinical Psychology, 188-92.

Berg, S. and Svensson, T. (1980) 'An Orientation Scale for Geriatric Patients', Age and Ageing, 9, 215-19.

Blessed, G.A., Tomlinson, B.E. and Roth, M. (1968) 'The Association between Quantitative Measures of Dementia and of Degenerative Changes in the Cerebral Grey Matter of Elderly Subjects', British Journal of Psychiatry, 114, 797-811.

Bolton, N., Britton, P.G. and Savage, R.D. (1966) 'Some Normative Data on the WAIS and its Indices in an Aged Population', Journal of Clinical Psychology, 22, 183-8.

Cantone, G., Orsini, A., Grossi, D. and De Michele, G. (1978) 'Verbal and Spatial Memory Span in Dementia', Acta Neurologia (Napoli), 33, 175-83.

Carroll, B.J. et al. (1981) 'A Specific Laboratory Test for the Diagnosis of Melancholia: Standardisation, Validation and Clinical Utility', Archives of General Psychiatry, 38, 15-22.

Cohen, J. (1968) 'Weighted Kappa: Nominal Scale Agreement with Provision for Scaled Disagreement or Partial Credit', Psychological Bulletin, 70, 213-20.

Cowan, D.W. et al. (1975) 'Cross-national Study of Diagnosis of the Mental Disorders: A Comparative Psychometric Assessment of Elderly Patients Admitted to Mental Hospitals', British Journal of Psychiatry, 126, 560-70.

Cyr, J. and Stones, M.J. (1977) 'Performance on Cognitive Tasks in Predicting the Behavioural Competence of the Institutionalised Elderly', Experimental Aging Research, 3, 263-64.

Davies, G., Hamilton, S., Hendrickson, D.E., Levy, R. and Post, F. (1978) 'Psychological Test Performance and Sedation Thresholds of Elderly Dements, Depressives and Depressives with Incipient

16

Brain Change', Psychological Medicine, 8, 103-9.

Erickson, R.S. and Scott, M.L. (1977) 'Clinical Memory Testing: A Review', Psychological Bulletin, 84, 1130-49.

Eysenck, H.J. and Halstead, H. (1945) 'The Memory Function', American Journal of Psychiatry, 102, 174-80.

Folstein, M.F., Goldstein, S.E. and McHugh, P.R. (1975) 'Mini-Mental State: A Practical Method for Grading the Cognitive State of Patients for the Clinician', Journal of Psychiatric Research, 12, 189-98.

Gibson, A.J. and Kendrick, D.C. (1980) Kendrick Battery for the Detection of Dementia in the Elderly, Manual, NFER, Nelson Publishing Co. Windsor.

Gilleard, C.J. (1980) 'Wechsler Memory Scale Performance of Elderly Psychiatric Patients', Journal of Clinical Psychology, 36, 958-60.

Goldfarb, A.L., Fisch, M. and Gerber, I. (1966) 'Predictors of Mortality in the Institutionalised Elderly', Diseases of the Nervous System, 27, 21-9.

Grossi, D., Orsini, A. and Ridente, G. (1977) 'Considerazioni Introduttive allo Studio Neuropsicologia delle Demense', Acta Neurologia (Napoli), 32, 682-5.

Gurland, B. (1980) 'The Assessment of Mental Health Status of Older Adults' in J.E. Birren and R.B. Sloan (eds.) Handbook of Mental Health and Aging, McGraw-Hill, New York, pp. 671-700.

Hanley, I.G. (1981) 'The Use of Signposts and Active Training to Modify Ward Disorientation in Elderly Patients', Journal of Behavior Therapy and Experimental Psychiatry, 12, 241-7.

Hare, M. (1978) 'Clinical Checklist for Diagnosis of Dementia', British Medical Journal, ii, 266-7.

Hemsi, L.K., Whitehead, A. and Post, F. (1968) 'Cognitive Functioning and Cerebral Arousal in Elderly Depressives and Dements', Journal of Psychosomatic Research, 12, 145-56.

Henshke, P.J. and Pain, R.W. (1977) 'Thyroid Disease in a Psychogeriatric Population', Age and Ageing, 6, 151-5.

Hetherington, R. (1965) 'A Neologism Learning Test', Bulletin of the British Psychological Society, 18, 21A-22A.

Hinton, J. and Withers, E. (1971) 'The Usefulness of the Clinical Tests of the Sensorium', British Journal of Psychiatry, 119, 9-18.

Hodkinson, H.M. (1972) 'Evaluation of a Mental Test Score for Assessment of Mental Impairment in the Elderly', Age and Ageing, 1, 233-8.

Holland, H.C. and Beech, H.R. (1958) 'The Spiral After-Effect as a Test of Brain Damage', Journal of Mental Science, 104, 466-71.

Inglis, J. (1957) 'An Experimental Study of Learning and Memory Function in Elderly Psychiatric Patients', Journal of Mental Science, 103, 796-803.

Inglis, J. (1958) 'Learning, Retention and Conceptual Usage in Elderly Patients with Memory Disorder', Journal of Abnormal and Social Psychology, 59, 210-5.

Inglis, J. (1959) 'A Paired Associate Learning Test for Use with

Elderly Psychiatric Patients', Journal of Mental Science, 105, 440-8.

Inglis, J., Shapiro, M. and Post, F. (1956) 'Memory Function in Psychiatric Patients over 60: the Role of Memory in Tests Discriminating between Functional and Organic Groups', Journal of Mental Science, 102, 589-98.

Irving, G., Robinson, R.A. and McAdam, W. (1970) 'The Validity of Some Cognitive Tests in the Diagnosis of Dementia', British Journal of Psychiatry, 117, 149-56.

Isaacs, B. and Walkey, F.A. (1964) 'Measurement of Mental Impairment in Geriatric Practice' Gerontologia Clinica, 6, 114-23.

Kahn, R.L., Goldfarb, A.L., Pollack, M. and Gerber, I.E. (1960a) 'The Relationship of Mental and Physical Status in Elderly Institutionalised Persons', American Journal of Psychiatry, 117, 118-24.

Kahn, R.L., Goldfarb, A.L., Pollack, M. and Gerber, I.E. (1960b) 'Brief Objective Measures for the Determination of Mental Status in the Aged'. American Journal of Psychiatry, 117, 326-8.

Kellett, J.M., Copeland, J.R.M. and Kelleher, M.J. (1975) 'Information Leading to an Accurate Diagnosis in the Elderly', British Journal of Psychiatry, 126, 423-30.

Kendrick, D.C. (1964) 'The Assessment of Premorbid Level of Intelligence in Elderly Patients Suffering from Diffuse Brain Pathology', Psychological Reports, 15, 188.

Kendrick, D.C. (1965) 'Speed and Learning in the Diagnosis of Diffuse Brain Damage in Elderly Subjects: A Bayesian Statistical Analysis', British Journal of Social and Clinical Psychology, 4, 63-71.

Kendrick, D.C. (1972) 'The Kendrick Battery of Tests: Theoretical Assumptions and Clinical Uses', British Journal of Social and Clinical Psychology, 11, 373-86.

Kendrick, D.C. and Post, F. (1967) 'Differences in Cognitive Status between Healthy, Psychiatrically Ill and Diffusely Brain Damaged Elderly Subjects', British Journal of Psychiatry, 113, 75-84.

Klinger, A., Kachanoff, R., Dastoor, D.P., Worenklein, A. et al. (1976) 'A Psychogeriatric Assessment Program: III Clinical and Experimental Psychologic Aspects, Journal of the Amercian Geriatrics Society, 24, 17-24.

Kral, V.A., Solyorn, I., Enescott, J. and Ledwidge, B. (1970) 'Relationship of Vitamin B12, and Folic Acid to Memory Function', Biological Psychiatry, 2, 19-26.

Kuriansky, J.B., Gurland, B.J. and Fleiss, J.L. (1976) 'The Assessment of Self-care Capacity in Geriatric Psychiatric Patients by Objective and Subjective Methods', Journal of Clinical Psychology, 32, 95-102.

Larner, S. (1977) 'Encoding in Senile Dementia and Elderly Depressives: A Preliminary Study', British Journal of Social and Clinical Psychology, 16, 379-90.

Logue, P. and Wyrick, L. (1979) 'Initial Validation of Russell's Revised Wechsler Memory Scale: A Comparison of Normal Aging versus Dementia', Journal of Consulting and Clinical Psychology, 47, 176-8.

McAllister, T.W., Ferrell, R.B., Price, T.R.P. and Neville, M. (1982) 'The Dexamethasone Suppression Test in Two Patients
18

with Severe Depressive Pseudo-dementia', American Journal of Psychiatry, 139, 479-81.

McDonald, C. (1969) 'Clinical Heterogeneity in Senile Dementia', British Journal of Psychiatry, 115, 267-71.

Meer, B. and Baker, J.A. (1965) 'Reliability of Measurements of Intellectual Functioning of Geriatric Patients', Journal of Gerontology, 21, 410-14.

Miller, E. (1977) Abnormal Ageing, John Wiley, Chichester.

Miller, E. and Lewis, P. (1977) 'Recognition Memory in Elderly Patients with Depression and Dementia: a Signal Detection Analysis', Journal of Abnormal Psychology, 86, 84-6.

Naguib, M. and Levy, R. (1982) 'Prediction of Outcome in Senile Dementia - a Computed Tomography Study' British Journal of Psychiatry, 140, 263-7.

Nott, P.N. and Fleminger, J.J. (1975) 'Presenile Dementia: the Difficulties of an Early Diagnosis', Acta Psychiatrica Scandinavica, 51, 210-17.

Orme, J.E. (1957) 'Non-verbal, and Verbal Performance in Normal Old Age, Senile Dementia and Elderly Depression', Journal of Gerontology, 12, 408-13.

Pattie, A.H. (1981) 'A survey Version of the Clifton Assessment Procedures for the Elderly (CAPE)', British Journal of Clinical Psychology, 20, 173-8.

Pattie, A.H. and Gilleard, C.J. (1976) 'The Clifton Assessment Schedule - Further Validation of a Psychogeriatric Assessment Schedule', British Journal of Psychiatry, 128.

Pattie, A.H. and Gilleard, C.J. (1979) Manual for the Clifton Assessment Procedures for the Elderly, Hodder & Stoughton Educational, Sevenoaks, Kent.

Pfeiffer, E. (1975) 'A Short Portable Mental Status Questionnaire for the Assessment of Organic Brain Deficit in Elderly Patients', Journal of the American Geriatrics Society, 23, 433-41.

Platt, S. (1980) 'On Establishing the Validity of "Objective" Data: Can We Rely on Cross-Interview Agreement?', Psychological Medicine, 10, 573-81.

Powell-Proctor, L. and Miller, E. (1982) 'Reality Orientation: A Critical Appraisal', British Journal of Psychiatry, 140, 457-63.

Priest, R.G., Tarighati, S. and Shariatmadari, M. (1969) 'A Brief Test of Organic Brain Disease: Validation in a Mental Hospital Population', Acta Psychiatrica Scandinavica, 45, 347-54.

Quresti, K.N. and Hodkinson, H.M. (1974) 'Evaluation of a Ten Question Mental Test in the Institutionalised Elderly', Age and Ageing, 3, 152-7.

Raven, J.C. (1956) Coloured Progressive Matrices, H.K. Lewis, London.

Roberts, M.A. and Caird, F.T. (1976) 'Computerised Tomography and Intellectual Impairment in the Elderly', Journal of Neurology, Neurosurgery and Psychiatry, 39, 986-9.

Robertson, R.J. and Malchik, D.L. (1968) 'The Reliability of Global Ratings versus Specific Ratings', Journal of Clinical Psychology, 23, 256-8.

Robinson, R.A. (1966) 'The Organisation of a Diagnostic and Treatment Unit for the Aged', in Psychiatric Disorders in the Aged, WPA Symposium, Geigy, Manchester.

Roth, M. and Hopkins, B. (1953) 'Psychological Test Performance in Patients over Sixty', Journal of Mental Science, 99, 439-50.

Russell, E.W. (1975) 'A Multiple Scoring Method for the Assessment of Complex Memory Functions', Journal of Consulting and Clinical Psychology, 43, 800-9.

Shapiro, M.B. (1953) 'Experimental Studies of a Perceptual Anomaly. III. The Testing of an Explanatory Theory', Journal of Mental Science, 99, 394-409.

Shapiro, M.B. and Nelson, E.H. (1955) 'An Investigation of the Nature of Cognitive Impairment in Co-operative Psychiatric Patients', British Journal of Medical Psychology, 4, 205-80.

Shapiro, M.B., Post, F., Lofiring, B. and Inglis, J. (1956) 'Memory Function in Psychiatric Patients over Sixty: Some Methodological and Diagnostic Implications', Journal of Mental Science, 102, 233-46.

Shraberg, D. (1978) 'The Myth of Pseudo-dementia: Depression and the Aging Brain', American Journal of Psychiatry, 135, 601-3.

Spar, J.E. and Gurney, R. (1982) 'Does the Dexamethasone Suppression Test Distinguish Dementia from Depression?', American Journal of Psychiatry, 139, 238-40.

Stefoski, D., Bergen, D., Fox, J., Morrell, F., Huckman, M. and Ramsey, R. (1976) 'Correlation between Diffuse EEG Abnormalities and Cerebral Atrophy in Senile Dementia', Journal of Neurology, Neurosurgery and Psychiatry, 39, 751-5.

Storier, P.M. (1974) 'Score Changes Following Repeated Administration of the Mental Status Questionnaire (MSQ)', Age and Ageing, 3, 91-6.

Walton, D. (1958a) 'The Diagnostic and Predictive Accuracy of the Wechsler Memory Scale in Psychiatric Patients over 65', Journal of Mental Science, 104, 1111-18.

Walton, D. (1958b) 'The Diagnostic and Predictive Accuracy of the Modified Word Learning Test in Psychiatric Patients over 65', Journal of Mental Science, 104, 1119-22.

Wechsler, D. (1945) 'A Standardised Memory Scale for Clinical Use', Journal of Psychology, 19, 87-95.

Wechsler, D. (1958) The Measurement and Appraisal of Adult Intelligence, Williams & Wilkins, Baltimore.

Weingartner, H., Kaye, W., Smallberg, S.A., Ebert, M.H., Gillin, J.C. and Sitaram, N. (1981) 'Memory Failures in Progressive Idiopathic Dementia', Journal of Abnormal Psychology, 90, 187-96.

Whitehead, A. (1973) 'Verbal Learning and Memory in Elderly Depressives', British Journal of Psychiatry, 123, 203-8.

Whitehead, A. (1976) 'The Prediction of Outcome in Elderly Psychiatric Patients', Psychological Medicine, 6, 469-79.

Whitehead, A. and Hunt, A. (1982) 'Elderly Psychiatric Patients: A Five-year Prospective Study', Psychological Medicine, 12, 149-58.

Williams, M. (1968) 'The Measurements of Memory in Clinical

Practice', <u>British Journal of Social and Clinical Psychology</u>, 7, 19-34.
Woods, R.T. and Holden, V.P. (1982) 'Reality Orientation', in B. Isaacs (ed.), <u>Recent Advances in Geriatric Medicine</u>, No. 2. Churchill Livingstone, Edinburgh.

Chapter Two

EVALUATION OF DISABILITY IN THE ELDERLY

Ron Lyle

Planning a rational programme of rehabilitation for the disabled elderly person involves not only a diagnostic assessment of the pathology present but also a functional evaluation of the degree and type of disability present. The process of predicting likely difficulties, and of devising ways of compensating for these, is likely to become even more necessary as, increasingly, elderly patients are unable to be accommodated within hospitals. The assessment of functional disability in the elderly is perhaps most usually the province of occupational therapists. Psychology may, however, be able to offer a useful contribution here in relation to the metrical aspects of disability assessment, and in the construction of assessment scales which yield a reliable and standardised score suitable for applied clinical and research purposes. Whereas physio-therapists tend to be interested in motor function <u>per se</u>, the occupational therapist seeks to measure and enhance the hemiplegic patient's competence in skills involving motor and cognitive components. One particular contribution is in the area of activities of daily living assessment (ADL). The format for assessment of ADL frequently differs from one occupational therapy department to another according to the needs of the patients and preferences of the departmental staff, however some published versions have acquired a certain prominence. Since publication of the earliest standard texts on this subject (Buchwald, 1952; Lawton, 1963) a range of alternative ADL tests have appeared, which have differed in the range of activities sampled, their degree of comprehensiveness within a general category of behaviour, and the scoring criteria adopted. As an example, one version by Carroll (1962) contained the twelve items shown in Table 2.1.

Nowadays it is an admitted requirement of many tests that they should possess to some degree the characteristics of validity and reliability. Validity refers to the usefulness of a test as a genuine measure of the functions being assessed, and includes consideration as to whether the test is detailed enough, or is an accurate indication of the patient's present or likely future abilities. Reliability is a different concept concerned with the repeatability or reproducibility of the test on the same patient with substantially the same result, by a different tester — barring, of course, anything having happened or changed in the patient in the interim. Thus, unless a test is reliable, it may give highly idiosyncratic results in the hands of different users: a source of variability which must detract from its eventual usefulness. Carroll provided no data on the <u>reliability</u> of the scoring system, but did present a classification of patients into six groups on the basis of ADL scores, as a means of predicting need for nursing care in an attempt to demonstrate the test's validity. The differentiation between patients afforded by the test was however rather coarse. One positive feature of Carroll's test was that patients were required to <u>attempt</u> the various activities in the presence of the examiner, and were not rated merely on the basis of the tester's vague recollection of the patient's level of competence. In general, such behavioural tests tend to have high validity.

Mahoney and Barthel's Barthel Index (1965) used criteria which related to the <u>degree of assistance</u> required by the patient in performing ten common activities of daily living. This must surely provide a good basis for planning individual care needs in the elderly. The activities assessed, although grouped differently from Carroll's (1962) evaluation, were essentially similar, except that communication, and the presence of decubitus ulcers and contractures, were not scored. The maximum score varied between 5 and 15 for independent completion of the activity, while completion with assistance received approximately half the maximum score. Mahoney and Barthel gave explicit criteria to be used in making the assessment, which was intended to be behavioural. The provision of scoring criteria would tend to increase reliability by reducing inter-rater variation in scoring practices. Whilst Mahoney and Barthel presented no evidence for the reliability of the measure, the Barthel Index was to an extent validated by Granger <u>et al</u>. (1977) who found admission Barthel Index scores to be related to prognosis for rehabilitation in stroke patients. The Barthel Index did however share, with Carroll's test mentioned above, the disadvantage of providing an assessment of only a limited range of activities.

The Kenny Self-Care Evaluation (Schoening and Iversen, 1968) employed a four-point rating scale, to assess six basic self-care activities: bed, transfers, locomotion, dressing, personal hygiene and feeding. The activities were subdivided into their constituent actions, and a score was assigned on the basis of the number of these which the patient could perform unaided. A fifth score point was allocated to performance which could not be otherwise classified. A particular strength of Kenny's study was that serial testing of patients was undertaken to compare curves depicting functional recovery across self-care activities. This produced interesting data regarding differences between left and right hemiplegics. For instance, right hemiplegics recovered competence in personal hygiene activities more rapidly than did left hemiplegics.

Katz et al. (1970) using an index of ADL virtually identical in skill coverage to the Kenny evaluation, but employing a three-point rating scale, drew attention to the sequence in which self-care capability was likely to return. They found that return of independence in feeding and continence preceded acquisition of competence in transfers and toileting, which in turn preceded recovery of independence in dressing and bathing, in a mixed group, including stroke patients. Katz et al. further produced evidence to demonstrate a statistical relationship between index of ADL score at discharge and an index of mobility two years later.

Halstead and Hartley (1975) placed emphasis on yet another aspect of assessment of the same six basic areas of self-care examined by the studies reviewed above. It is sometimes not enough to know only the degree of assistance required by a patient in carrying out some act of daily living. The Time Care Profile quantified dependency by using a diary method to record both the frequency and duration of acts of assistance to the patient by care staff. Hence the patient's needs, and their cost to others, might be evaluated. Consider, for instance, the example of two patients both incontinent, once per day in one case, and twelve times in the other: the latter poses a considerably greater potential demand on staff time. Importantly, Halstead and Hartley also found that there were discrepancies in the same self-care skills as performed at different times of day - due in part to the effects of fatigue - and further argued that tests of ADL frequently elicited an atypically optimal performance from the patient, because of a sense of occasion: hence observation over a period of time should be preferred. Halstead and Hartley investigated agreement between raters on recorded duration and frequency of assistive acts for various categories of ADL but found this to range somewhat alarmingly between 37 and 80 for the former, and 51 and 97 for the latter.

Lawton and Brody (1969) made the distinction between a scale of activities necessary for physical self-maintenance (PSMS) and instrumental activities of daily living (IADL). The PSMS assessed basic self-care activities such as toileting, feeding, dressing, grooming, walking and bathing, whereas the IADL was concerned with activities such as use of the telephone, shopping, preparation of meals, housework, laundry, use of transport, self-administration of medicines and financial competence, subdivided into gradations of dependence, and scored in yes/no format. Within activity categories, patients able to perform more difficult items could also reliably perform all items of lesser difficulty. Reliability was found to be high and the physical self-maintenence scale correlated +0.61 with the instrumental activities of daily living, and each was correlated to a lesser, but yet significant extent with physical classification, rated mental status, and rated behaviour and adjustment. An advantage of Lawton and Brody's scales is that the differentiation between PSMS and IADL might allow preselection of the appropriate skill range and thus promote efficiency in assessment.

But the IADL was still restricted in breadth of skill coverage by comparison with the ADL of Donaldson et al. (1973), which was a comprehensive ADL test, adapted for computerisation. From entries describing the patient's performance on 150 variables, reflecting competence in 14 categories of ADL, computer programs were devised to yield equivalent Kenny, Katz and Barthel indices from the same data base. Data from 100 medical rehabilitation patients allowed a comparison to be made between these three alternative measures, from which it was concluded that the Kenny self-care evaluation was more sensitive to change than the Katz Index, with the Barthel Index being intermediate between the two. The Donaldson ADL evaluation would, however, require an inordinate amount of time were each item to be

administered behaviourally, and this must effectively rule it out from more widespread use.
Accordingly, Donaldson advocated completion of the
assessment by staff already familiar with the
patient's capabilities, in other words, by recall.
This is, of course, less than satisfactory as scores
are likely to be less accurate.

An evaluation of activities of daily living must
involve, as we have seen, some degree of compromise
between rapidity of administration and completeness
of skill coverage. Reduced availability of staff may
encourage a preference for rating scales of
proficiency in place of actual behavioural tests, but
it should not be assumed too readily that assessments
obtained in this way are a valid indicator of the
patient's competence, although they may range over
wide areas of behaviour.

There may, however, be a way of reconciling
these conflicting demands of rapidity and
comprehensiveness. Let us consider first that the
grouping of ADL activities by categories such as
toileting, feeding, housework, although superfic-
ially logically appealing, does not appear to relate
to any underlying similarities in the patterns of
movement involved. Since it is patterns of movement,
and functions such as balance which are commonly
impaired in physical disability, and amongst stroke
patients in particular, it seems appropriate to ask
whether there are potential ways of grouping ADL
items which might reflect such an underlying
classification of disability. Secondly, if such
groupings could be identified, it might well be found
that their constituent items formed a hierarchy of
difficulty, sufficient to constitute what is called a
Guttman scale. It is a property of Guttman scales
that successful completion of more difficult items
predicts success with items of lesser difficulty; and
that failure on easier items predicts failure on the
more difficult. If ADL assessment could be structured
in this way, testing time might be considerably
reduced without any corresponding loss in
comprehensiveness of the range of skills over which
prediction could be made. A further advantage
accruing from groupings of ADL items reflecting
similarities in underlying function might be that
corrective therapy, or use of prosthetic devices for
a defective movement pattern or function might
facilitate performance over a wider range of
activities, as compared with the current tendency to
teach specific skills in a piecemeal fashion. One
consequence of this line of thought was that use of

assistive devices should perhaps be incorporated within the ADL assessment, and analysed together with unassisted and personally assisted performance. For reasons of validity, it seems desirable that ratings should continue to be based upon the behaviour of the patient in a behavioural test.

A recent study (Lyle, 1980) sought to overcome some of the difficulties in the previous work outlined above, in developing a more rapid and logical way of assessing ADL making use of Guttman scale structures and functional groupings of ADL items. The study was conducted with hemiplegic patients, but the same principles of test instruction are potentially applicable to other standardisation groups with different diagnoses.

Twenty patients were assessed and the results are shown in Table 2.2.

Common brands of goods were used to allow replication elsewhere. The 109 items were drawn from a range of ADL protocols from a variety of centres, and were selected to cover in some depth as wide a range of activities as possible. A system of scoring was devised as depicted in Table 2.3 on the basis of the degree of supervision which the patient required in performing the relevant task.

The use of this relatively objective criterion, in addition to being more meaningful for discerning the patient's needs (e.g. self-sufficient, requires mechanical aids, home-help) was intended to increase agreement on ratings.

The patients were tested on each applicable item by one of two experienced occupational therapists. A correlation matrix was next computed using the data obtained to identify test items closely correlated across the patient population. Groups of items forming natural, _functional_ sub-scales, involving similar movements, were thus detected in place of the logical, _a priori_ scales (e.g. dressing, bathroom, etc.) which currently predominate.

The groupings of correlated items were next examined to determine whether they fulfilled the stringent criteria for Guttman scales. When the term cutting score is used below, this means that a patient was deemed to have passed an item when his score equalled or exceeded that score. Since ability or otherwise to function independently is frequently a meaningful basis for classification of the disabled for the purposes of discharge, a minimum cutting score of 3 is appropriate as it represents the minimum level of competence to perform an individual test item without assistance.

Twenty-three items were discarded as being insufficiently widely applicable or not suitably correlated for inclusion in a Guttman scale. Eight non-scale items were discarded since all patients scored at least 4 on them, and six items (see Table 2.4) consisting of male and female variants of similar activities were condensed into three.

The remaining 75 items were arranged into an ADL protocol of twelve Guttman scales, shown in Table 2.5. Within each scale, the number in brackets indicates the cutting score applied. The items in each scale are arranged in descending order of difficulty, with the exception of the second item in each scale which is empirically the easiest. In addition, for each scale two statistics were determined, namely the coefficient of reproducibility, which is a measure of the predictability of a respondent's response pattern on the basis of his total score on that scale; and secondly, the coefficient of scalability. Nie et al. (1975) recommend that a coefficient of reproducibility of above 0.9 and a coefficient of scalability of well above 0.6 be taken to indicate that a Guttman scale is valid. All scales amply fulfil these criteria.

It is worth noting that many of the Guttman scales appear to represent the use of a particular limb, or a particular pattern of movement or skill. These functional scales are contrasted with the groupings of items by location (bathroom, kitchen) or type of activity (cleaning, dressing) which appear to be the norm in current ADL tests.

A move towards functional groupings of items would offer some advantages. First, identification of particular defective patterns of movement may allow improvement on a wider number of ADL items by directing therapy at the defective pattern. Secondly, knowledge of performance on a handful of items may enable predictions to be made over a larger range of activities. Thirdly, there may implications for the design and prescription of aids. On the basis of economy of effort, the case can readily be justified. Let us assume that a patient is first tested on the most difficult item within each scale, and if he passes that item, is credited with having passed the remaining items within that scale. Should he fail the most difficult by scoring below the specified cutting score, the least difficult item is next administered. Should he fail that, he is regarded as having failed all items contained in that scale. Should the individual pass the least difficult, the remaining items could be administered sequentially in increasing difficulty, until a failure occurred. Assuming this latter convention, a reworking of the data reveals that, on the patient sample studied, the Guttman scales would effect a saving of 53 per cent on the number of items which would require to be administered.

It must be admitted that the number of patients tested was relatively small (n=20). This was because of the time required to administer all items to each patient. Replication on a further group of hemiplegic patients is awaited, although, in further support of the above findings, it must be stated that the criteria for Guttman scales are very strict, and that it is to be expected that the scales should survive cross-validation.

Although the new ADL test will have been validated on hemiplegics it is likely that other groups of physically disabled for whom a particular limb or pattern of movement is impaired may produce Guttman-type scales of ADL too. Further studies are needed to ascertain this.

Relevance of Cognitive Factors

The assessment of physical disability is a relatively new area of interest for psychologists, who have more traditionally been associated with assessing cognitive function per se. Since this subject is dealt with more extensively elsewhere in this book, no attempt will be made here to present an overview of the kinds of cognitive assessments which are likely to be encountered currently. However, cognitive assessments are only useful in so far as they allow us to predict an individual's likely behaviour, and although cognitive testing is relatively well developed and established within clinical psychology there has been little attempt so far to use this information systematically to predict the individual patient's ability to survive independently within society. Thus, although we might be able to say that a patient had an IQ at the 40th percentile, we would be unable to predict with any confidence whether he might be able to use a bank account, or to organise shopping and self-care activities.

One of the best-known memory tests, the Wechsler Memory Scale, for instance, simply allows us to compute a 'memory quotient', but leaves us in the dark as to how to use this in predicting the patient's ability to cope with everyday tasks. Just

29

how much memory does a patient require in order to be able to cope with independent existence? And how can he be taught to compensate for this difficulty? For this reason I think it is necessary that we begin to develop measures of cognitive function which are more directly related to competence in activities of daily living. Typical defects which we would wish to identify amongst the elderly would be degrees of apraxia and confusional states, which might impede the performance of certain self-care activities of which the patient might otherwise be physically capable. Broadbent has made a step in this direction with his Cognitive Difficulties Questionnaire (1979). This is basically a checklist of symptoms which the patient himself (perhaps rather ill-advisedly) is asked to complete as they describe his own difficulties. A complicating factor here might be lack of insight, or even memory failure, such that deficits in performance were not even recollected! What is really required is perhaps a memory or more general cognitive assessment, correlated with a measure of performance in activities of daily living. Thus it would be possible to determine at what levels of cognitive impairment various activities began to become impaired. Such knowledge might be useful in deciding whether a patient were fit to return to live alone, or whether, and to what extent, the services of a home-help might be required. It had been hoped to identify statistically cognitive dimensions of ADL within the study described above. Happily, at least one scale so derived appears to test for degrees of ideational apraxia. Research to establish the validity of neuropsychological assessment procedures as predictors of coping behaviour has been insufficient to date, and might repay detailed study by yielding substantial benefits in improving the effectiveness of current rehabilitative practices. One example might be the enhancement of a range of activities by provision of an external prosthetic memory, where apraxic difficulties were evident.

All these approaches represent something of a departure from the almost pure-science approach to cognitive testing which has tended to be the norm so far. It is obvious, however, that our ways of testing individuals will have to change in this direction if we wish to make predictions about their ability to cope with the demands of life.

TABLE 2.1: Test Items (Carroll, 1962)

	Permissible grades			
Bowel and bladder control	0		5	10
Decubitus ulcer	0		5	
Contractures	0		5	
Communication	0	3	5	
Feeding and personal toilet	0		5	10
Dressing	0			10
Propel wheelchair	0		5	10
Move from bed to wheelchair	0			10
Move from wheelchair to bed	0			10
Get on and off toilet	0			10
Walk 100 feet	0			10
Ascend and descend steps	0		5	10

TABLE 2.2: Full List of ADL Items Tested (Lyle, 1980)

1	Standing balance
2	Walk 20 metres
3	Propel wheelchair
4	Operate door lever
5	Operate light switch
6	Operate door knob and key
7	Wash, rinse and wring teatowel
8	Place on pulley and raise
9	Fetch and assemble ironing board
10	Iron towel
11	Sweep with long brush
12	Sweep with short brush and dustpan
13	Wet mop part floor
14	Move bin across floor
15	Operate coin meter
16	Ascend and descend 5 steps
17	Get on and off bus
18	Get into and out of car
19	Upper garment on and off over head
20	Upper garment on and off front opening
21	Lower garment on and off over feet
22	Fit and remove appliance
23	Shoes on and off
24	Dressing gown on and off
25	Socks on and off
26	Stockings or tights on and off

TABLE 2.2 (cont)

27	Menstrual hygiene
28	Empty and change catheter bag
29	(Standing) get stick from floor
30	On and off chair
31	Get up from floor
32	In and out of bed (taking down cover)
33	Tie shoelaces (using board)
34	Take gloves on and off
35	Fasten tie
36	Fasten scarf
37	Fasten buttons (on board)
38	Fasten hooks (on board)
39	Fasten buckles (on board)
40	Fasten zip (on board)
41	Wind watch
42	Take money from purse
43	Produce coins to order
44	Operate telephone
45	Sign name
46	Sew button
47	Use scissors
48	Electric shave
49	Apply lipstick
50	Cut toe and finger nails
51	Brush and comb hair
52	Strip and make bed
53	Plug in to low point and switch on
54	Carry coal bucket
55	Prepare open fire
56	Strike match
57	Dust windowsill
58	Open window
59	Use carpet sweeper
60	Get on and off toilet
61	Use toilet paper
62	Flush toilet
63	Manage clothes at toilet
64	Feel hot and cold taps
65	Simulate wash and dry face
66	Simulate wash and dry neck
67	Simulate washing arms to nails
68	Simulate washing body and back
69	Simulate washing legs and feet
70	Simulate wash and dry hair
71	Brush teeth
72	In, out and soak dentures
73	Wet shave

TABLE 2.2 (cont)

74	In and out bath
75	Drink from mug or straw
76	Sup with spoon
77	Butter bread
78	Cut and eat bread (knife and fork)
79	Eat with fork
80	Eat boiled egg
81	Take plate from high press
82	Open jar
83	Lift bag of tins across room
84	Open tin
85	Turn gas hotplate on and off
86	Fill kettle
87	Put kettle on hotplate
88	Plug kettle in level socket
89	Pour hot water into teapot
90	Pour tea into cup
91	Carry laden tray to low top
92	Put cup and plates on trolley
93	Wheel trolley to sink
94	Turn taps on and off
95	Wash up crockery
96	Dry crockery
97	Take pan and dish from low press
98	Read recipe
99	Peel and cut potatoes
100	Grate and weigh cheese
101	Break eggs
102	Beat eggs
103	Drain potatoes
104	Beat all together
105	Light oven
106	Insert dish in oven
107	Take hot dish from oven
108	Serve onto plate
109	Clean utensils

<u>TABLE 2.3</u>: Scoring Criteria (Lyle, 1980)

0   Can perform no part of the test

1   (If applicable) Performs test partially - can
     complete only with major assistance

2   (If applicable) Completes test with slight
     help or supervision recommended for safety

3   (If applicable) Completes test with specified
     mechanical aid

4   Completes test safely and independently but
     takes a long time or has some difficulty

5   Performs test normally

<u>TABLE 2.4</u>: Equivalent Male and Female ADL Items

25   Socks on and off (men)

26   Stockings or tights on and off (women)

35   Fasten tie (men)

36   Fasten scarf (women)

48   Electric shave (men)

49   Apply lipstick (women)

TABLE 2.5: Guttman-scaled ADL Protocol for Hemiplegia

Patient .... Date ....

Examiner .... Side Impaired ....

Scoring 0 Can perform no part of test.
        1 If applicable - performs test partially, can complete only with major assistance.
        2 If applicable - completes test with slight help or supervision recommended for safety.
        3 If applicable - completes test with specified mechanical aid.
        4 Completes test safely and independently but takes a longer time or has some difficulty.
        5 Performs test normally.

Instructions to Examiner:

This ADL measure has been specially constructed to speed up testing time. It is divided into twelve sub-scales. Items within each sub-scale are credited as passes, if the patient attains or exceeds the score point indicated in brackets following that item. Items within each sub-scale are ordered in such a way that if the patient passes the first item (the most difficult) he would almost certainly pass every other item at the score levels indicated. Thus, if a pass is obtained on Item 1 the patient is credited as having passed all items of that sub-scale, at least at the score levels indicated, without having to be tested on the remaining sub-scale items. Items so credited should be indicated by a tick. If the patient scores a fail on Item 1, then Item 2 is next administered. Item 2 is the easiest item in that sub-scale, and if the patient fails to pass that item at the specified score level, then he is unlikely to achieve a pass on any item in that sub-scale. Thus, he is credited with a zero score for that sub-scale, and you should move to the next sub-scale.

    Should the patient who has failed to pass Item 1 at the specified level, succeed in passing Item 2, then subsequent items within the sub-scale should be administered in the order laid out in the form. Testing on that sub-scale can safely be terminated when the patient fails to pass an item at the specified score level.

    This sounds complicated to explain, but is easy in practice. The result is an average saving of approximately 50 per cent in testing time.

Examples:

Example 1:

(5)

✓	ADL
✓	ADL
✓	ADL
✓	ADL
4	Total

ADL	26	(4)	Stockings tights or socks on and off
ADL	49	(4)	Elecshave or lipstick
ADL	44	(4)	Operate telephone
ADL	96	(4)	Dry crockery

The patient scored (5) for item one, and hence was credited as having passed all other items in the sub-scale.

Example 2:

(2)
(2)

✗	ADL
✗	ADL
✗	ADL
✗	ADL
0	Total

ADL	52	(4)	Strip and make bed
ADL	95	(4)	Wash up crockery
ADL	109	(4)	Clean utensils
ADL	97	(4)	Take pan and dish from low press

The patient scored (2) on Item (1), and (2) on Item (2). Thus he is considered to have failed all items in the sub-scale.

Example 3:

(3)
(3)

✗	ADL
✓	ADL
✗	ADL
✗	ADL
✗	ADL
✗	ADL
✗	ADL
1	Total

ADL	60	(4)	Get on and off toilet
ADL	60	(3)	Get on and off toilet
ADL	105	(4)	Light oven
ADL	12	(4)	Sweep with short brush and dustpan
ADL	11	(4)	Sweep with long brush
ADL	13	(4)	Wet-mop part floor
ADL	31	(4)	Get up from floor

The patient scored (3) on Item (1), and (3) on Item (2), but failed subsequent items on the sub-scale.

Guttman Scale: Balance
(cutting scores in brackets)

ADL	9	(4)	Fetch and assemble ironing board
ADL	1	(3)	Standing balance
ADL	2	(3)	Walk 20 metres
ADL	1	(4)	Standing balance
ADL	29	(4)	(Standing) get stick from floor
ADL	81	(4)	Take plate from high press
ADL	16	(3)	Ascend and descend 5 steps
ADL	16	(4)	Ascend and descend 5 steps
ADL	17	(4)	Get on and off bus
ADL	2	(4)	Walk 20 metres
ADL	50	(4)	Cut toe and finger nails
Total			

Guttman Scale: Two Hands

ADL	84	(4)	Open tin
ADL	40	(4)	Fasten zip on board
ADL	39	(4)	Fasten buckle on board
ADL	107	(4)	Take hot dish from oven
ADL	80	(4)	Eat boiled egg
ADL	91	(4)	Carry laden tray to low top
Total			

Guttman Scale: One Hand

ADL	84	(3)	Open tin
ADL	108	(3)	Serve onto plate
ADL	104	(3)	Beat all together
ADL	79	(3)	Eat with fork
ADL	37	(4)	Fasten buttons on board
ADL	30	(4)	On and off chair
ADL	15	(4)	Operate coin meter
ADL	21	(4)	Lower garment on and off over feet
ADL	20	(4)	Upper garment (front opening) on and off
ADL	10	(4)	Iron towel
Total			

Guttman Scale: Two Wrists

ADL	99	(4)	Peel and cut potatoes
ADL	79	(4)	Eat with fork
ADL	104	(4)	Beat all together
ADL	7	(4)	Wash, rinse and wring teatowel
ADL	60	(4)	Get on and off toilet
Total			

Guttman Scale: Shoulders

ADL	60	(4)	Get on and off toilet
ADL	60	(3)	Get on and off toilet
ADL	105	(4)	Light oven
ADL	12	(4)	Sweep with short brush and dustpan
ADL	11	(4)	Sweep with long brush
ADL	13	(4)	Wet-mop part floor
ADL	31	(4)	Get up from floor
Total			

Guttman Scale: Arms

ADL	8	(4)	Place on pulley and raise
ADL	82	(4)	Open screw top jar
ADL	69	(4)	Simulate washing, legs and feet
ADL	86	(4)	Fill kettle
ADL	51	(4)	Brush and comb hair
ADL	42	(4)	Take money from purse
ADL	3	(4)	Propel wheelchair
ADL	19	(4)	Upper garment on and off over head
ADL	24	(4)	Dressing gown on and off
ADL	14	(4)	Move bin across floor
Total			

Guttman Scale: Pinch

ADL	78	(4)	Cut and eat bread (knife and fork)
ADL	77	(3)	Butter bread
ADL	100	(3)	Grate and weigh cheese
ADL	67	(3)	Simulate washing arms to nails
ADL	67	(4)	Simulate washing arms to nails
ADL	100	(4)	Grate and weigh cheese
ADL	77	(4)	Butter bread
ADL	78	(3)	Cut and eat bread (knife and fork)
Total			

Guttman Scale: Gripforce

ADL	54	(4)	Carry coal bucket
ADL	90	(4)	Pour tea into cup
ADL	57	(4)	Dust windowsill
ADL	89	(4)	Pour hot water in teapot
ADL	85	(4)	Turn gas hotplate on and off
ADL	62	(4)	Flush toilet
ADL	106	(4)	Insert dish in oven
ADL	87	(4)	Put kettle on hotplate
ADL	83	(3)	Lift bag of tins across room
ADL	59	(4)	Use carpet sweeper
ADL	6	(4)	Operate door knob and key
ADL	83	(4)	Lift bag of tins across room
Total			

Guttman Scale: Adroit

ADL	26	(4)	Stockings tights or socks on and off
ADL	49	(4)	Elecshave or lipstick
ADL	44	(4)	Operate telephone
ADL	96	(4)	Dry crockery
Total			

Guttman Scale: Complex 'A'

ADL	52	(4)	Strip and make bed
ADL	95	(4)	Wash up crockery
ADL	109	(4)	Clean utensils
ADL	97	(4)	Take pan and dish from low press
Total			

Guttman Scale: Complex 'B'

ADL	70	(4)	Simulate wash and dry hair
ADL	92	(4)	Put cup and plates on trolley
ADL	103	(4)	Drain potatoes
ADL	53	(4)	Plug in to low point and switch on
ADL	72	(4)	In, out and soak dentures
Total			

Guttman Scale: Plan

ADL	18	(4)	Get in and out of car
ADL	43	(4)	Produce coins to order
ADL	55	(4)	Prepare open fire
ADL	47	(4)	Use scissors
ADL	98	(4)	Follow recipe
ADL	56	(3)	Strike match
Total			

References

Buchwald, E. (1952) Physical Rehabilitation for Daily Living, McGraw-Hill, New York.

Carroll, D. (1962) 'The Disability in Hemiplegia Caused by Cerebrovascular Disease: Serial Studies of 98 Cases', Journal of Chronic Diseases, 15, 179-88.

Donaldson, S.W., Wagner, C.C. and Gresham, G.E. (1973) 'Unified ADL Assessment Form', Archives of Physical Medicine and Rehabilitation, 54, 175-9.

Granger, C.V., Sherwood, C.C. and Greer, D.S. (1977) 'Functional Status Measures in a Comprehensive Stroke Care Program', Archives of Physical Medicine and Rehabilitation, 58, 555-61.

Halstead, L. and Hartley, R.B. (1975) 'Time Care Profile: An Evaluation of a New Method of Assessing ADL Dependence', Archives of Physical Medicine and Rehabilitation, 56, 110-15.

Katz, S., Downs, T.D., Cash, H.R. and Grotz, R.C. (1970) 'Progress in Development of the Index of ADL', Gerontologist, 10, 20-30.

Lawton, E.B. (1963) Activities of Daily Living for Physical Rehabilitation. McGraw-Hill, New York.

Lawton, M.P. and Brody, E.M. (1969) 'Assessment of Older People: Self-maintaining and Instrumental ADL', Gerontologist, 9, 179-86.

Lyle, R.C. (1980) Functional Assessment and Biofeedback Treatment of the Upper Limb in Hemiplegia, unpublished PhD thesis, University of Edinburgh.

Mahoney, F.I. and Barthel, D.W. (1965) 'Functional Evaluation: The Barthel Index', Maryland Sate Medical Journal, 14, 61-5.

Nie, N.H., Hull, C.H., Jenkins, J.G., Steinbrenner, K. and Bent, D.H. (1975) Statistical Package for the Social Sciences (2nd edn), McGraw-Hill, New York.

Schoening, H.A. and Iversen, I.A. (1968) 'Numerical Scoring of Self-care Status', Archives of Physical Medicine and Rehabilitation, 49, 221-9.

Chapter Three

ASSESSMENT OF BEHAVIOURAL IMPAIRMENT IN THE ELDERLY: A REVIEW

Chris Gilleard

Introduction

Growth in the numbers of elderly infirm residents in both the community and in health and social service institutions since the last world war continues to be a matter of national concern. The factors determining admission and continued residency in institutions, as well as the costs of community health and social services, are increasingly being seen in terms of level of disability or functional competence of the individual (Lowenthal, Berkman and associates, 1967; Wright, 1974; Opit, 1977). Socialised medicine and public accountability require a continual monitoring of services and service users, an important part of which involves the quantification of demand. One element in this process is the evaluation of 'functional status' or 'behavioural competence' in elderly people.

In this chapter the three main approaches to measuring behavioural impairment in the elderly will be described, namely, survey indices, global ratings of impairment and behaviour rating scales. Following this descriptive outline, I shall consider in some detail the content of the various measures, in particular the distinct content areas of behavioural disability versus behavioural disturbance. This reflects the two backgrounds of chronic illness and psychiatry, the former dealing mostly with 'acts of omission', and the latter concentrating on 'acts of commission'. Finally, I hope to bring out two of the central issues concerning these types of assessment – the scaling of disability as a unidimensional construct, and the limitations in the search for an adequate dimensional structure in rating scales for the elderly. The summary at the end offers an ecological alternative.

Survey Methods

Most surveys of the elderly have included some index of health status or functional incapacity, often relying upon questions directed to the older person regarding his abilities to perform key activities of daily living (ADL function). One of the early examples was Townsend's index of incapacity, which listed such questions as 'Can you get out of doors?', 'Can you wash and bathe yourself?', and 'Can you cut your own toe nails?' (Townsend, 1962, 1963). Each question is then scored according to the degree of difficulty/assistance needed for each activity. Such surveys of the elderly in the community have tended to assume the accuracy of the person's self-reported incapacity, conditions which may be better met in the community than in residential settings where a significant proportion of elderly people may be confused and unreliable recorders of their present functional status. More recently, attempts have been made to check the validity of such self-reports with mixed results (Garrad and Bennett, 1971; Kuriansky et al., 1976). The parallel that exists between such inventories and observer-completed rating scales is quite close, but at present there is little evidence to support the equivalence of data generated by these two means. In the related field of rehabilitation, Safilios-Rothschild (1970) has reviewed several studies indicating 'interesting and little understood discrepancies between objective and subjective evaluations' (p.218). Kuriansky et al. (1976) have pointed out that important discrepancies exist between self-report, observer-report, and performance-based report in evaluating ADL function in the elderly.

Global Ratings

In the field of chronic disease, early attempts were made to rate disability status by simplified unidimensional rating schemes (cf. Zeman, 1947; Steinbrocker et al., 1949). Considerable unreliability has been demonstrated for such procedures (Hutchinson et al., 1979), and even when detailed rating point instructions are given, global judgements of disability or self-sufficiency remain extremely unreliable (Robertson and Malchik, 1968). Agreement between professionals, and agreement between professionals and relatives is equally affected (cf. Safilios-Rothschild, 1970). Attempts to encapsulate more than one simple dimension have been made (e.g. Krauss, 1962; Gordon et al., 1962), but by maintaining the same level of generality these methods remain equally subject to the criticisms of the single global rating.

Behaviour Ratings

In psychiatric settings, early behaviour rating scales attempted considerable specificity by including a large number of items in the scales, each with a 'yes/no' response format (see Hall, 1980, for a review). This style of nurse-completed rating scale was taken over and applied to geriatric settings or chronic medical illness wards by a number of researchers (Burdock et al., 1960; Shatin et al., 1961). Since the majority of geriatric mental patients involved in these early studies were long-stay, chronically-ill psychotics, the items specified in the ratings were often irrelevant as behavioural descriptions for the present psycho-geriatric and geriatric residents in institutional care. Nevertheless, because of the instability of psychopathology and attendant concern over diagnostic reliablity in psychiatry, more emphasis was placed upon specification and reliability in the development of these scales.

The Content of Behaviour Assessment Measures

It is in the last two decades that measurement concerns have produced, albeit slowly, an increasing convergence between these three styles of evaluation. Global ratings have been increasingly replaced by staff-completed detailed ADL scales in the field of geriatrics and rehabilitation medicine. Nevertheless, the satisfactoriness of such a unidimensional approach to the measurement of disability and change has itself come under criticism (Albrecht and Higgins, 1977). In the psychiatric area, presumably as a result in the shift from graduate to psychogeriatric patients in hospitals, the content of rating scales has shifted from the psychopathology toward the self-care-impairment axis (cf. Honigfeld, 1981). In addition to the developments in the content of these measures, there has been increasing interest in the scaling and construct validity of these scales. This interest has focused on identifying sources of variance in rating

scales of disability (cf. Gurel et al., 1972), and
identifying the developmental scaling of disability
(cf. Williams et al., 1976). Each of these issues
will be reviewed in turn.

Content Analyses and the Dimensions of Disability

Donaldson et al. (1973) reviewed the content of 25
scales developed to evaluate 'activities of daily
living' (ADL). Although these scales are not confined
in their application to elderly populations, they are
all of direct relevance to this age group. Almost
three-quarters (71 per cent) of the scales included
the following items: ability to dress; to walk; to
bathe; to eat; to visit the toilet; to transfer from
bed to chair and from a chair to standing up. Items
relating more directly to cognitive status were
infrequent (about one-quarter included items
relevant to communication, memory, orientation and
'grasp'). One half included items on continence.
Aspects of social and emotional behaviour are notably
absent.

Honigfeld (1981) has recently reviewed
geriatric ward behaviour rating scales, most of which
were derived from an earlier review by Salzman et al.
(1972), and then updated. While not providing much
detail of their content, he argued that most of the
items could be divided into two groups, those
referring to psychopathology and interpersonal
functioning, and those referring to self-care-
impairment (a term obviously allied to ADL content).

A more satisfactory approach to identifying the
axes of behavioural impairment in the elderly is to
consider studies which have factor analysed rating
scale data from evaluation of elderly residents in
care. Several such studies have been carried out
(Meer and Baker, 1966; Pichot et al., 1970; van der
Kam et al., 1971; Gurel et al., 1972; Lawson et al.,
1977; Smith et al., 1977; Wimmers and Van Eckelen,
1978; Csapo, 1981; Twining and Allen, 1981).
Although, as Smith (1979) has pointed out, factor
analytic techniques remain tied to the choice of
items employed, and the group from which the results
are obtained, such a review provides a handy
starting-point to examine content areas. (Table
3.1).

Consideration of such factor analytic studies
indicates that three consistent sources of
disability emerge, reflecting physical disability or
self-care impairment, impairment of cognitive
functions, and social-emotional behaviour disturbance (dimensions I, II and III). A fourth source of

variance, 'apathy' or 'withdrawal', is identifiable, while disturbance of communication and mood appear in only one or two studies.

It is apparent, however, than even when fairly similar rating scales are used, the structure is not always constant. Pichot et al. (1970) in their analysis of the Stockton Geriatric Rating Scale (Meer and Baker, 1966) failed to find evidence of a 'communication failure' dimension, while Twining and Allen (1981), in a study of a modified version of the same scale, failed to identify an 'apathy' dimension. Different multivariate analyses of the same scale have also led to different interpretations. Wimmers and Van Eckelen (1978), in an analysis of the Rating Scale for Older Patients (BOP), observed a two-dimensional solution from ratings of nursing home residents using Smallest Space Analysis techniques (Bailey, 1974), contrasting with the four-dimensional structure originally derived from the factor analysis of the scale, reported by van der Kam et al. (1971) while 'the most important scale, Scale I, General Need of Help (Dependency) did not appear to form a distinct cluster' (Wimmers and Van Eckelen, 1978, p.8). As Smith (1979), Gilleard and Pattie (1980) and Twining and Allen (1981) have all recently pointed out, dimensions of disablity may not be invariant across differing populations of elderly people, with the clustering of items varying according to the health characteristics of the subject populations.

The present author has carried out a survey of some 28 rating scales developed for use with elderly patients. After listing the content of these scales, in terms common to two or more scales, ten clinical psychologists, working with the elderly, were asked to allocate each item into one of the six areas identified from the factor analyses given in Table 3.1. Forty-nine out of 67 items were allocated to the content area judged by the author to be the most appropriate in 80 per cent or more instances, and only four items had less than 50 per cent agreement. A summary of the scales, their number of items, response points and content areas are indicated in Appendix 3.1.

Apart from purely descriptive information, it is apparent that scales with few (less than 12) items have a wide response format (four or more response points) while those scales with many (more than 36) items invariably have a yes/no response format. Secondly, scales with few items tend to focus upon physical disability/self-care impairment, while those with many items focus more on social interaction/disturbance and mood-related items. This can be seen as reflecting the distinction between defined psychiatric statements of pathological behaviour, and global, chronic illness statements of disability. At the same time, scales developed since 1970 can be seen as having a broader, more evenly spread set of items, compared with those developed prior to 1970, suggesting that the convergence of a multidimensional framework for evaluating disability attended to earlier is becoming apparent from the activities of scale constructors. Nevertheless, there remains a discrepancy between the ADL approach and the behaviour rating scale approach, reflected in the continued separation of ADL scales and general behaviour rating scales, and the retained interest in a single construct of disability, compared with multivariate conceptions of disability.

ADL Scales: Specifying the Steps in Disability Scaling

Employing a single construct of disability or ADL dependency has led to some methodological and theoretical consideration of the development and course of disability in the elderly. Katz et al. (1963) formulated the principle of 'an ordered regression as part of the natural process of ageing' paralleling a primary biological and psychosocial pattern of child development. This intrinsic pattern of disability has been recently further explored by Williams (Williams et al., 1976; Williams, 1979), who sees both the development of disability and recovery from disability as following a cumulative and unidimensional pattern, appropriately measured by Guttman Scale techniques. Measures which follow a Guttman Scale pattern allow one to identify which disablities are present, from a knowledge of how many disabilities are present. For example, Katz et al. (1963) reported that 86 per cent of the 1,001 elderly patients rated on their scale fell into a single pattern, ranging from independence, through dependency in bathing, then dressing, going to the toilet, transferring, continence, and finally feeding. Patients unable to feed themselves, therefore, could not remain continent, could not move in or out of a bed or chair, could not manage going to the toilet, could not dress themselves, nor bathe themselves. Such intrinsic patterning of disability according to Guttman Scale criteria has been proposed to provide an effective index of the construct validity of ADL rating schemes. More recently,

Williams (1979) has suggested that such patterns demonstrate not a biological, mechanistic relationship between physical impairment and disability, but the effect of socialisation, which he argues determines the choice of activities given up or taken on following illness and impairment. Williams suggests that this deviancy model of disability applies much more to the pattern of recovery from illness or impairment than to the pattern of deterioration, which he suggests is less susceptible to social control.

An important consequence of this model is the assumed influence of the patient's social group on the normative expectations regarding what activities should or should not be taken on or given up during the course of illness or recovery. A good Guttman Scale therefore will not be universally applicable across all social groups, since any pattern will be socially selected. Such hypotheses have been examined primarily from the results of interview-based scales of disability, relying upon what people say they can or cannot do. It remains open whether either the methodology or the theory apply to the observed ratings of behaviour carried out on institutionalised populations. Demonstrated Guttman Scale patterns in the behaviour ratings of psychogeriatric patients have, for example, been taken to reflect the biological/mechanical influences of progressive dementia (Gilleard and Pattie, 1980), and such patterns may be restricted equally by diagnostic specifications as by specifications of sociocultural sub-groups. Perhaps the importance of Williams' work for assessment of behaviour in the elderly is that it emphasises the danger of assuming an absolute invariance to scales designed to assess the elderly, and the need to be aware of the influence of environmental factors in determining not only the level of impairment, but the form that impairment takes. The work of Willems (Willems, 1974, 1977) is also relevant here in demonstrating the socio-ecological variability in patients' level of functioning. This fact is well recognised clinically by hospital and other personnel involved in the institutional care of the elderly. A frequent comment is made to the effect that even some quite demented patients, who appear to require the assistance of two nurses to visit the dining-room occasionally will be spotted shuffling along the corridor, with only the help of somebody else's Zimmer.

Such factors have been emphasised recently in a

slightly different context by Dunt et al. (1980). These authors have pointed out that besides issues of 'type of scaling', scales of disability may have their validity impaired by the variability in response format. For any given aspect of ADL performance, they identify three sources of variation. First, whether 'usual' or 'optimal' performance is being considered - 'Do you/does he/she' versus 'Can you/can he/she ...'; secondly, the regularity of performance - 'Every day' versus 'Some days'; thirdly, nature of assistance 'With aids' versus 'With help'. When performance of ADL items is recorded in unspecified or variable circumstances, they demonstrate that the resulting scores obtained from ratings can vary quite considerably, emphasising the need for precise specification of the conditions under which any given disability may manifest itself. One further point, not made by these authors but of obvious relevance, is that the very existence of aids or appliances may vary according to the environment in which the elderly person is living, thus altering the context of the disability and its consequent validity. Is an elderly person living at home, unable to walk about the house, and without sticks or a Zimmer, or a son or daughter, as disabled as an elderly person who possesses a Zimmer, or who lives with a daughter? The former cannot walk (she has no daughter to lean on, the house or flat will not allow her the space to learn to use the Zimmer) the latter can.

Clearly, it is not only the social environment that influences disability, but the broader ecological context. Increasing specifications of items, as suggested by Dunt et al. (1980), will go some way to sharpening the assessments made, but even such an increase in precision will not completely alleviate the problems. The psychological truism 'behaviour is the function of person, environment and person environment interaction' (cf. Lawton, 1977) is unavoidable, and the reduction of disability to either a biological or a social construct is unsatisfactory. Under these circumstances, despite the value of recent methodological developments, it seems unlikely that a single 'disability' scale will prove adequate for either clinical or research needs.

Multi-dimensional Behaviour Ratings: The Limits of a Dimensional Model of Impairment

While the preceding section has tried to illustrate some of the advantages and hazards in the use of single indices of disability, a similar pattern of more sophisticated developments and an accompanying awareness of methodological problems can be noted in recent research upon multidimensional rating scales. Most recent reviews have recognised the importance of the Stockton Geriatric Rating Scale in the development of an age-appropriate, multidimensional rating scale for elderly institutionalised people (cf. Salzman et al., 1972; Honigfeld, 1981). It has been translated into many languages (Pichot et al., 1970; Van der Kam et al., 1971; Asanc et al., 1981) cross-validated (Taylor and Bloom, 1974; Dastoor et al., 1975) and variously modified (Plutchik et al., 1970; Gilleard and Pattie, 1977).

The fact that there continues to be development of new rating scales for use with the elderly in institutional care however, may indicate the dissatisfaction felt with the SGRS and its derivations. Various criticisms have been made of the scales, including their over-generality (Wilkinson and Graham-White, 1980), the instability of the dimensional structure (Twining and Allen, 1981) and the over-reliance on quantification of aggregated disabilities (Powell-Proctor et al., 1981). Smith (1979) has suggested that the GRS (Geriatric Rating Scale, a modified version of the SGRS) is insensitive to change, while Pablo (1976) has reported that the PAMIE (Physical and Mental Impairment-of-Functional Evaluation, a scale similar to the SGRS in its multidimensional framework) has low inter-rater reliability.

It can be argued that, as with single ADL scales, no completely satisfactory multidimensional scale can be produced. Specific itemised behavioural deficits may reflect a diverse number of influences, including the degree of CNS, musculo-skeletal and other systemic deficits, the richness or poverty of institutional environments, social expectations and norms in such settings, and the cognitive-perceptual frameworks of staff in differing settings, each of which will lead to different and varying patterns of aggregated disability. A relevant case in point can be seen in the present interest in the dimension of 'engagement' applied to the behaviour of elderly people in institutions (Blunden and Kushlik, 1975). While bearing some similarity to the factor analytic dimension of 'apathy/withdrawal versus socialisation' (see Table 3.1), this construct has recently been emphasised because it offers a clear separation from more biologically-oriented impairments. Thus, McFadyen et al., (1980) speak of 'the advantages of focusing on engagement (which) lies in the possibility of improving the quality of life in the institutionalised elderly even if we cannot substantially reverse the behavioural consequences of the pathology'. An important and distinctive feature of studies on engagement in the institutionalised elderly has been the use of direct behavioural observation, in contrast to observer completed rating scales (cf. McCallahan and Risley, 1975; Jenkins et al., 1977; Burton, 1980; McFadyen et al., 1980). While quantifying in detail the effects of specified interventions, this approach leaves open the problem of validating the choice of behaviour recordings being made. What precisely is engagement? Does the same act or activity have similar behavioural experiential correlates across both persons and situations, and what is the normative significance of activity levels in old age?

The validity of the equation active = happy, inactive = sad/unhealthy will not be considered in great detail here. However, it should be pointed out that several studies have emphasised that generalised level of activity/engagement is not significantly related to subjective well-being in the institutionalised aged (e.g. Simpson et al., 1981). Even if there were no problems with its measurement, the clinical significance of the construct is not free from criticism. Certainly, the behaviour analytical approach has contributed to a move away from the pitfalls of generalised ratings to concentrate upon observed recordings of ongoing activity in the institutionalised elderly. The point made by McFadyen et al. (1980) that records of engaged behaviour may be independent of pathologically-determined behaviour deficits, and hence be more open to intervention, is one which helps shift the emphasis on disability. Jenkins et al. (1977) suggest that 'low levels of observed activity may be as much a function of very limited opportunities to engage in activities, as of the characteristics as disabilities of the residents.' Unfortunately, this lack of separation between person and environment variables is itself problematic, especially when, as most studies to date seem to have done, engagement or activity level is treated as a linear quantitative construct, i.e. one is more or less engaged/active. There may be, for example, important qualitative distinctions between passive engagement and active engagement, between goal-directed and diffuse activity, and between self-selected and externally imposed engagement. Willems (1974) has outlined a more detailed critique of the lack of ecological context in much of behaviour analysis methodology which may reduce the validity of such measurement approaches.

Perhaps the most important contributions made by this move towards detailed behaviour recording of activity levels, are the de-emphasising of pathological constructs of disability in evaluating the behaviour of the institutionalised elderly, and recognition of the importance of environmental manipulations in enhancing the quality of life for such populations. Although it is necessary to recognise the effects of ageing and disease on the behavioural competence of the elderly, it is important to recognise that there are other dimensions of behaviour which require attention and intervention, and that even in those areas of behaviour traditionally assumed to bear the closest relationship with impairment - the ADL measures - social and physical environmental features contribute in significant ways to the level of attained competence.

In short, the multidimensional analysis of persons may be seen as providing only half the solution, and further directions may arise from similar multidimensional analyses of environments and care settings. The work of Moos and colleagues in the Social Ecology Laboratory at Stanford represents an important advance in devising assessments of care settings for the elderly (Moos and Lemke, 1979, 1980), developments which can be seen in other related health care areas such as mental handicap (Raynes, et al., 1979; Pratt et al., 1980). The numerous intervention studies which have failed to produce significant behavioural change, measured by multidimensional ratings of the residents' or patients' disabilities which in turn have led some to advocate a more critical approach to the possibilities of change in the elderly impaired, (cf. Wershow, 1977) could be replaced by a different type of evaluative study. For example, evaluating the impact of 24-hour Reality Orientation programmes could involve measuring the behaviour of staff towards patients, and changes in how staff perceive (construe) their patients. If the eyes of the behavioural observer can be switched from steadily following the elderly patient around the ward, to viewing the social and physical environment of the ward itself, a more valid perspective in health care evaluation may thus be achieved.

Summary

The present chapter has reviewed methods currently employed to measure behavioural competence in the elderly, particularly the elderly in need of care. It seems clear that such measurement involves statements about acts which should not occur - like incontinence, shouting, wandering - and acts which should, but in some cases do not occur - like dressing oneself, walking about a room and cutting one's toe nails. Emphasis on the latter tends to produce single indices of disability, based on a score-card of acts of omission, while emphasis on the former produces a multidimensional charting of acts of commission. It seems likely that both measures are subject to biological/mechanical and social/environmental influences. A measure of incompetence is not therefore the constitutional possession of an elderly patient, and is consequently capable of being altered by both positive and negative medical and environmental interventions. The limits of such interventions remain unknown challenges, to future researches into environmental, psychological and medical management approaches to impaired elderly persons.

Note

1. Raskin, A. and Crook, T.H. (1981) Nurses' Assessment of Global Symptomatology - Elderly (NAGS-E) Rating Scale, Psychopharmacology Research Branch, NIMH.

TABLE 3.1: Factor Analytic Studies of Behaviour Rating Scales for the Elderly

Studies	Dimensions					
	1	2	3	4	5	6
Meer and Baker (1966)	physical disability	apathy	socially irritating behaviour	-	communication failure	-
van der Kam et al. (1971)	general dependency	inactivity	aggressiveness	mental vs. physical disability	-	-
Gurel et al. (1972)	physical infirmity	-	psychological agitation	psychological deterioration	-	-
Lawson et al. (1977)	motor ability	-	emotional control	disorientation	communication	-
Smith et al. (1977)	deficits in acts of daily living	withdrawal/ apathy	anti-social disruptive behaviour	-	-	-
Csapo (1981)	self-care impairment	withdrawal	interpersonal behaviour	disorientation	-	mood
Twining and Allen (1981)	physical impairment	-	social impairment	mental impairment	-	-

APPENDIX 3.1: Content Analysis of Behaviour Rating Scales for use with the Elderly

Authors	No of items	Response points	Physical disability	Social activity	Communication difficulties	Cognitive dysfunction	Social disturbance	Mood	Other
Robinson (1961)	10	5	4	1	1	1	0	2	1
Shatin et al. (1961)	82	2	11	43	5	7	4	7	-
*Kelman and Muller (1962)	5	5	5	0	0	0	0	0	0
Krauss (1962)	3	4	2	0	0	0	1	0	1
*Gordon et al.	3	4	2	1	0	0	0	0	0
Katz et al. (1963)	6	3	6	0	0	0	0	0	0
Meer and Krag (1964)	15	3	9	1	2	0	1	0	2
Burdock et al. (1966)	110	2	6	38	4	8	19	7	-
Freeman and Murray (1966)	12	4	1	2	1	2	2	3	1
Meer and Baker (1966)	33	3	8	7	3	2	8	0	5
Linn (1967)	16	3	8	1	2	1	1	2	0
Watson and Fulton (1967)	5	8	5	0	0	0	0	0	0
Gottfries and Gottfries (1968)	126	2	45	17	2	31	0	23	0
Trier (i)	8	V*	4	2	1	0	0	0	1
(ii)	13	4	0	0	0	8	0	4	1
Lawton and Brodie (1969)	6	5	6	0	0	0	0	0	0

APPENDIX (Continued)

Authors	No of items	Response points	Physical disability	Social activity	Communication difficulties	Cognitive dysfunction	Social disturbance	Mood	Other
Plutchik et al. (1970)	31	3	7	9	2	0	8	0	5
van der Kam et al. (1971)	35	3	7	6	3	3	8	3	5
Gurel et al. (1972)	77	2	22	10	3	4	11	19	17
Waldton (1973)	29	V*	12	5	0	1	3	1	7
Ferm (1974)	13	6	6	3	1	2	0	0	1
Miller and Parachek (1974)	10	5	7	3	0	0	0	0	0
Dastoor et al. (1975)	28	2	2	20	1	0	0	0	5
Grauer and Birnbom (1975)	26	V*	4	0	3	4	2	0	13
Lawson et al. (1977)	27	2	-	-	-	-	-	-	-
Clarke et al. (1979)	5	V*	5	0	0	0	0	0	0
Wilkinson and Graham-White (1980)	39	V*	12	0	2	10	13	1	1
Csapo (1981)	40	4	8	8	2	6	4	11	1
Raskin and Crook	21	5	2	2	1	4	3	7	2

Note *V = variable response format.

References

Albrecht, G.L. and Higgins, P.C. (1977) 'Rehabilitation Success: the Inter-relationships of Multiple Criteria', Journal of Health and Social Behaviour, 18.

Asano, H., Maeda, D. and Yagrehi, K. (1981) 'Subjective Well-being of the Residents in Old People's Homes', paper presented at the 12th International Congress of Gerontology, 12-17 July, Hamburg.

Bailey, K.D. (1974) 'Interpreting Smallest Space Analysis', Sociological Methods and Research, Vol. 3, No. 1.

Blunden, R. and Kushlik, A. (1975) 'Looking for Practical Solutions', Age Concern Today, 13, 2-5.

Burdock, E.J., Elliot, H.E., Hardesty, A., O'Neill, F.J. and Sklar, J., (1960) 'Biometric Evaluation of an Intensive Treatment Program in a State Mental Hospital'. Journal of Nervous and Mental Diseases, 130, 271-7.

Burton, M. (1980) 'Evaluation and Change in a Psychogeriatric Ward through Observation and Feedback', British Journal of Psychiatry, 137, 566-71.

Clarke, M., Hughes, A.O., Dodd, K.J., Palmer, R.L., Brandon, S., Holden, A.M. and Pearce, D. (1979) 'The Elderly in Residential Care: Patterns of Disability', Health Trends, 11, 17-20.

Csapo, K. (1981) 'Development of a Functional Rating Scale for Institutionalised Elderly', paper presented at the 12th International Congress of Gerontology, 12-17 July, Hamburg.

Dastoor, D.P., Norton, S., Boillat, J., Minty, J., Papadopdou, F. and Muller, H.F. (1975) 'A Psychogeriatric Assessment Program 1. Social Functioning and Ward Behaviour', Journal of the American Geriatrics Society, 23, 465-9.

Donaldson, S.W., Conlin, C.W. and Gresham, G.E. (1973) 'A unified ADL Form', Archives of Physical Medicine and Rehabilitation, 54, 175-9.

Dunt, D.R., Kaufert, J.M., Corkhill, R., Creese, A.L., Green, S. and Locker, D. (1980) 'A Technique for Precisely Measuring Activities of Daily Living', Community Medicine, 2, 120-5.

Ferm, L. (1974) 'Behavioural Activities in Demented Geriatric Patients', Gerontologia Clinica, 16, 185-94.

Freeman, H. and Murray, P. (1966) 'Treatment of Aged Psychotic Patients with Hydergine', Gerontologia Clinica, 8, 279-86.

Garrad, J. and Bennett, A.E., (1971) 'A Validated Interview Schedule for Use in Population Surveys of Chronic Disease and Disability', British Journal of Preventitive and Social Medicine, 25, 97-102.

Gilleard, C.J. and Pattie, A.H. (1977) 'The Stockton Geriatric Rating Scale: a Shortened Version with British Normative Data', British Journal of Psychiatry, 131, 90-4.

Gilleard, C.J. and Pattie, A.H. (1980) 'Dimensions of Disability in the Elderly: Construct Validity of Rating Scales for Elderly Populations', paper presented at the annual conference of the British Psychological Society, April, Aberdeen.

Gordon, E.E., Kohn, K., Sloan, J. et al. (1962) 'A Study of Rehabilitation Potential in Nursing Home Patients over 65 Years' Journal of Chronic Diseases, 15, 311-26.

Gottfries, C.G. and Gottfries, I. (1968) 'Psykogeriatriskt Skaltming-schema' (stencil), St Lars Hospital, Lund, Sweden. (English translation, in Adolfsson R. et al. (1981) Acta Psychiatrica Scandinavica, 63, 225-44.)

Grauer, H. and Birnbom, F. (1975) 'A Geriatric Functional Rating Scale to Determine the Need for Institutional Care', Journal of the American Geriatrics Society, 23, 472-6.

Gurel, L., Linn, M.W. and Linn, B.S. (1972) 'Physical and Mental Impairment of Functional Evaluation in the aged: The PAMIE Scale', Journal of Gerontology, 27, 83-90.

Hall, J.N. (1980) 'Ward Rating Scales for Long-stay Patients: A Review', Psychological Medicine, 10, 277-88.

Honigfeld, G. (1981) 'The Evaluation of Ward Behaviour Rating Scales for Psychogeriatric Use', paper presented at the FDA Bureau of Drugs Symposium in the Development of Psychopharmacologic Drugs for the Cognitively and Emotionally Impaired Elderly, Rockville, Maryland, March.

Hutchinson, T.A., Boyd, N.E. and Feinstein, A.R. (1979) 'Scientific Problems in Clinical Scales as Demonstrated in the Karnofsky Index of Performance Status', Journal of Chronic Diseases, 32, 661-6.

Jenkins, J., Felce, D., Lunt, B. and Powell, L. (1977) 'Increasing Engagement in Activity of Residents in Old People's homes by Providing Recreational Materials', Behaviour Research and Therapy, 15, 429-34.

Katz, S., Ford, A.B., Moskowitz, R.W., Jackson, R.A. and Jaffe, M.W. (1963) 'Studies of Illness in the Aged: The Index of ADL', Journal of the American Medical Association, 185, 914-91.

Kellman, H.R. and Wilner, A. (1962) 'Problems in Measurement and Evaluation of Rehabilitation', Archives of Physical Medicine and Rehabilitation, 43, 174-80.

Krauss, T.C. (1962) 'Use of a Comprehensive Rating Scale System in the Institutional Care of Geriatric Patients', Journal of the American Geriatric Society, 10, 95-102.

Kuriansky, J.B., Gurland, B.J. and Fleiss, J.L. (1976) 'The Assessment of Self-care Capacity in Geriatric Psychiatric Patients by Objective and Subjective Methods', Journal of Clinical Psychology, 32, 95-102.

Lawson, J.S., Rodenberg, M. and Dykes, J.A. (1977) 'A Dementia Rating Scale for Use with Psychogeriatric Patients', Journal of Gerontology, 32, 157-9.

Lawton, M.P. and Brodie, E. (1969) 'Assessment of Older People: Self-maintaining and Institutional Activities of Daily Living', Gerontologist, 9, 179-86.

Lawton, M.P. (1977) 'The Impact of the Environment on Aging and Behaviour' in J.E. Birren and K.W. Schaie (eds.), Handbook of Psychology of Aging, Van Norstrond, New York.

Linn, M.W. (1967) 'A Rapid Disability Rating Scale', Journal of the American Geriatrics Society, 15, 211-14.

Lowenthal, M.F., Berkman, P.F. and associates (1967) Ageing and Mental Disorders in San Francisco, Joseey, Bass Inc., San Francisco.

McClannahan, L.E. and Risley, T.R. (1975) 'Design of Living Environments for Nursing Home Residents: Increasing Participation in Recreational Activities', Journal of Applied Behaviour Analysis, 8, 261-8.

McFadyen, M., Prior, T. and Kindness, K. (1980) 'Engagement: an Important Variable in Institutional Care of the Elderly', paper presented at the annual British Psychological Society Conference, Aberdeen, March.

Meer, B. and Baker, J.A. (1966) 'The Stockton Geriatric Rating Scale', Journal of Gerontology, 21, 392-403.

Meer, B. and Krag, C.L. (1964) 'Correlation of Disability in a Population of Hospitalised Geriatric Patients', Journal of Gerontology, 19, 440-6.

Miller, E.R. and Parachek, J.F. (1974) 'Validation and Standardisation of a Goal-oriented Quick Screening, Geriatric Scale', Journal of the American Geriatrics Society, 22, 278-83.

Moos, R.H. and Lemke, S. (1979) Multiphasic Environmental Assessment Procedure: Preliminary Manual, Social Ecology Laboratory, Stanford University School of Medicine, Palo Alto, California.

Moos, R.H. and Lemke, S. (1980) 'The Multiphasic Environmental Assessment Procedure: a Method for Comprehenively Evaluating Sheltered Care-settings' in A. Jeger, and B. Slotnik (eds.), Community Mental Health: A Behavioural/Ecological Perspective, Plenum Press, New York.

Opit, L.J. (1977) 'Domiciliary Care for the Elderly Sick: Economy or Neglect?', British Medical Journal, 30-3.

Pablo, R.Y. (1976) 'The Evaluation of the Physical and Mental Impairments of a Long-term and Rehabilitation Hospital Patient Population', Canadian Journal of Public Health, 67, 305-13.

Pichot, P., Girard, B. and Dreyfus, J.C. (1970) 'L'echelle d'Eppreciation Geriatrique de Stockton (SGRS): Etude de sa Version Francaise' Revue de Psychologie Appliqué, 20, 245-54.

Plutchik, R., Conte, H., Leiberman, M., Bakur, M., Grossman, J. and Lehrman, N. (1970) 'Reliability and Validity of a Scale for Assessing the Functioning of Geriatric Patients', Journal of the American Geriatrics Society, 18, 491-500.

Powell-Proctor, L., Chege, N. and Savage, G. (1981) 'Creating and Working with Small Groups in a Psychogeriatric Hospital Ward', Nursing Times, vol. 77, 1679-82, September.

Pratt, M.W., Luszcz, M.A. and Brown, M.E. (1980) 'Measuring Dimensions of the Quality of Care in Small Community Residences', American Journal of Mental Deficiency, 85, 188-94.

Raynes, N., Pratt, M.W. and Roses, S. (1979) Organisational Structure and the Care of the Mentally Retarded, Croom-Helm, London.

Robertson, R.J. and Malchik, D.L. (1968) 'The Reliability of Global Ratings versus Specific Ratings', Journal of Clinical Psychology, 23, 256-8.

Robinson, R.A. (1961) 'Problems of Drug Trials in Elderly People', Gerontologia Clinica, 3, 247-57.

Safilios-Rothschild, C. (1970) The Sociology and Social Psychology of Disability and Rehabilitation, Random House, New York.

Salzman, C., Shader, R.I., Kochansky, G.E. and Cronin, D.M. (1972) 'Rating Scales for Psychotropic Drug Research with Geriatric Patients. I. Behaviour Ratings', Journal of the American Geriatrics Society, 20, 209-14.

Shatin, L., Brown, P. and Loizeaux, M. (1961) 'Psychological Remotivation of the Chronically-ill Medical Patient', Journal of Chronic Disease, 14, 452-68.

Simpson, S., Woods, R. and Britton, P.G. (1981) 'Depression and Engagement in a Residential Home for the Elderly', Behaviour Research and Therapy, 19, 435-8.

Smith, J.M. (1979) 'Nurse and Psychiatric Aide Rating Scales for Assessing Psychopathology in the Elderly: a Critical Review', in A. Raskin and L.F. Janik (eds.), Psychiatric Symptoms and Cognitive Loss in the Aged, Halstrad Press, New York.

Smith, J.M., Bright, B. and McCloskey, J. (1977) 'Factor Analytic Composition of the Geriatric Rating Scale (GRS)', Journal of Gerontology, 32, 58-62.

Steinbrocker, O., Traeger, C.H. and Balterman, R.C. (1949) 'Therapeutic Criteria in Rheumatoid Arthritis', Journal of the American Medical Association, 140, 659-63.

Taylor, H.G. and Bloom, L.M. (1974) 'Cross Validation and Methodological Extension of the Stockton Geriatric Rating Scale', Journal of Gerontology 29, 190-3.

Townsend, P. (1962) 'Measuring Incapacity for Self-care', Appendix 2, in The Last Refuge, Routledge & Kegan Paul, London.

Townsend, P. (1963) 'Measuring Incapacity for Self-care' in R.H. Williams, C.Tibbitts and W.Donahue (eds.), Processes of Ageing II, p. 272. Atherton Press, New York.

Trier, T.R. (1968) 'A Study of Change among Elderly Psychiatric Inpatients During their First Year of Hospitalisation', Journal of Gerontology, 23, 354-62.

Twining, T.C. and Allen, D.G. (1981) 'Disability Factors among Residents of Old People's Homes', Journal of Epidemiology and Community Health, 35, 205-7.

van der Kam, P., Mol, F. and Wimmers, M.F.H.G. (1971), Beoordelingschael voor Ouden Patienten, (BOP) Van Loghum Slaterus, Deventer, Netherlands.

Waldton, S. (1973) 'Psykiatriska Undersokningar', in S. Waldton (ed.), Dementia Senilis: Sjukdomsbild och Forlopp has 66 Krimliga Patientes (stencil), Karolinska Institute, Stockholm.

Watson, C.G. and Fulton, J.R. (1967) 'Treatment Potential of the Psychiatrically Medically Infirm. I. Self-care Independence', Journal of Gerontology, 22, 449-56.

Wershow, H.J. (1977) 'Comment: Reality Orientation for Gerontologists: Some Thoughts about Senility', Gerontologist, 17, 297-302.

Wilkinson, I.M. and Graham-White, J.G. (1980) 'Dependency Rating Scales for Use in Psychogeriatric Nursing', Health Bulletin (Edinburgh), 38, 36-41.

Willems, E.P. (1974) 'Behavioural Technology and Behavioural Ecology', Journal of Applied Behavioural Analysis, 7, 151-65.

Willems, E.P. (1977) 'Ecological Psychology' in D. Stokols (ed.),

Perspectives on Environment and Behaviour, Theory, Research and Applications, Plenum Press, New York.

Williams, R.G.A. (1979) 'Theories and Measurement in Disability', Journal of Epidemiology and Community Health, 33, 32-47.

Williams, R.G.A., Johnston, M., Willis, L.A. and Bennett, A.E. (1976) 'Disability: a Model and Measurement Technique', British Journal of Preventitive and Social Medicine, 30, 71-8.

Wimmers, M.F.H.G. and van Eckelen, C.W.J.M. (1978) 'The Rating Scale for Older Patients as an Instrument for the Assessment of Nursing Home Residents', Internal Report, 78, 1SG 01, Psychologisch Laboratorium, Katholieke Universiteit Nijmegen, Netherlands.

Wright, K.G. (1974) 'Alternative Measures of the Output of Social Programs: the Elderly', in Culyer, A. (ed.), Economic Policies and Social Goals: Aspects of Public Choice, Martin Robinson, Bath, pp. 239-72.

Zeman, F.D. (1947) 'The Functional Capacity of the Aged, its Estimation and Practical Importance', Journal of the Mount Sinai Hospital, 14, 721-28.

Chapter Four

TOWARDS A BEHAVIOURAL ANALYSIS OF DEMENTIA

John Hodge

Introduction

The behaviour modification approach has proved
itself as a powerful therapeutic tool for many
patient groups. Ullman and Krasner (1975) have
summarised the essential nature of the behavioural
approach as utilising 'systematic environmental
contingences to alter directly the subject's
reactions to situations' (p. 233). Thus changes in
behaviour are effected by the application of the
general principles of operant conditioning.
Behaviour analysis consists of a detailed objective
examination of the situational context of the
behaviour (antecedents), the behaviour itself, and
the consequences of the behaviour for the individual.
This allows problem behaviour to be modified to be
more socially acceptable by manipulating either the
situational context or the consequences. The same
procedures also enable low-frequency adaptive
behaviours to become more firmly established in the
patient's repertoire, thereby aiding the rehabilitative process.
     The effectiveness of this approach has been
demonstrated with chronic schizophrenics (Hall and
Baker, 1973; Kazdin, 1977), autistic children
(Lovaas and Koegel, 1973), the mentally handicapped
(Tennant et al., 1981), brain-damaged individuals
(Peck, 1975; Wood and Eames, 1981) and in the elderly
(Libb and Clements, 1969; Hoyer, 1973; Geiger and
Johnson, 1974). Despite these wide ranges of
application, a recent review of behavioural studies
in the elderly concluded that 'in relation to
dementia ... behaviour modification is an extremely
promising approach, but as yet there remains a lack
of convincing evidence for its effectiveness'
(Holden and Woods, 1982, p. 47). In fact, these same

authors also point out that 'there is disappointingly little research in the use of behaviour modification per se with patients clearly diagnosed as having dementia' (p. 33).

Such a lack of basic knowledge about the applicability of this potentially powerful therapeutic tool to problems of the demented elderly is difficult to justify in view of the size of the dementing population (Arie and Isaacs, 1978), and the fact that dementia often brings with it behaviour changes which often cause significant problems to care-givers both in the community (Gledhill et al., 1982; Gilhooly, Chapter 5, below) and in the hospital (Miller, 1977). The importance of gaining information concerning the utility of behavioural techniques is underlined by recent trends which show that the numbers of the elderly (especially those over 75) are increasing markedly, and, with them, the number of demented elderly (Arie and Isaacs, 1978). If behavioural techniques do prove useful, then their early implementation is esssential, not only to improve the quality of life of the demented patients themselves, but also to relieve the strain suffered by the care-givers (Bergmann et al., 1978; Gilhooly, Chapter 5). A recent study examining the effects of looking after a demented relative at home on the supporter, using Goldberg's (1972) General Health Questionnaire found that over 70 per cent of supporters scored above the threshold, indicating the presence of a clinical level of psychiatric disturbance (Whittick et al., 1982). If behavioural techniques prove to be ineffective or of only limited use, then we must accept that priority should be given to research on other forms of management and support to alleviate this immense problem.

The purpose of this chapter is to examine some of the reasons why there is not already clear-cut evidence as to the effectiveness or otherwise of the behavioural model, and then to suggest a possible paradigm on which to base research to establish the utility or otherwise of this approach.

Lack of Available Evidence for Effectiveness

There seem to me to be four possible, interlocking explanations for the paucity of research in this large clinical area and for the lack of available evidence as to the effectiveness of behavioural approaches. First, lack of research can, to some extent, be explained by geriatrics not being seen as a priority area for clinical psychologists until relatively recently. Secondly, since one of the primary characteristics of dementia is a memory or learning deficit, it may have been assumed that a behavioural approach based as it is on learning would be totally inappropriate to this condition. Thirdly, since dementia is well recognised to be a progressive condition, it may have been felt that any gains achieved would be unlikely to be worth the effort, since they would be likely to be of only transitory benefit. Finally, when appropriate research has been done, it has been undermined by diagnostic problems and marked lack of homogeneity within the experimental groups.

The relatively recent development of geriatrics as an area of clinical interest is fairly easy to explain, at least in the United Kingdom, in terms of the development of clinical psychology as a profession. In the 1940s and 1950s, the main remit of clinical psychologists was test administration and interpretation. Provision of a clinical service beyond psychometric assessment was rare. It was only in the late 1950s and 1960s, associated mainly with the advent and development of behaviour therapy, that clinical psychologists began to provide a therapeutic service. Initially, this service was directed at mainly neurotic problems, only becoming more oriented towards the chronic patient population with the development of ward-wide behavioural programmes such as the Token Economy (Ayllon and Azrin, 1968). Seen in this context, the necessity of establishing priority areas for provision of clinical psychology services has developed only relatively recently in the United Kingdom and then only after the initial necessity to develop the therapeutic techniques themselves. This development has been accelerated recently by the setting-up, within the profession, of special interest groups focusing on the problems of the elderly. The Scottish special interest group, PACE (Psychology Applied to the Care of the Elderly) was established in 1978, and the English group, PSIGE (Psychologists' Special Interest Group in the Elderly) was formed in 1980. Although much valuable work was done by individuals prior to the establishment of these groups, they now provide a forum for the encouragement of research and service provision in geriatrics. More behavioural work with the elderly has been undertaken in the United States (e.g. Hoyer, 1973), but its relevance to the applicability of behavioural techniques to demented patients is in question due to differences in diagnostic practices. This will be discussed later.

The evidence that one of the primary characteristics of dementia is an impairment of new learning ability (Miller, 1977; Holden and Woods, 1982) may well have led to an attitude amongst practitioners that behavioural approaches, based on learning principles, would be inappropriate in this condition. This attitude may have been reinforced by early studies on operant learning in demented subjects by MacKay (1965). MacKay found that as compared to elderly controls, demented subjects were seriously impaired in operant learning with lower, more variable response rates, together with little response to changes in schedules of reinforcement, the implication being that normal operant procedures are unlikely to be of much use in shaping their social behaviour. However, later studies have shown that brain damage per se in the elderly is not a bar to operant learning (Halbertsam and Zaretsky, 1969; Halbertsam et al., 1971). Halbertsam's studies, however, used patients who had had cerebrovascular accidents, and who were not necessarily dementing, thus limiting the applicability of his results in demented populations.

Ankus and Quarrington (1972) used memory-disordered patients as subjects in their study to assess whether MacKay's results could be attributed to inadequacy or inappropriateness of the reinforcers he used. They concluded that appropriateness of reinforcement is very important, and that with appropriate reinforcers their 48 memory disordered subjects could learn a lever-pulling task almost normally. While these results are encouraging, caution must be used in their interpretation. Ankus and Quarrington's subjects were not described as 'demented', but as 'memory-disordered'. While this probably implies that many were, in fact, demented, it is possible that some may have been memory-disordered for other reasons, e.g. in association with depression (Holden and Woods, 1982) or as an amnesic syndrome (such as Korsakoff's syndrome) and therefore not necessarily experiencing the more general intellectual deterioration found in dementia (Walsh, 1978). In view of the looser diagnostic criteria for dementia used in the United States as compared with the United Kingdom (Copeland et al., 1975; see below), it is very possible that Ankus and Quarrington's groups comprised of patients of whom up to 50 per cent would not be considered to be dementing using a stricter diagnostic system.

Despite their use of the Paired Associate Learning Test (Inglis, 1959) as an objective index of memory disorder, which might reduce the likelihood that their subjects were depressed rather than dementing (Inglis, 1959; Irving et al., 1970), it would certainly not rule out organic amnesic syndromes other than dementia. Since no other studies of operant learning in dementia have as yet been reported, it is not possible to make any definitive statement about the learning abilities of demented patients. However, two clinical studies, Hanley (1981) and Gilleard et al., (1981), both with better specification of their experimental subjects, have independently shown that disoriented dementing patients can be oriented to their ward environment, using an instructional training format within the context of a reality orientation programme, providing some evidence that a behavioural or learning-based treatment approach could be successful.

A third possible reason for the lack of appropriate behaviour research in dementia, is that many practitioners may feel that any gains achieved would be quickly lost within the context of a progressive deteriorating disease. However, the lack of available research on the establishment of new behaviour in demented people makes it difficult to evaluate this belief. Certainly, early stimulation studies (e.g. Cosin et al., 1958) tended to support the idea. They found that increased sensory and social stimulation effected a number of improvements in their patients in the realms of purposefulness, activity and communicativeness. Their study lasted over the period of one year, was designed around a reversal model of repeated four-week treatment blocks, alternating with two-week 'rest' (base-line) blocks. They found that the gains made during the treatment blocks tended to be lost during the two-week rest periods, and that the overall gradual improvement seen in the patients during the first six months reversed to become a gradual decline over the second six months. The authors interpreted this to mean that a peak had been reached in improving their patients' clinical state, after which the effects of the continued deterioration due to the progressive nature of the illness, again became manifest. However, an alternative interpretation might simply be the notorious difficulty in keeping going even a successful ward programme over such a long period. The problem of long-term maintenance of changed staff behaviour (essential to implement new ward programmes) has recently been reviewed by Wood and Cullen (1983).

On the positive side of the progressive deterioration argument, a paper by Christie (1982) has shown that demented patients are now surviving much longer than they did 30 years ago. This may imply that the rate of any deterioration has been slowed by better medical and nursing care and therefore, perhaps, any subsequent deterioration of behavioural gains would be correspondingly slowed down.

On the other hand, deterioration may be as speedy as hitherto, with patients simply surviving longer once they have reached their personal limit. Evidence against this possibility is provided by Hanley (1981), who found that two of the patients he was able to orient to their ward environment performed on the Koskella Test (Ferm, 1975) as 'gravely demented'. If patients with this severity of dementia still retain some learning capacity then surely it should be possible to construct an environment which will maximise the probability of less severely-demented patients retaining behavioural gains? This might be done, for example, by use of a 24-hour reality orientation approach, as described by Hanley (Chapter 1). At present, however, this is purely speculative and, in view of the difficulties associated with maintaining a 24-hour reality orientation programme in the long term (q.v. Hanley, 1983), it may not be practical. In conclusion, it must be stated that at the present time there is little evidence either to support or reject the idea that any behavioural changes achieved will be quickly lost.

A fourth difficulty in obtaining the evidence necessary for the proper evaluation of the effectiveness of behavioural approaches with demented patients is the already cited differences in diagnostic practices between the UK and the USA, which until recently was the scene of almost all the behavioural work undertaken with the elderly. The differences in diagnostic practice between the two countries can be illustrated by examining the subject sample in a paper by Mishara and Kastenbaum (1973) establishing the effects of a token economy on self-injurious behaviour. The authors described 60 per cent of their elderly sample as having a diagnosis of 'chronic brain syndrome' (dementia), yet the sample had an average age of 69 years, and an average length of current hospitalisation of 21½ years. In a British hospital, such a population would almost certainly be found in a graduate or long-term ward with few, if any, patients diagnosed as demented. In the UK, demented patients are more typically admitted to hospital late in life and have a much briefer length of current hospitalisation. (They would also probably be older.)

That there is a difference between Britain and America in diagnostic practices has been shown recently by the US/UK Diagnostic Project (Copeland et al., 1975; Copeland, 1978). This project demonstrated that American psychiatrists diagnose dementia in their elderly patients about one-third again more often than do British psychiatrists. They were able to establish that this was not a function of the composition of the patient groups themselves, but rather of the different diagnostic practices between the two countries. In fact, the project psychiatrists disagreed with 48 per cent of the US psychiatrists' diagnoses of dementia (Copeland, 1978). In practical terms this means that up to about half of an American sample carrying a diagnosis of chronic brain syndrome might well be given a functional (non-organic) diagnosis in the UK. This would have two implications: first, in American studies, dementing samples of patients are likely to be less homogeneous than they would be in the UK; secondly, when a proportion of patients in an American sample responds to any specific management programme, it may be the (UK diagnosis) 'functional' portion which responds while the (UK diagnosis) 'demented' portion remains totally unaffected. Obviously, this makes research findings very difficult to interpret unless the study has gone further than simple diagnosis as a method of describing its subject sample. Unfortunately, very few studies have done so. Since the UK diagnostic criteria are the stricter, it may be that a UK diagnosis of dementia may be a more acceptable description (in terms of group homogeneity) than a US diagnosis of 'chronic brain syndrome'. However, the diagnosis of dementia itself carries with it the implication of considerable heterogeneity of the nature of the specific deficits suffered by these patients (Pierce and Miller, 1973; Miller, 1977).

It would seem necessary, then, to tighten up group comparison research by insisting on more detailed matching of subject characteristics such as neuropsychological functioning and/or specific behavioural characteristics. Alternatively, a greater use of single case studies with individuals whose functional assets and deficits are tightly

67

specified (Hersen and Barlow, 1976) could overcome many of the difficulties inherent in comparison of patient groups. Such an approach would fit much more appropriately into the behavioural paradigm, which generally tends to reject diagnosis by itself as a useful description of individuals.

These explanations of the abysmal lack of behavioural research interest in the field of dementia do not make up the whole picture, however. Where behavioural approaches have been used with demonstrably dementing patients, results have proved equivocal unlike their obvious success with other patient groups (e.g. Ayllon and Azrin, 1968, with chronic schizophrenics). A close analysis of one such study (Pollock and Liberman, 1974) provides some explanations for these equivocal results.

The Pollock and Liberman Study

Pollock and Liberman published a therapeutic study in 1974 entitled 'Behaviour Therapy of Incontinence in Demented In-patients'. While acknowledging that incontinence can occur through multiple pathways, including damage to or infection of various parts of the nervous system or urinary tract, and can also occur in dementing patients because of confusion and memory loss, they hypothesised that some incontinence can be maintained by social reinforcement - specifically, individual attention from staff members. They suggested that incontinence governed by such contingences should be modifiable using a behavioural programme, such as has been successful in chronic psychotics and retarded patients. In order to test their hypothesis they chose six male patients from a 50 patient geriatric unit, each with a diagnosis of chronic brain syndrome, each incontinent, and each able to carry on a simple conversation. No other selection criteria were recorded. Four of the patients had a diagnosis of arteriosclerotic dementia (although two of these had secondary diagnoses, one of schizophrenia and one of epilepsy), the remaining two patients were diagnosed as organic brain syndrome due to alcoholic degeneration.

The behavioural programme consisted of three phases. First, a baseline period (one week) in which the men's pants were checked every two hours. During the second phase (one week), patients had to mop up their incontinence, and were only changed if they requested it (punishment for incontinence). These contingencies were continued throughout the third phase (one week) during which were added positive reinforcement for having dry pants at check-time. Reinforcement consisted of sweets or cigarettes, with a few minutes' conversation including praise for continence and reminders to visit the toilet.

Of the five patients remaining at the end of the study, none showed significant improvements in continence, three had lower scores, two had higher scores (one of which followed a change in medication). In an attempt to explain the poor results of this study, Pollock and Liberman pointed to the inconsistency of reinforcement provided by the staff. One patient followed up after the study became continent within two weeks when staff consistently provided him with cigarettes only when he was dry. Further analysis of their data, however, showed no relation between improvement in continence and frequency of reinforcement in the patient group as a whole. Other explanations supplied by the authors were, first, memory deficits preventing the patient from benefiting from reinforcing techniques; and, secondly, the probable delay between the act of wetting and the pants check, leading to inevitable delays in applying the reinforcement contingencies. Perhaps the most significant explanation for failure they offered, however, is that two of their patients were unable to find the toilet, and therefore unable to complete the complex chain of behaviours necessary to become continent. When they placed a white line on the floor from the dayroom to the toilet, and showed these patients the line's function, one of the two patients was able to make use of this afterwards to find the toilet (and one assumes, although the authors do not mention this, thereby became more continent).

This study has been described in detail to illustrate three main points which, I think, are typical of the inappropriate application of behavioural programmes to dementia. (Incidentally, how many of these patients were actually dementing is open to question. Two could have had amnesic (Korsakoff) syndromes and at least one of the others seemed to be a chronic schizophrenic.) The first point is illustrated by the patient who did not show significant improvement in his incontinence during the three weeks of the study, but who continued to improve to the point of total continence by the staff continuing the reinforcement for dry pants for two weeks after the study. Demented patients represent a mentally handicapped population and, like other mentally handicapped populations, they learn very slowly (Tennant et al., 1981). The most powerful reinforcement contingency used in this study (reward for dryness) only lasted one week. This is an inappropriately short time to train mentally handicapped people in such a complex skill.

Secondly, the authors found that two of their patients were unable to find the toilet and therefore unable to complete the chain of behaviours required for continence. They propose two solutions to this, first a 'quick' solution, i.e. that of providing an environmental prop — a white line between the dayroom and the toilet — which worked for one patient; and, secondly, they recommend a backwards-shaping programme similar to that prepared for the mentally handicapped by Azrin and Foxx (1971). The point is that these individuals had deficits in neuro-psychological functioning which prevented their achieving the goals of their behavioural programme. In this case the deficits were in memory and in ward orientation. However, it is well known that demented patients can also suffer from a wide range of other neuropsychological function impairment, including agnosia (Rochford, 1971), spatial difficulties (Miller, 1977), dyspraxia (Pierce and Miller, 1973) and problems associated with damage to the frontal lobes such as personality changes, perseveration and — what may be of particular importance here —deficits in their ability to plan a series of actions and carry it through (Miller, 1977; Walsh, 1978). In other words, behavioural programmes for demented patients cannot assume that the patient has the neuropsychological capabilities necessary to be able to perform all the necessary steps required to achieve the target. It follows also that the more complex the behavioural target, the more likely is the dementing subject to fail. Finally, it also follows that any neuropsychological deficit which interferes with achieving the behavioural goal should be identified, and the means to overcome it, if this is possible, should be incorporated within the behavioural programme. Pollock and Liberman, themselves, provide an excellent example of this by their use of the white line to overcome the inability of one of their patients to find the toilet.

The third, and from the point of view of this chapter, main point, is related to the previous one. Pollock and Liberman start well by discussing some of the multiple pathways which can lead to incontinence in dementing patients, one of which could be the social reinforcement of incontinence by staff attention. However, when it comes to selecting patients to test their social reinforcement hypothesis, they make no attempt to select for this variable. The result is that only one of their patients (eventually) becomes continent through changes in reinforcement contingencies, and at least two are found to be incontinent for an entirely different reason to that originally hypothesised, i.e. an inability to find the toilet. It is unlikely that simply modifying the reinforcement contingencies to reward dryness would ever have helped these two patients to become continent. This emphasises the pointlessness of designing behavioural programmes for demented patients without first undertaking a thorough behavioural analysis which should include assessment of any neuropsychological function necessary for achieving the final behavioural goal. It also emphasises the interaction between any functional deficit and the environment in which the behaviour takes place. Without such a problem analysis, any behavioural programme is likely to succeed only by chance. A medical analogy would be to treat all cases of incontinence with antibiotics to find later that a substantial proportion were due to lesions of the spinal cord, and not to a localised infection. The idea of basing behavioural programmes on a detailed behaviour analysis is not new (Blackman, 1981). Indeed, detailed behaviour analysis is, or should be, a basic component of all behavioural treatments. However, most analyses tend to assume an intact organism, especially in cases where there is evidence that the behaviour to be trained was previously a part of the patient's repertoire. This assumption cannot be made in demented patients, where indeed it is almost safe to assume that some neuropsychological deficits exist which might inhibit treatment effectiveness unless taken into account from the start.

What is needed with these patients is a methodology to identify the relevant interactions between functional capacity and the environmental factors more traditionally associated with behaviour analysis. An excellent account of such a methodology of experimental behaviour analyses in dementia which takes into account both a neuropsychological deficit and the situational context of the behaviour is provided in a classic paper by Cameron (1941).

The Cameron (1941) Study

Cameron addressed himself to the problem of senile nocturnal delirium, i.e. the tendency for some demented patients to become agitated and to wander, especially at night. He hypothesised that this may either be due to fatigue or to have something to do with the onset of darkness itself. To test the alternative hypothesis he placed a number of patients who demonstrated the problem in a dark room, early in the day, long before fatigue would be likely to be a factor. He found that:

> In every instance delirium appeared within an hour after the patient had been put into the dark room, and in some cases a degree of agitation also had become apparent. This subsided again in about an hour after the patient was brought back into the light. The 'dark room' delirium appeared earlier and was more marked in those patients in whom it was most severe during the night hours.

He concluded that the relevant stimulus was darkness rather than fatigue. He related the problem to the demonstrable impairment in recent memory which characterised these patients and suggested that their orientation in space depended much more on continual visual scanning than in normal individuals, who can retain an internal picture of their surroundings even in the dark. He checked this hypothesis by demonstrating that when these patients are blindfolded they quickly forget the location of significant features in their immediate surroundings. He concluded that nocturnal delirium was a direct result of this loss of spatial orientation concomitant with the reduction in visual cues brought about by darkness. This disorientation leads to anxiety, which in turn will serve to further increase the confusion.

Cameron's study seems to me to be an excellent example of what the experimental analysis of behaviour should comprise for demented patients. He not only demonstrates experimentally the functional relationship between the behaviour and its situational context (darkness), but also takes into account the interaction between this and the impairment of neuropsychological function in the individual (recent memory deficit). His further analysis relating the loss of spatial orientation to the anxiety and panic demonstrated by these patients suggests that, in less ambulant patients, the same interaction would lead to nocturnal agitation alone, without the wandering. Gilhooly (Chapter 5) has indeed found that sleep disturbance is a problem frequently identified by caretakers of elderly demented patients at home.

The implication of Cameron's behavioural analysis is that, since nocturnal wandering is brought about by the interaction between darkness and the memory deficit, then preventing the darkness by leaving on a light, for example, might be sufficient to prevent it. I have been unable to trace any reference in the literature in which this simple approach has been systematically tried with these patients. My own opinion is, however, that it would be unlikely that leaving a light on in itself would be sufficient to overcome the problem in all patients. The reason for this is that Cameron's problem analysis, though excellent, ignores the social dimension. The onset of darkness is usually accompanied by social isolation as well as by spatial disorientation. This would occur either by the patient being alone in a bedroom, or, if in a dormitory of a ward, by other patients being hidden by darkness or in unfamiliar positions in their beds. While Cameron's account of his experiments do not indicate clearly whether his patients were also subjected to social isolation, that this is probably a relevant variable is indicated by the frequent complaints by relatives that much wandering also occurs in daytime (Gilhooly, Chapter 5).

In addition to daytime wandering, caretakers often complain of being followed wherever they go and of being unable to leave their dependant alone for any length of time (Whittick et al., 1982). Since, as Cameron has shown, these patients have considerable short-term memory defects, it is probable that these other problems are also brought about by the interaction of the neuropsychological deficit and environment (i.e. the short-term memory deficit and the absence of the caretaker). These patients would have no recollection of how long the caretaker has been gone or of any message to the effect that the absence is temporary and short term. This lack of awareness of when the caretaker is likely to return could lead to anxiety (in much the same way as did Cameron's spatial disorientation) which would lead to agitation and purposeful wandering, seeking the reassuring presence of the caretaker. Even though the purpose of the wandering may itself be quickly forgotten, the agitation itself is likely to maintain it. Alternatively, since some learning does occur in demented patients (Greene <u>et al</u>., 1979; Hanley, 1981) avoidance of agitation may lead to preventative measures such as not allowing the caretaker to get out of sight, and constantly following him or her. If we term this process social disorientation, then we might reasonably expect that the additional factor of spatial disorientation created by darkness would serve to increase agitation and make it more likely that the patient will go to seek help, thereby making wandering or disturbance more likely at night.

Although Cameron's experiment may not have gone far enough, his creative approach to the experimental analysis of the behaviour of his dementing patients cannot be faulted. A more modern knowledge about single-case experimental design (Hersen and Barlow, 1976) would add more powerful research techniques to this basic paradigm, thereby facilitating the experimental analysis of problem behaviour in the demented patient. Such analyses could obviously have direct implications for developing specific treatment programmes for individual patients. For example, Cameron's analysis of nocturnal wandering in terms of the agitation created by spatial disorientation would imply that the target for intervention in his subject sample should have been the spatial disorientation rather than the wandering <u>per se</u>. This inference is testable and would imply that maintaining illumination above a certain minimal level should lead to considerable amelioration of both the wandering and its associated agitation. As I have already mentioned, to the best of my knowledge this has never been systematically tested. However, if we add the social isolation factor to the behaviour analyses, then we would predict that simple maintenence of the illumination level would be insufficient and that some reminder of the proximity of the caretaker may be necessary. This could take the form of a tape-recorded message in the caretaker's voice, perhaps switched by a pressure pad so that it comes on when the patient rises from the bed. Alternatively, in patients whose reading skills are largely intact, a simple message in a prominent position may suffice. With the advent of cheaper home video systems, perhaps a videotape of the primary caretaker, switched on by some sort of arrangement as described above, may be found to be effective. Indeed, such a memory prosthetic may also ameliorate daytime wandering and provide the caretaker with some additional freedom. The main difficulty with such prosthetic memories is not only to ensure that they are effective, but to ensure that they are used. Unless they can be switched on automatically, as suggested, the patient will almost certainly require to be trained fairly intensively how to use them. However, Hanley's (1981) success in training demented patients to use signposts to improve their ward orientation suggests that training patients to use prosthetics may well have some useful potential.

Wandering is not the only problem behaviour of dementing patients capable of a functional analysis within a framework which takes into account both the neuropsychological state of the patient along with his immediate environment. Other possibilities, discussed in more detail below, are agitation, aggression and incontinence. Yet other behaviour may well be attributable to neuropsychological impairment alone, such as inability to dress and some eating problems, both probably being attributable to dyspraxia, or loss of ability to carry out well-rehearsed tasks involving spatial skills and manual coordination.

Where neuropsychological deficits are identified as contributing to the behavioural problem, there is a tendency to be pessimistic about the possibility of amelioration. This is probably due to the recognition of the central importance of memory disorder in dementia and the assumption that this implies that the person is incapable of acquiring new skills necessary to overcome the deficit. However, much recent work, as summarised in Powell (1981), has shown that functional deficits attributable to brain lesions can be ameliorated or compensated for using behavioural techniques in the rehabilitation process. Luria (1966) has proposed a model of neuro-retraining which capitalises on cognitive strengths to compensate for deficits arising from regions of cerebral damage, while Diller (1976) has suggested a 'Cognitive Retraining' model aimed at improving specific impaired skills. While these models have been designed for patients with (usually) specific, traumatic lesions, and are therefore likely to have only limited application to dementia, which is characterised by multiple cognitive deficits together with intellectual decline, they do suggest rehabilitative procedures if there is sufficient plasticity of function remaining in some demented patients to ameliorate the specific neuropsychological deficits underlying some of their problem behaviour.

Behaviour Analysis in Dementia

Nelson and Hayes (1981) describe behavioural assessment (behaviour analysis) as 'the identification and measurement of meaningful response units and their controlling variables (both environmental and organismic) for the purposes of understanding and altering human behaviour' (p.3). They go on to define organismic variables to be past learning, genetic variables and current physiology. Such a definition is in keeping with the S-O-R-K-C model of behavioural analyses proposed by Kanfer and Saslow (1969), and Kanfer and Phillips (1970). In this model, S refers to the antecedent events, O to the biological condition of the organism, R to the response, K to the contingency, and C to the consequences. Other authors (e.g. Goldfried and Sprafkin, 1974) have proposed similar models for behavioural analyses. However, although much has been written about methods of observing and specifying S, R, K and C, relatively little space in textbooks of behavioural assessment has been devoted to evaluating O, with the exception of when O refers to a mood state, such as anxiety or arousal, or to past learning, such as a well-established habit pattern. Apart from these examples, generally speaking behavioural analysts tend to assume that O is almost a constant in their analyses and have concentrated most of their efforts on the more directly observable variables.

Even when it is recognised that organismic variables may be important, as for example in the analysis of 'psychotic' behaviour such as hallucinations, the bulk of the behavioural literature tends to emphasise the environmental relationships, and to exclude consideration of the biological aspects. Although in some cases this has still resulted in therapeutic success (Butcher and Fabricatore, 1970; Slade, 1972) such incomplete analyses do not contribute to our understanding of the behaviour or to its future prevention. On the other hand, it is quite obvious that raw biological data would contribute little to behavioural analyses. It is impossible to interpret directly into behavioural terms the implications of a deficiency or excess of a specific neurotransmitter substance or even the implications of an area of damaged brain tissue. Organismic variables have to be couched in terms of psychological functioning in order to be of use in behaviour analysis.

One recent, notable example of behavioural

assessment involving the integration of biological variables with environmental factors has been the work of Green and his co-workers in the field of auditory hallucinations (Green et al., 1979). They have hypothesised that auditory hallucinations occur in individuals with a lesion of the corpus callosum, the brain tissue interconnecting the two cerebral hemispheres. This leads to difficulties in transferring information, particularly auditory information, from one hemisphere to the other. Individuals with auditory hallucinations have been shown to suffer from this cognitive impairment or information transfer deficit. These authors have demonstrated the relationship between this cognitive deficit, certain stimulus conditions, and the production of auditory hallucinations in a number of single case studies. The implications of this analysis for our understanding of auditory hallucinations and their treatment has been fully discussed by Green et al. (1979) and would seem to provide a model of what is required for our understanding of some of the behaviour of dementing patients.

There is little doubt that biological factors are of considerable importance in determining much of the behaviour of demented people. Simple behavioural analysis which either ignores or plays down these factors, while occasionally leading to some therapeutic success, is unlikely to do so consistently and will certainly contribute little to our understanding of their behaviour. Only by taking into account the biological changes in terms of psychological functioning are we likely to develop appropriate strategies for management and retraining.

So what kind of changes in psychological functioning should we expect to have to take into account in our analysis of demented patients' behaviour? Cameron's study has highlighted the importance of memory impairment and intellectual decline (which in itself is too diffuse to be of much value in behavioural assessment), but there has been relatively little study of other forms of neuropsychological impairment. Language problems have been demonstrated in a number of studies (summarised by Miller, 1977), but there is some controversy as to whether demented patients are truly dysphasic or have difficulty in naming objects due to difficulties in recognising them (visual agnosia) (Rochford, 1971). There does seem to be some poverty of speech which, however, may be due to frontal lobe lesions (Walsh, 1978) rather than the more usual forms of dysphasia which reflect more posterior lesions. Frontal lesions also probably form the neurological basis of a number of other characteristic changes, such as perseveration, personality changes, disinhibition, etc. Perceptual and spatial problems occur, such as dyspraxia (constructional dyspraxia and dressing dyspraxia being common examples). In fact, as Miller (1977) himself concludes, dementia probably creates changes in every aspect of behaviour or psychological functioning. However, the important point is that different dementing individuals will show different degrees of impairment in different psychological functions, and for many there may be sufficient residual learning capacity or intact functional capacity in other areas to compensate for specific functional impairments. Thus we might expect, as indeed happens, that we get different forms of behavioural problems in different dementing individuals. However, we might also expect that the same behavioural topography may have different underlying roots in different patients, where different functional deficits interact with different environmental conditions.

Behavioural Analysis of Specific Problems

Cameron's (1941) experimental analysis of nocturnal wandering has already been discussed in detail and modified to take into account the possible influence of social isolation. However, as Cameron pointed out, this behaviour was accompanied by considerable agitation on the part of the patients. Where the patient is less ambulant it is likely that the same stimulus conditions would tend to simple noctural restlessness and sleep disturbance, probably accompanied by verbal attempts to re-establish contact with the caretaker, such as shouting or calling for help. While this behaviour is topographically dissimilar to wandering, if it results from the same stimulus conditions then it could be considered to be functionally identical and treated in the same way.

My expansion of Cameron's analysis to include the 'social disorientation' factor may help to explain daytime as well as nocturnal wandering in some patients. However, other functional deficits may well also contribute to wandering. Visual agnosia, in which the patient is unable to recognise the caretaker (even a close relative) may well precipitate agitated wandering even in the presence of the caretaker, or alternatively, precipitate aggressive outbursts (see below).

Snyder et al. (1978) conducted a study of wandering in which they compared matched pairs of wandering with non-wandering residents of a nursing home. In addition to confirming Cameron's finding that wandering is often associated with spatial disorientation, they identified three types of wandering behaviour using a behavioural-mapping observational technique. These three types consisted of:

(1) Overtly goal directed/searching behaviour in which the resident constantly searched for somebody or something (often unobtainable, e.g. mother).

(2) Overtly goal directed/industrious behaviour in which the resident seemed to be driven to do things or remain busy (e.g. housework tasks).

(3) Apparently non-goal directed behaviour in which the resident seems aimlessly drawn to one stimulus or another and seldom follows through to any goal. (p.275)

The authors examined the social histories of their study residents and concluded that 'at least three psychosocial factors may influence the tendency to wander':

(1) Search for security.

(2) Previous work roles. (To this I would also add well-established habits such as going for a walk after tea, etc.)

(3) Lifelong patterns of coping with stress, such as becoming restless or taking a brisk stroll.

Each of these factors would obviously carry with it quite different implications for rehabilitation or management. Factor two, for example, may best be managed by providing appropriate work (dusting, cleaning, sewing, etc.) while factor three may best be dealt with by reducing the level of environmental stimulation and therefore stress, or alternatively, by occasional quiet conversation with a staff member or caretaker to reassure and reduce anxiety levels. Snyder et al. suggest a number of rehabilitative and compensatory approaches to deal with wandering, linked to the nature of the underlying cause. Other relatively frequent problems encountered in dementing patients are capable of similar kinds of analysis.

Aggression is a fairly common problem in the demented elderly which is often found to be rated as a severe problem by caretakers (Whittick et al.,

1982). This could be the direct result of disinhibition of aggressive behaviour due to organic damage (frontal lobe lesions) and perhaps maintained by attention from caretakers, or alternatively, an indirect result of visual agnosia where the patient is unable to recognise his family and friends and may resent their intimate behaviour towards him. In the first instance the aggressive behaviour may respond to direct modification by manipulation of contingent attention (an example of this approach is quoted by Horton <u>et al</u>., 1981), while in the second instance a more appropriate strategy might be to retrain the patient to recognise his caretakers. If the patient finds it impossible to relearn to recognise complex visual patterns such as a face, perhaps he could be taught to recognise that a specific feature (e.g. spectacles) represented the appropriate person.

Incontinence is a particular problem which can cause considerable problems both in the home and in the ward. It is a much more complicated problem to analyse as being continent involves a complex chain of behaviours, the loss of any one of which will result in incontinence. For example, the patient needs to recognise the need to micturate or defecate; he needs to know how to find the toilet; he must be able to move well enough to get there in time; and he needs to be able to recognise the toilet and to undress appropriately. In addition, there may be motivational problems either of apathy or of incontinence being maintained by inappropriate attention from staff or caretaker. Finally, there may be a specific medical condition which either by itself or interacting with any of the other factors may lead to incontinence. Each of these problems requires an individual solution.

If incontinence is due to non-recognition of need, then, at least in the case of urinary incontinence, a portable enuretic alarm may supply the biofeedback necessary for retraining to occur. At the very least, use of such a device would enable staff to determine if the incontinence were associated with any particular environmental stimulus and thereby enable a more detailed behaviour analysis to take place. If the problem is inability to find the toilet then either reorientation training, whether or not with easily identified signposts (Hanley, 1981), or marking a coloured track on the floor between day-area and toilet (Pollock and Liberman, 1974) would be more appropriate. Research into the most appropriate form of signposting could be very useful here. In the case of a physical problem which makes the patient unable to get to the toilet quickly enough, obviously either placing him nearer the toilet or supplying a nearby commode would help considerably. If, however, the problem is an inability to recognise the toilet (visual agnosia), then the most likely approach would either be to retrain him to recognise the stimulus configuration of the toilet or to associate it with some particular stimulus he can recognise (e.g. sound, colour) and train him to form the association. If dressing apraxia is the problem, then easily opened fasteners plus training in how to use them, or perhaps readily available step-by-step verbal instructions and training to use them may work. Apathy may well respond to a general stimulation programme together with the introduction of reinforcement contingent on appropriate use of the toilet. This may consist simply of manipulating the contingency of the caretaker's attention so that more attention was available for continence than incontinence where this is important. Where a medical condition co-exists with any of these other problems, then obviously it should be treated concurrently.

These examples should suffice to underline the need for comprehensive behavioural analysis, taking into account all the various possibilities, both organismic and environmental which may interact to lead to the specific behaviour under review. A major problem which is created by the need for such a comprehensive assessment is in discriminating between the various possible organismic factors which may be involved so that the most appropriate therapeutic strategy will be selected. One possibility might be to undertake a complete neuropsychological assessment of psychological functioning. This would have the advantage of not only showing up areas of deficient functioning but also of identifying relatively intact abilities which might be used in a treatment plan to support impaired abilities (Luria, 1966). However, the expertise to undertake such an assessment is not always readily available and, furthermore, such assessments take considerable time which might be difficult to afford in a busy geriatric unit. Provided the various possibilities are well recognised, it should be possible in many cases to come to some fairly accurate conclusion based on close observation of the patient's behaviour in the ward or home. Perhaps this too could be illustrated by using the example of incontinence.

The various possible breaks in the behaviour

chain which were identified are listed in Table 4.1.

TABLE 4.1 Behaviour Change in Incontinence

Inability to recognise need.
Inability to find toilet.
Too slow to get there in time.
Inability to recognise toilet.
Inability to undress appropriately.
Apathy.
Incontinence maintained by contingent staff attention.
Medical problems.

Some of these problems will be almost immediately obvious, e.g. physical slowness on moving, or difficulties with undressing, will be fairly obvious even to a casual observer, while medical problems will probably be assessed routinely by the responsible medical officer. Some of the other problems should be identifiable by closer observation of the patient. For example, where the patient is suffering from an inability to find the toilet, he will show other signs of disorientation such as being unable to find the dining-area or his bed. He may be difficult to distinguish from the patient who cannot recognise the toilet in that both may urinate in various parts of the ward; however, a simple test of taking the patients to the toilet and allowing them freedom to use it as they wish should quickly identify those with recognition problems from those with memory problems. Where undressing is a difficulty this will also be apparent if the patient is observed dressing or undressing on rising or at bedtime. The remaining three headings are more difficult, but again should be capable of being distinguished by close observation. Incontinence due to apathy and that due to contingent staff attention should be relatively easily identified by analysing the consequences of incontinence and the patient's response to these. The apathetic patient is unlikely to attract staff attention to his incontinence or show much response to their attending to him. Discriminating patients who are simply unable to tell when they need to micturate again may be difficult to identify unless they become agitated at having accidents.
While observation will help identify the root

problem in many cases, in many others, especially where a mixture of reasons apply, the most appropriate method may be by experimentally testing hypotheses in succession until the proper solution or combination of solutions are found. This could be started by using an enuretic alarm to identify quickly the environmental aspects of discrete episodes of incontinence and thereby facilitate the behavioural assessment, followed by treatment procedures consistent with what seem to be the most likely reasons for the incontinence.

Conclusion

This chapter has not attempted to describe a general approach suitable either to deal with all problems of the demented elderly patient or to design an ideal living environment for them. Rather, it has tried to identify ways in which behavioural approaches, which have been found so successful with other groups of patients, can be used with demented patients despite their multiple handicaps. It has found that one impediment to the use of the behavioural approach is the failure to take into proper account the many deficits in neuropsychological functioning seen in these patients and has suggested ways in which this omission can be remedied. Given that the majority of dementing elderly patients have multiple deficits, it is likely that many may well not respond completely as the same problem may occur in the same person at different times for different reasons. However, since the goal with most dementing patients is to maximise their quality of life, rather than expect a return to predemented levels of functioning, even small gains may be of considerable importance to the individual. Agitated wandering or incontinence are probably just as unpleasant to demented patients as they would be to people with more intact cognitive functioning.

References

Ankus, M. and Quarrington, B. (1972) 'Operant Behaviour in the Memory-Disordered', J. Geront., 27, 500-10.

Arie, T. and Isaacs, A.D. (1978) 'The Development of Psychiatric Services for the Elderly in Britain', in Isaacs, A.D. and Post, F. (eds.), Studies in Geriatric Psychiatry, John Wiley, Chichester.

Ayllon, T. and Azrin, N.H. (1968) The Token Economy: A Motivational System for Therapy and Rehabilitation, Appleton Century Crofts, New York.

Azrin, N.H. and Foxx, R.M. (1971) 'A Rapid Method of Toilet Training in the Institutionally Retarded'. J. App. Beh. Anal. 4, 89-99.

Bergmann, K., Foster, E.M., Justice, A.W. and Matthews, V. (1978) 'Management of the Demented Elderly Patient in the Community', Brit. J. Psychiat., 132, 441-9.

Blackman, D. (1981) 'The Experimental Analysis of Behaviour and its Relevance to Applied Psychology', in Davey, G. (ed.), Applications of Conditioning Theory, Methuen, London.

Butcher, B. and Fabricatore, J. (1970) 'Use of Patient-Administered Shock to Suppress Hallucinations' Beh. Ther. 1. 382-5.

Cameron, D.E. (1941) 'Studies in Senile Nocturnal Delirium', Psychiat. Quart., 15, 47-53.

Christie, A.B. (1982) 'Changing Patterns in Mental Illness in the Elderly', Brit. J. Psychiat., 140, 154-9.

Copeland, J.R.M. (1978) 'Evaluation of Diagnostic Methods: An International Comparison', in Isaacs, A.D. and Post, F. (eds.), Studies in Geriatric Psychiatry, John Wiley, Chichester.

Copeland, J.R.M., Kelleher, M.J., Kellett, J.M. et al. (1975) 'Cross-national Study of Diagnosis of the Mental Patients Admitted to Mental Hospitals serving Queens County, New York, and the former Borough of Camberwell, London', Brit. J. Psychiat., 126, 11-20.

Cosin, L.Z., Mort, M., Post, F., Westrop, C. and Williams, M. (1958) 'Experimental Treatment of Persistent Senile Confusion', Internat, J. Soc. Psychiat. 4, 24-42.

Diller, L.A. (1976) 'Model for Cognitive Retraining in Rehabilitation', The Clinical Psychologist, 29, 13-15.

Ferm, L. (1975) 'Changes of Intellectual Functioning and Nursing Dependency in Institutionalized Old People', paper presented at a domestic symposium, Koshela Geriatric Hospital, Helsinki.

Geiger, O.G. and Johnson, L.A. (1974) 'Positive Education for Elderly Persons: Correcting Eating Through Reinforcement', Gerontologist, 14, 432-6.

Gilleard, C., Mitchell, R.G. and Riordan, J. (1981) 'Ward Orientation Training with Psychogeriatric Patients', J. Adv. Nurs. 6, 95-8.

Gilleard, C.J., Watt, G. and Boyd, W.D. (1981) 'Problems of Caring for the Elderly Mentally Infirm at Home', paper presented to the 12th International Congress of Gerontology, 12-17 July, Hamburg.

Gledhill, K.J., Mackie, J.E. and Gilleard, C.J. (1982) A Comparison of Problems and Coping Reported by Supporters of Elderly Day Hospital Patients with Similar Ratings Provided by Nurses', paper presented at British Psychological Society Annual Conference, April.

Goldberg, G.P. (1972) 'The Detection of Psychiatric Illness by Questionnaire', Maudsley Monograph No. 21, Oxford University Press, London.

Goldfried, M.R. and Sprafkin, J.N. (1974) 'Behavioural Personality Assessment', in Spence, J.T., Carson, R.C. and Thibaut, J.W. (eds.), Behavioural Approaches to Therapy, General Learning Press, New Jersey.

Green, P., Glass, A. and O'Callaghan, M.A.J. (1979), 'Some Implications of Abnormal Hemisphere Interaction in Schizophrenia', in Cruzelier, J.H. and Fler-Henry, P. (eds.), Hemisphere Assymetries and Psychopathology, Macmillan, London.

Greene, J.G., Nicol, R. and Jamieson, H. (1979) 'Reality Orientation with Psychogeriatric Patients', Beh. Res. Ther. 17, 615-7.

Halbertsam, J.L. and Zaretsky, H.H. (1969) 'Learning Capacities of the Elderly and Brain-Damaged', Arch. Phys. Med. & Rehab., 50, 133-9.

Halbertsam, J.L., Zaretsky, H., Brucker, B.S. and Guttman, A.R. (1971) 'Avoidance Conditioning of Motor Responses in Elderly Brain-Damaged Patients', Arch. Phys. Med. & Rehab. 52, 381-27.

Hall, J. and Baker, R. (1973) 'Token Economy Systems: Breakdown and Control', Behaviour Research and Therapy, 11, 253-63.

Hanley, I.G. (1981) 'The Use of Signposts and Active Training to Modify Ward Disorientation in Elderly Patients', J. Beh. Ther. & Exp. Psychiat., 12, 241-7.

Hanley, I.G. (1983) 'Theoretical and Practical Considerations in Reality Orientation Therapy with the Elderly', in Hanley, I.G. and Hodge, J.E. (eds.) Psychologicial Approaches to the Care of the Elderly, Croom Helm, Beckenham.

Hersen, M. and Barlow, D.H. (1976) Single Case Experimental Designs: Strategies for Studying Behaviour Change, Pergamon Press, New York.

Holden, U.P. and Woods, R.T. (1982) Reality Orientation: Psychological Approaches to the Confused Elderly, Churchill-Livingstone, Edinburgh.

Horton, A.M., Wedding, D. and Phay, A. (1981) 'Current Perspectives on Assessment and Therapy for the Brain-Damaged Individual', in Golden, C.J. et al. (eds.), Applied Techniques in Behavioural Medicine, Grune and Stratton, London.

Hoyer, W.J. (1973) 'Application of Operant Techniques to the Modification of Elderly Behaviour', Gerontologist, 13, 18-22.

Inglis, J. (1959) 'A Paired Associate Learning Tests for Use with Elderly Psychiatric Patients', J. Ment. Sci., 105, 440-8.

Irving, G., Robinson, R.A. and McAdam, W. (1970) 'The Validity of Some Cognitive Tests in the Diagnosis of Dementia', Brit. J. Psychiat., 117, 149-56.

Kanfer, F.H. and Phillips, J.S. (1970) Learning Foundations of Behaviour Therapy, John Wiley, New York.

Kanfer, F.H. and Saslow, G. (1969) 'Behavioural Diagnosis', in Franks C.M. (ed.), Behaviour Therapy, Appraisal and Status, McGraw

Hill, New York.

Kazdin, A.E. (1977) The Token Economy, Plenum Press, New York.

Libb, J.W. and Clements, C.B. (1969) 'Token Reinforcement in an Exercise Program for Hospitalized Geriatric Patients', Percept. Mot. Skills., 28, 957-8.

Lovaas, O.I. and Newsom, C.D. (1976) 'Behaviour Modification with Psychotic Children', in H. Leitenberg, (ed.), Handbook of Behaviour Modification and Behaviour Therapy, Prentice-Hall, New Jersey.

Lovaas, O.I. and Koegel, R.L. (1973) 'Behaviour Therapy with Autistic Children', in C.E. Thoreson (ed.), Behaviour Modification in Education, National Society for the Study of Education, 72nd Yearbook, University of Chicago, Chicago, pp.230-58.

Luria, A.P. (1966) Higher Cortical Functions in Man, Basic Books, New York.

MacKay, H.A. (1965) 'Operant Techniques Applied to Disorders of the Senium', unpub. PhD. thesis, Queen's University, Kingston, Ontario.

Miller, E. (1977) Abnormal Ageing: The Psychology of Senile and Presenile Dementia, John Wiley, Chichester.

Mishara, B.L. and Kastenbaum, R. (1973) 'Self-Injurious Behaviour and Environmental Change in Institutionalized Elderly', Intl. J. Ageing & Hu. Dev., 4, 133-45.

Nelsen, R.O. and Hayes, S.C. (1981) 'Nature of Behavioural Assessment', in Hersen, M. and Bellach, A.S. (eds.), Behavioural Assessment: A Practical Handbook (2nd edn.), Pergamon Press, New York.

Peck, D.F. (1975) 'Behaviour is Behaviour is Behaviour', in Bregelmann, J.C. (ed.), Progress in Behaviour Therapy. Springer-Verlag, Amsterdam.

Pierce, J. and Miller, E. (1973) Clinical Aspects of Dementia, Bailliere Tindall, London.

Pollock, D.D. and Liberman, R.P. (1974) 'Behaviour Therapy of Incontinence in Demented In-patients', Gerontologist, 14, 488-91.

Powell, G.E. (1981) Brain Function Therapy, Gower, Aldershot, England.

Rochford, G. (1971) 'A Study of Naming Errors in Dysphasic and Demented Patients', Neuropsychologia, 9, 437-43.

Slade, P.D. (1972) 'The Effects of Systematic Desensitization on Auditory Hallucinations', Beh. Res. Ther. 10, 35-91.

Snyder, L.H., Rupprecht, P., Pyreck, J., Brekhus, S. and Moss. T. (1978) 'Wandering', Gerontologist, 18, 272-80.

Tennant, L., Cullen, C. and Hattersley, J. (1981) 'Applied Behaviour Analysis: Intervention with Retarded People', in Davey, G. (ed.), Applications of Conditioning Theory, Methuen, London.

Ullman, L.P. and Krasner, L. (1975) A Psychological Approach to Abnormal Behaviour (2nd edn.), Prentice-Hall, New Jersey.

Walsh, K.W. (1978) Neuropsychology: A Clinical Approach, Churchill Livingstone, Edinburgh.

Whittick, J.E., Gledhill, K. and Gilleard, C.J. (1982) 'Problems and Strain Among Supporters of the Elderly Mentally Infirm: Effects of Sex, Age, Living Arrangements and Relationship to Patient', paper presented at the British Society of Gerontology's Annual

Conference, September.

Wood, R. and Eames, P. (1981) 'Application of Behaviour Modification in the Treatment of Traumatically Brain-Injured Adults', in Davey, G. (ed.), <u>Applications of Conditioning Theory</u>, Methuen, London.

Woods, P.A. and Cullen, C. (1983) 'Determinants of Staff Behaviour in Long-Term Care', <u>Behav. Psychother.</u> <u>11</u>, 4-17.

Chapter Five

THE SOCIAL DIMENSIONS OF SENILE DEMENTIA

Mary L. M. Gilhooly

Introduction

There are three ways of looking at the social
dimensions of senile dementia: first, one can ask if
social and psychological factors are significant in
the aetiology of dementia; secondly, one can ask
about the social and psychological consequences of
senile dementia for the sufferer; and thirdly, one
can enquire as to the social and psychological
consequences of dementia for those who give care to
the dementing elderly in the community. All three
issues will be examined in this chapter. The first
two questions will be answered by drawing on
published literature in the first two sections, while
the examination of the social and psychological
consequences for supporters will rely heavily on
unpublished findings from my own research on
supporters of the dementing elderly in the third
section. To a certain extent the first sections are
an introduction to the third, and, as this section is
more or less self-contained, readers interested
mainly in the consequences for supporters can begin
there.

Before considering the questions raised above,
it is necessary to make a brief statement about what
is, and is not, being discussed in this chapter, and
about the use of terms. This chapter is about senile
dementia, and not about the reversible dementias or
acute confusional states. Two main forms of
irreversible senile dementia exist - senile dementia
of the Alzheimer type, and multi-infarct dementia.
Neither form has a known cure, and it is often
difficult to distinguish between the two from a brief
clinical encounter with the sufferer as both involve
the progressive loss of memory and intellect, with
ultimate disintegration of both personality and

social orientation. However, changes such as high blood pressure and the occurrence of 'stepwise' rather than gradual deterioriation indicate multi-infarct dementia (Medical Research Council, 1983). It has become fashionable to use terms other than senile dementia since dementia is regarded as having such negative connotations. Various terms have been offered as replacements, e.g. elderly mentally infirm (IMI), and confused and Alzheimer's disease. (1) However, it is my belief that whatever word is chosen it will come, in time, to have the same connotations. Furthermore, it is rather cumbersome to use words like 'elderly mentally infirm', and such expressions do not convey progressive deterioration in the same way as 'dementing'. So, in this chapter dementia will be used, as will dementing.

The Social and Psychological Causes of Senile Dementia

Although there is now considerable evidence to support the view that senile dementia is a 'disease' caused by biological disturbances, it is worthwhile considering (1) why social and psychological variables have been thought to be of significance in the aetiology of dementia; (2) what kind of evidence has been, or could be used to support the argument that dementia is caused by social and psychological factors; and (3) in what way social and psychological factors influence dementia, i.e. the role of such variables in symptom formation and the course of a dementing disorder.

The fashion for stressing social-psychological factors in the aetiology of senile dementia stems from early studies in which brain atrophy was not precisely paralleled by clinical changes. Gruenthal (1927), for example, found a positive association between the degree of senile deterioration and the severity of neuropathological changes, but there were a number of subjects in whom atrophy did not closely match clinical changes. Gruenthal, therefore, suggested that senile changes and cerebral atrophy occurring in the old person were not 'sufficient causes of senile dementia, but that unidentified, pathogenic factors had to be present as well.' Ten years later Rothschild (1937, 1942) also suggested that the severity of dementia was not closely related to the extent of cerebral damage.

In other words, patients with senile or arteriosclerotic psychoses should not be regarded merely as passive carriers of a morbid anatomic process. One should attempt to estimate to what extent more personal factors are concerned in each case. In many cases, such a study suggests that the qualities of the living person and his life experiences are the most important factors in the origin of the mental breakdown ...

Thus, there emerges a more meaningful picture of the psychosis as an end state in a long process which has its roots not just in certain impersonal tissue alterations, but in psychological stresses and in special problems which affect the ageing population.
                    (Rothschild (1956) in Post (1965) p.69)

Note, however, that Post (1965), following Corsellis (1962), has pointed out that Rothschild over-emphasised the occasional case where there had been a serious disagreement between clinical assessment and severity of anatomical change.

Morgan (1965) was one of the first theorists to argue that dementia is a psychogenic disorder. Morgan described the features of senility as being a 'senescent defence against a personal and inevitable death'. The loss of recent memory (the primary disturbance in senile dementia) was, according to Morgan, representative of the defence mechanism repression. It was suggested that recent memories constantly remind the old person of his age, increasing infirmity, and impending death.

More recently, Meacher (1972) again put forward the view that 'confusion' in old people was the result of adjustments to the 'painful' experiences of 'isolation, impotence, and hopelessness' (p.38). By showing that confused people in residential care were capable of registering the significance of events around them, and responding to them in an interpretative manner, Meacher claimed that he would demonstrate that confused behaviour was not the 'irrational excrescence of a deranged mind'. He found that confused people in his study, which compared the experiences of confused old people in special homes with those in ordinary old people's homes, could perceive their own and other's loss of sensory powers, recognised their facetiousness, retained a sense of humour, were capable of responding to incentives, were distressed by rejection and neglect, and could in general identify the subtle significances of social events. Thus, he argues, such findings, demonstrate that confused behaviour is a logical adjustment to a distressing environment.

At about the time that Meacher was collecting data, Folsom (1967, 1968), the originator of reality orientation, suggested that disorientation in elderly people arose from loss of purpose and sense of identity which are exacerbated by other people's attitudes and actions.

Although the idea that dementia is a defence against constant reminders of death, experiences of isolation and feelings of hopelessness is an interesting one, such theories are open to a number of serious criticisms. First, such approaches tend to account only for memory loss or disorientation, and have nothing to say about the large numbers of other changes that occur in dementia. Furthermore, there is experimental evidence that in dementia new information fails to be acquired rather than acquired and then repressed. Finally, it is interesting that no one appears to have considered it worth while conducting experiments to test, for example, Morgan's ideas (Miller, 1977).

Life Events
The relationship of life events and crises to dementia has also been investigated. Garside et al. (1965), as part of the Newcastle survey, investigated the association of bereavement and dementia, but found that they were not significantly related. In a study of 25 female demented patients and a similar number of non-demented elderly people, Amster and Krauss (1974) found that the dementing women had double the number of life crises in the five years before the study. Amster and Krauss were cautious in interpreting the results, pointing out that mental deterioration could have begun before it was noticed by relatives and friends and the women could, therefore, have been predisposed to a greater frequency of crises than the controls. It is also possible that once dementia begins the individual is likely to be less able to cope with the stresses and strains of normal life and these then become elevated to the level of a major crises.

If senile dementia is caused by social factors, then it is reasonable to expect that there would be class and sex differences in the prevalence of dementia. Age difference could, of course, be attributed to biological and/or social causes.

Social-Demographic Variables

Age. The one factor which has been clearly demonstrated to be related to dementia is age. Epidemiological studies (e.g. Adelstein et al., 1968) have shown that as age increases, the percentage of subjects with dementia in each age cohort increases. Kay et al. (1970), using a stringent criterion of dementia, reported the prevalence rates shown in Table 5.1. More recently, Gurland et al. (1980), discussing findings from the United States-United Kingdom Cross-National Geriatric Community Study, reported the prevalence rates for dementia among old people in New York City (see Table 5.2). As can be seen, the oldest age cohort has the highest rates, rates increase with age, and the largest increase occurs across the boundaries of 75 and 80 years.

Although the literature indicates that as age increases the prevalence of dementia increases, evidence is beginning to accumulate which suggests that after the age of 90 there is minimal risk of developing dementia. Tomlinson and Kitchener (1972) reported that the prevalence of senile brain disease identified at autopsy levelled off during the ninth decade of life.

Sex. Table 5.2, from the study by Gurland et al., shows a sex difference in the prevalence rates of dementia among the elderly in New York City. In the paper from which the table was extracted, findings indicating whether or not the sex differences were significant were not presented, although Gurland commented upon the sex difference. However, replying to questioning about the sex difference, he explained it as due to (a) female dements surviving for longer than male dements and/or (b) male dements being removed from a community sample by institutional admission sooner than female dements. He also speculated that it might be possible that there is a higher incidence of dementia among females than among males, but did not go on to say why there might be a difference.

Adelstein et al. (1968) found that women had a somewhat higher rate of senile psychoses than men, and Kay et al. (1970) also reported differences in the prevalence rates for males and females. Although Kay and his colleagues did not report results from significance tests of the differences, it is stated in the the Office of Health Economics Document Dementia in Old Age, when referring to the data, that 'it is clear that the rates for males and females do not differ significantly confirming that the apparently higher prevalence among females is a selection of the more favourable survival they experience in old age' (p.10).

Social Class. The evidence for social class differences in prevalence rates is either very weak or only indirect. The only influence of social class that emerged in the extensive investigations of Larsson et al. (1963) was in the case of single females with dementia who were on average of lower socio-economic status. Parsons (1965), in his community study in Swansea, Wales, found that social class and educational attainment were not significantly associated with cognitive state in his sample of 271 persons aged 65 and over.

However, rates and severity levels of dementia have varied with sociocultural factors when psychological tests have been used to assess dementia. For example, Kahn et al. (1961) report that mental functioning as measured by the Mental Status Questionnaire (MSQ) in a sample of 605 old people residing in institutions in New York was significantly correlated with number of years of education - the fewer the years of education the poorer the test performance. Pfeiffer (1975) has reported a similar association between level of education and test performance in a study of 997 elderly in North Carolina. Gurland (Gurland et al. 1978; Gurland, 1981) reports that high scores (more errors) on the dementia scale used in the US-UK Cross-National project were 2.5 times more frequent in the low education group (17 per cent) than in the high education group (7 per cent); this sample was of non-institutionalised elderly.

Although the number of errors on a test like the MSQ is predictive of the clinical diagnosis of dementia or organic brain syndrome (Gurland, 1981) a strong correlation between MSQ score and education does not necessarily mean that dementia is more common in those with a low level of education. Performance on psychological tests could be influenced by both dementia and sociocultural factors like education, class and race. However, Gurland (1981) believes that 'it is still an open matter whether there is an important sociocultural contribution to the prevalence of Alzheimer's and related forms of dementia occurring in the senium (and) ... the evidence now available is sufficiently intriguing to warrant further study of this issue.' While not everyone would agree that the association between dementia and sociocultural factors is an open question (see, for example, comments by Roth and Bergmann on Gurland's 1981 paper), there seems to be less dispute over the role of social factors in referral and institutionalisation. Sainsbury et al. (1965) found that there was a strong relationship between social class and referral, with elderly psychiatric patients from classes I and II having higher referral rates. However, Adelstein et al. (1968), in their study of inception rates - those seeking psychiatric care for the first time - in Salford, England, found no social class gradient for organic and senile psychoses.

Area of residence and social isolation. In the 1940s and 1950s a number of studies examining the relationship between areas of residence and hospitalisation for psychiatric disorders were conducted. Studies such as that by Faris and Dunham (1939), showing that the incidence (as assessed by hospitalisation rates) of schizophrenia, senile and arteriosclerotic dementia was highest in the central areas of low social and economic status and lowest in the affluent residential districts, were often interpreted as evidence that social isolation (it was argued that in the central areas of a city a person tended to become cut off from intimate and lasting emotional relations) was a causal element in mental disorders. Although it is impossible to separate cause from effect in such studies, those showing an association between areas of residence and/or social isolation and hospitalisation rates are today interpreted as indicating that such factors are determinants of hospitalisation or consequences, rather than causes of mental disorders. Therefore, the studies of census tracts, social isolation and marital status will be reviewed in the next section.

The Role of Personality in the Aetiology of Senile Dementia
There has been much speculation, but little research, on the role of personality in either the aetiology of dementia or in symptom formation. One of the earliest studies on personality was by Williams et al. (1942). They made a distinction between arteriosclerotic dementia and senile dementia and found that the arteriosclerotics were (as a group) well adjusted socially and domestically, while most of the senile dements had become socially deteriorated or isolated. It was concluded that senile dementia developed in the wake of long standing social

deterioration which was primarily a consequence of earlier personality defects. They argued further that cerebroarteriosclerotic damage was a physiogenic event, relatively independent of personality or environmental variables.

In another early study of personality, Post (1944) found that amongst 79 consecutive admissions for senile and arteriosclerotic dementia, only 30 had 'normal' previous personalities, and only eight of the group with normal personalities had psychotic symptoms in addition to dementia. Rigidity and obsessional trends were prominent among the abnormal personality traits. Oakley (1965), investigating Noyes and Kolb's (1958) view that dements have a characteristic pre-morbid personality which is obsessional and rigid, also found that, compared to non-dementing patients (Oakley interviewed relatives), dementing patients exhibited more obsessional characteristics.

Studies using retrospective accounts of the personalities of dementing old people are, of course, open to the criticism that the relatives' accounts are coloured and distorted by reactions to the dementing process. Their attempts to make sense of the disorder may also cause them to look for personality characteristics which could be viewed as causal.

The Role of Socio-psychological Factors in Symptom Formation

The psychosomatic approach. To begin, let us briefly consider the view of dementia as a psychosomatic illness. This view was put forward by Wilson in 1955.

Wilson argued that the pathological changes within the brain were the direct cause of the symptoms seen in senile dementia, but the pathological changes were, in turn, the result of psychological features. It was suggested that when an old person's life became meaningless and narrow this led to a restricted view of life, a restricted lifestyle, and then restricted blood flow. Restricted blood flow in turn leads to the observed and pathological features of dementia. Miller (1977), commenting on this approach to dementia, says:

> Needless to say, it is the psychosomatic approach at its most naive. The nature of the mechanism which could link a restricted life-style with a restricted blood flow is unspecified and to claim that restriction of one thing claims to restriction in another surely descends to the

level of argument by 'clang association'.

(p.95)

Personality and symptom formation. Although there
has been little research on the association between
personality and symptom formation, it seems logical
to assume that personality is influential in the
course of dementia. Post (1965) referring to Hughling
Jackson's distinction between 'negative' symptoms
(those directly attributable to loss of function) and
'positive' symptoms (phenomena newly produced or
released because higher integrating controls have
been abolished) puts this view:

> People with personality weaknesses and
> character defects who have earlier in life
> responded to stresses with minor and major
> psychiatric symptoms, might be expected to be
> especially prone to show 'positive' symptoms in
> the course of a dementing illness in old age ...
> Dements with ill-adjusted difficult personal-
> ities and with disorders of mood, behaviour and
> experiencing - are more likely to find their way
> into mental hospitals than old people with
> lovable personalities and only 'negative'
> symptoms of dementia.

More recently, Verwoerdt (1981), citing Gianturco et
al. (1974) and Goldstein (1959), stated that patients
whose pre-morbid personality is characterised by
versatility in adaptation tend to have relatively
less intellectual impairment in association with a
certain amount of neuronal loss. He argues further:

> It is, indeed, reasonable to expect that any
> pre-morbid behavioural style involving aggres-
> sive and 'high energy' defences is especially
> vulnerable to the psycho-trauma of loss of
> mastery (resulting from organic changes): and
> that compulsive, rigid individuals are prone to
> react with profound anxiety, when faced with the
> necessity to change their habitual style, and
> accommodate themselves to ego-alien const-
> raints.

(p.60)

Gurland (1981) cites two studies which indicate that
pre-morbid personality may influence adaptation to
the changes brought about by dementia. In the first,
Gianotti (1975) described a personality type which
predicted the tendency to confabulate. Gianotti

argued that confabulation was more adaptive than admitting a failure of memory. The confabulators were characterised as ambitious, hard-driving, independent, upwardly-mobile and more often in the higher social classes. The second study cited is that by Sinnott (1977), who claimed that flexibility in the assumption of roles is the crucial adaptive quality.

Summary

Two of the three questions asked at the beginning of this section - why have socio-psychological factors been considered important in the aetiology of dementia, and what kinds of evidence could be, or have been used to support the view that such factors are important in aetiology - have been examined. The lack of a perfect match between brain atrophy or cerebral damage and clinical changes in dementia seems to have been responsible for the interest in social and psychological factors as primary causative agents. The factors which have been examined in relation to dementia have included, life events, personality, age, sex, social class and isolation. Apart from age, there is little evidence that such factors are significant in the aetiology of dementia. However, even though we know a lot about the causes of senile dementia and even though almost everyone would agree that the primary cause is biological, there is still not a perfect match between brain changes (e.g. neurofibrillary tangles and senile plaques) and clinical changes. There is, thus, good reason to believe that social and psychological factors influence symptom formation and the course of dementia.

The Consequences of Dementia For The Dementing Elderly

Although this section is concerned with the consequences of dementia for the dementing person, the typical psychological changes that take place - changes that are regarded as the signs and symptoms of senile dementia - will not be outlined. The general characteristics of senile dementia were noted at the beginning of the chapter. However, it seems worth while to mention what is known about how old people react to the onset of a dementing disorder. To a certain extent this was done when considering the role of personality characteristics in symptom formation, and one certainly would not

expect all old people to react in exactly the same
manner to the onset of dementia. Nevertheless, a
search of the literature indicates: (1) that little
is known about the dement's view of what is
happening, what meaning the symptoms have for the
individual; and (2) that anxiety is reported as an
immediate response by most writers. Ann and Stephen
Newroth (1980) regard fear as one of the features of
the personality changes that accompany Alzheimer's
disease. They state:

> Early in the course of Alzheimer's disease, fear
> becomes an increased part of the life of the
> person who has the disease ... In some cases,
> this increased feeling of fear is not an ongoing
> characteristic, but rather comes and goes
> periodically. The intensity of the fears is not
> diminished, however, and it is important that
> support is provided for these periods of anxiety
> when they occur .... This fear may be due to a
> growing awareness by the person that he can no
> longer function as before. The only appropriate
> response to this increase of fear and anxiety is
> for others to develop a sensitivity to the
> reality of his emotional expression and his
> inability to understand the changes that are
> happening with him.
>
> (p.6)

The Newroths do not base their statement on findings
from research projects, but presumably on clinical
experience or discussions with clinicians. Of
course, it may be that research on the meaning of
dementia for the dementing elderly is difficult to
conduct because of the anxiety engendered during
discussions of dementia. However, Meacher (1972),
Carter (1981) and Hirschfeld (1978) have managed to
interview confused old people and discuss their
perceptions of the changes taking place.

In his attempt to substantiate the claim that
confusional behaviour represents a series of logical
adjustments to a distressing environment, rather
than the irrational excrescence of a deranged mind,
Meacher (1972) interviewed confused residents in old
people's homes. Many examples of insight into the
residents' own loss of reactions to their sensory and
mental powers are provided by him. For example, an
85-year-old man said, 'That's a bit of a tease. I'm
going soft, I suppose. 'Course my memory for various
things has got weak on account of age' (p.285).
Meacher also provides examples of confused

residents' feelings about living in an old people's home - feelings mainly of alienation and deep dissatisfaction.

Hirschfeld (1979), in a study of supporters of old people with senile brain disease, also interviewed the dement for purposes other than an assessment of cognitive functioning, but she was forced to report many of these findings from the viewpoint of the supporter. For example, the results concerning activities which the dement enjoyed was reported as information gleaned from comments by supporters. What is important for the discussion here is that when discussing activities enjoyed by the impaired old person, Hirschfeld indicates that supporters/relatives in many cases assume that when there is cognitive impairment, the old person becomes incapable of having a good time. Yet Hirschfeld found examples of old people who could play bridge and chess, even though they could not remember what they had for breakfast. For example:

> Mr. Green's cognitive functioning has been severely impaired for the last two to three years. My husband does not remember if he eats or what time of the day it is, he doesn't recognize the neighborhood we lived in for 20 years, but sometimes he plays not badly bridge .... And he plays pretty good chess; that is unbelievable. He plays with me canasta and he beats me quite often.
>
> (p.135)

Carter (1981) notes that it is often assumed that elderly confused persons do not 'suffer' from the distress of the mental problems of old age. It is assumed that because they are dementing they lack sentience and insight completely. However, in her study of day hospitals she found that painful feelings were experienced by some of the confused old people in day services. She reports that about half admitted to being depressed in the previous month and over two-fifths said that they wished that they were dead. Interestingly, Carter found that the despair of the users of psychogeriatric day services appeared to be more self-directed than aimed at relatives, but users understood very well that a disruption had taken place in the family. In comparison, elderly patients in geriatric day hospitals were more prone to dwell on the vicissitudes created by their illness for the immediate family.

Social Isolation

So little is known about the interaction between dementing old people and their supporters and friends that it would be premature to suggest that when the first signs of dementia occur the old person is labelled as senile and treated as such. However, some of the research on isolation indicates that the dementing elderly are socially isolated and it might be reasonable, therefore, to assume that one of the consequences for the sufferer (even for those living with family) is lack of social stimulation and a decrease in meaningful contact.

Early studies, as noted before, of the social correlates of mental illness in old age have indicated a strong association between mental illness and social isolation. For example, Berkman (see Lowenthal, 1965), in his analysis of the correlates of psychiatric disability in a community sample of 600, found that at all age levels over the age of 60, those suffering from moderate or severe psychiatric disability were living a more restricted social life than those who were psychiatrically healthy.

Lowenthal (1965), in a study investigating the hypothesis that social isolation is a significant intervening variable between pre-disposing personality and related social factors on the one hand, and the development of mental disorders on the other, found that isolation was related to mental illness in old age, but argued that it was a consequence rather than a cause of mental illness.

Kay et al. (1964), in their community survey of psychiatric disturbance in the elderly in Newcastle upon Tyne, found that those with organic mental syndromes, like the functionally ill, had fewer daily contacts, were more often unemployed for at least five years, and had poorer amenities in their homes than the normals. They state: 'Perusal of the list of items found to be associated with the organic mental syndromes shows that, without much doubt, many of them were consequences rather than causes of mental and physical disabilities brought about by the underlying cerebral degeneration.'

Institutionalisation

Besides the risk of becoming socially isolated when suffering from dementia, there is a greater chance of having to move permanently into some form of institutional care. Kay et al. (1970), reporting on the follow-up of three groups of old people living in Newcastle upon Tyne, one group with a diagnosis of

chronic brain syndrome (CBS), one with a functional syndrome, and a group without significant psychiatric abnormality, found that at follow-up 19 per cent of the 'normal' group, 25 per cent of the functionally disordered group, and 61 per cent of the chronic brain syndrome subjects had been admitted to an institution of some kind (a difference significant at $p < 0.01$). Although smaller in number, the CBS subjects accounted for 46 per cent of patients admitted to geriatric wards, and also a relatively large proportion (36 per cent) of those entering institutions.

Thinking that the greater hospital and residential home usage by those with CBS might have been a consequence of their greater age, and hence greater likelihood of being physically ill, widowed or lacking domestic support, Kay and his colleagues matched the CBS subjects by age and sex with a group of 'normals'. They then found that 55 per cent of the CBS subjects, compared to 22 per cent of the matched controls, were admitted to hospital beds at some time during the follow-up, and 17 and 4 per cent, respectively, to residential care. The chronic brain syndrome subjects were also found to have spent four times as long in hospital (7½ years) and ten times as long in homes (11½ years) as the controls. Most of the chronic brain syndrome subjects had been in geriatric wards, while the controls had spent most of their time in acute medical or surgical wards. Carter (1981) also notes that evidence suggests that once admitted to mental hospitals, patients with a diagnosis of dementia rarely come out.

Although it has been argued that those who enter institutional care are apathetic and withdrawn before institutionalisation (Tobin and Lieberman, 1976), social withdrawal amongst old people in institutional settings has been widely reported (Gottesman and Brody, 1975; Jenkins et al., 1977). It seems to be generally accepted that life in an institution is so lacking in stimulation that the symptoms of dementia can be and are exacerbated. Also, removing a confused old person from familiar surroundings is believed to increase disorientation. Hence, besides a greater likelihood of becoming institutionalised, another consequence of dementia for the dement may be an exacerbation of confusion and disorientation.

This section cannot be ended without reference to the benefits of institutionalisation for the dementing old person. Although current social policy is premised on the belief that family care is best for dependency groups, including the frail elderly, many dementing old people live alone and are only visited by caregiving family members. Thus, they remain alone and at risk for large periods of the day. The tensions that can, and do, build up when a dementing old person lives with a caregiver lead to an increased likelihood of 'granny-battering'. Thus, institutionalisation, by increasing contacts with other people and reducing the risks of home accidents and granny-battering, do have some benefits. 'Good' institutions also have therapies which may remove excess disabilities, the discrepancy which exists when the individual's functional incapacity is greater than that warranted by the actual impairment, (Brody et al., 1971).

Social Factors Influencing Institutionalisation and Hospitalisation

Although the results from Kay et al.'s (1970) follow-up, and the heavy hospital usage by old people with organic brain syndromes (2) suggests that for the old person the onset of dementia greatly increases his or her chances of ending up as a permanent resident of a hospital or nursing home, it is well known that other social factors are strong determinants of the likelihood of institutionalisation. It therefore seems worth while to digress somewhat and briefly review some of the research concerned with institutionalisation.

The literature relating social-demographic factors and hospitalisation falls into two categories - studies examining residential areas and studies examining the characteristics of individuals. Research on residential areas and hospitalisation was, as noted earlier, quite popular in the 1940s and 1950s. More recent research has been primarily on the individual social characteristics of old people admitted to hospitals and institutions. The shift in emphasis is probably due to the increased use of sophisticated research methodology and statistics.

The research on residential areas suggests that people in economically poor areas, living alone or in boarding houses are more likely to be admitted to hospitals with the onset of dementia. Faris and Dunham (1939), in a study in Chicago, found that census tract first mental hospital admission rates for senile and arteriosclerotic psychoses were similar to, but less marked than that of schizophrenics. In other words, the rates were highest in central areas of low social and economic status and lower in the affluent districts. Gruenberg (1953) in a study in Syracuse, however, did not find that hospital admissions were related to the economic level of the census tract. What Gruenberg did find was that vulnerable census tracts were characterised by an agglomeration of tenements and boarding houses. With the aim of testing the observations of Faris and Dunham, Hare (1956) studied admission rates in the 28 wards of Bristol, England and found that senile dementia showed no association with living alone, the mean rateable value of housing in the ward, or the population density. Hare offered the following as an explanation for the differences between his results and those of Faris and Dunham and Gruenberg:

> It is not hard to find reasons why the distribution of senile and arteriosclerotic dementia in Bristol should be different from that in American cities. The more even distribution of wealth and the facilities for free treatment under the National Health Service in Britain will tend to lessen the difference between rich and poor in their methods of seeking medical attention for permanently disabled relatives.
>
> (p.355)

Studies in the United States of the individual characteristics of those admitted to hospital have shown that factors involved in low social status -low level of education and low income - are associated with hospitalisation for psychiatric disorders in old age (Fisch et al., 1968). Locke et al. (1960) have also reported that urban, compared to rural residents, negroes and the divorced and separated are more likely to be admitted to hospital.

Single status, widowhood and low socio-economic status also make it more likely that a demented old person will move into an institution in Britain (Jolley and Arie, 1978). Family support is extremely important in maintaining viability in the community.

Bergman et al. (1978), in one of the few studies concerned solely with the dementing elderly patient in the community, examined 83 consecutive patients on their first admission to a psychiatric day hospital assessment unit in a general hospital. They found that at the end of 12 months, nearly 46 per cent of those living with their adult children remained resident in the community. Patients living only with an elderly spouse were more vulnerable, while those who lived alone were most vulnerable of all. More recently, however, Gilleard et al. (1981), reporting preliminary findings from a study in Edinburgh of the impact of psychogeriatric day care on primary supporters of the elderly mentally infirm, noted that for dementing patients living with a spouse was an important factor in determining continued community life, whilst living with a son or daughter(s) was much less likely to lead to successful community maintenance. Living alone, but supported, did not seem to lead to a much higher rate of institutionalisation.

Summary
Very little has been written and hence is known about the dementing person's perceptions of the changes consequent upon dementia. Fear and anxiety have been discussed by writers and clinicians as immediate responses, and it is probably correct to say that this is as much a response to dementia, as a sign or symptom.

Social isolation has been found to be associated with dementing disorders; most investigators regard this as a consequence of dementia. As the dementing person loses the ability to carry on normal conversation, becomes apathetic, irritable, or exhibits a loosening of inhibitions, friends may find visits less rewarding. In the early stages the dementing person may go out less often for fear of getting lost or falling, thus further restricting social contact and stimulation.

Besides a reduction in social stimulation and meaningful contact dementia brings with it, from the dement's viewpoint, an increased probability of permanent institutionalisation. Social factors have been found to be very important in the management of the confused elderly; widowhood, single status and low socio-economic status made a move to permanent institutional care more likely.

'Bad' institutions no doubt exacerbate the symptoms of dementia and make residents unhappy, but 'good' institutions — those providing therapies and an atmosphere which reduces anxiety — may be better for dementing old people than remaining in the community.

The Consequences of Senile Dementia For Supporters

So far in this chapter it has been argued that social, psychological and demographic factors (other than age) have not been convincingly shown to be implicated in the aetiology of senile dementia, but that there are social consequences, namely increased social isolation and an increased probability of a permanent move to some form of institutional care. What must now be considered are the social and psychological consequences of dementia for those who support or 'prop' (Bree, 1960) the dementing elderly in the community.

As mentioned in the introduction, this section relies heavily on the present author's unpublished findings from a study of family care of the dementing elderly. The focus of this study is on the principal supporter, and the aim is to describe problems arising from: (1) the dependant's mental state or behaviour patterns; (2) the supporter's physical and psychological resources and limitations; and (3) environmental and social conditions.

The sample is drawn from day hospital records and the case-load of a community psychiatric nurse. All the patients/dependants have a primary diagnosis of senile dementia. As noted above, the principal supporter (in most cases next of kin) was the focus of the study. To date 52 interviews have been conducted, but of these six are incomplete. Most of the data were gathered via intensive (interviews last about 6 hours) semi-structured interviews with supporters. The dependant was also assessed at the day hospital and the staff filled in ratings forms about the patient's functioning in a number of areas. The data are being analysed both quantitatively and qualitatively.

As this study is still ongoing and only partially analysed, discussion points will consider findings from other studies on supporters. Before beginning, however, a brief look at the size of the problem is worth while.

Who Gives Care?

Although, as noted in the previous section, dementia carries with it an increased risk of hospitalisation, this does not mean that the majority of the elderly with dementia are in institutions. Quite the contrary has been found to be the case. Kay et al., (1964), for example, in their community survey in Newcastle reported that there were 14 times more old people in private households with senile or arteriosclerotic dementia than in welfare homes. Taking the figures for those with 'severe brain syndromes' gives a ratio of 6.5 in the community for every one in any type of institution. Parsons (1965) in a community study in Swansea found that 4.4 per cent of his sample of 228 persons over the age of 65 years were 'demented', giving a ratio of 6.3 demented living in private households for every one in hospital (figures calculated by Meacher, 1972).

Looking at the population figures gives an idea of the actual numbers of old people living in the community with senile dementia. The mid-year estimate of the numbers of people over 75 years (the most vulnerable group) for 1979 was 3,059,300 (Central Statistical Office, 1981). The projected figures for the United Kingdom for 1991 for the over 75 age group is 3,621,000 (Office of Population Census and Surveys, 1980). Using 3 million as a convenient and conservative base-line and a conservative estimate of 10 per cent (see Table 5.1) gives a figure of 300,000 with dementia. Based on Kay et al.'s (1964) report that one in five of the elderly with dementia are in institutions leaves 240,000 demented old people living in the community – in my opinion quite a staggering figure.

Although the community care movement has aimed at government support for this section of the population, the burden of care for the infirm elderly still falls primarily on relatives. Some, but by no means all, of these people live with caregiving relatives. Carter (1981), in a study on day units, found that in units for the confused elderly just over half said they lived alone, while 40 per cent lived with relatives. Of these latter, 17 per cent lived with a spouse, 12 per cent with adult children and 10 per cent with other relatives. Of those users aged 70 or over there was a marked increase in the numbers living alone – nearly threefold. Carter argued that this implies that the death of a spouse may uncover cases of mental disorders which would otherwise remain contained within the family for longer periods.

In an earlier study of 83 consecutive admissions of people suffering from organic psychiatric disorders, Bergmann et al. (1978) found that 34 per cent had been living alone, 23 per cent living with a spouse, 29 per cent living with other relatives and 14 per cent had been in residential care. In the general population aged 65 years and over, 52 per cent live with a spouse, 14 per cent live with others, and 34 per cent live alone (Social Trends, Central Statistical Office, 1981). There are also fairly marked sex differences: 74 per cent of men, compared to 37 per cent of women live with a spouse, and 17 per cent of men compared to 45 per cent of women live alone. When working out the numbers of

dementing old people living alone, with a spouse, or
with others in the community, one must therefore take
into account these differential rates in household
type, as well as the fact that the ratio of women to
men in the 75 and over age group is approximately
68:32 (Social Trends, Central Statistical Office,
1981).

Extrapolating from these figures and excluding
those over 75 living in institutions produces the
following: around 36,800 (46 per cent) of men and
16,000 females (10 per cent) with dementia live with
a spouse; 21,600 males (27 per cent) and 52,800
females (33 per cent) live with others; 21,600 males
(27 per cent) and 91,200 females (57 per cent) live
alone. Looking at the problem in another way, these
estimates indicate that 52,800 spouses care for a
dementing person, and 74,400 other relatives (mainly
adult children) care for a dementing person.

Two things should be kept in mind when
considering these very rough calculations: (1) the
estimates of dementia are based on a very
conservative figure of 10 per cent of the over 75s;
(2) those giving support in the community to the
dementing elderly are primarily females (Hunt 1978;
Equal Opportunities Commission, 1980).

Because of the increase in the proportion of the
very old, combined with government policy
encouraging community rather than hospital care for
the mentally ill and aged, more and more relatives
will find themselves in the position of looking after
a mentally-impaired old person. Professionals have,
therefore, begun to take a keen interest in the
effects on supporters and many investigations on the
care of the elderly have been conducted recently.
Most of these studies have focused on the degree of
burden experienced and the psychological well-being
of the supporter.

The Psychological Well-being of the Supporter

Most of the literature to date has shown that caring
for the elderly mentally-impaired is stressful and
leads to psychological distress in supporters.
Isaacs et al. (1972), reporting on a study of the
reasons for admission of 280 patients to a geriatric
unit in Glasgow, noted that the presence of mental
abnormality created an immeasurably greater amount
of strain on supporters than that produced by
physical symptoms.

Supporters I interviewed often said spontaneously that caring for someone who was physically
ill, no matter how ill, would be easier. Gilleard,

for example (1982), in a study of supporters of the
elderly mentally infirm, reports that in his pilot
sample of 40 supporters the prevalence of significant
psychological disturbance (as measured by the GHQ)
exceeded 50 per cent. Wheatley (1979) in an in-depth,
intensive study of seven supporters of dementing old
people found that all supporters suffered from
emotional distress, nervous strain and anxiety.
Hirschfeld (1978), in a study of 30 supporters living
with a dementing person, reported that 60 per cent of
the supporters rated themselves 'low' to 'fair' on
life satisfaction. The morale of supporters in my
study was very 'low' (using the Kutner Morale Scale,
1956), but there was little evidence of psychiatric
'caseness' using scales from the Present State
Examination (PSE) schedule. Nevertheless, 40 per
cent of co-resident supporters, and 30 per cent of
non-resident supporters experienced mild to moderate
depressed mood; 65 per cent of co-resident and 47 per
cent of non-resident supporters reported mild
feelings of nervous tension. Only 20 per cent of the
co-resident supporters experienced feelings of
hopelessness and none in the non-resident group. My
own findings are not particularly surprising
considering the nature of the sample. Those who cope
well and experience no anxiety, worry, depression,
etc. probably do not come into contact with the
psychiatric services. Those supporters who are
seriously depressed or who have clinically
significant symptoms probably do not cope at all and
the dementing relatives therefore end up in an
institution at an earlier stage. However, broader
based studies should shed further light on this
matter.

Stressful Features of Caregiving
What is it about senile dementia that produces such
strain and distress? Is it the loss of memory,
disorientation, progressive dependency for self-care
and activities of daily living? Is it the personality
or emotional changes or the loosening of inhibitions?
What about incontinence? Or, is the strain due to
features only indirectly related to the symptoms of
dementia, that is, the strain due to the supporters'
attitudes to caregiving, to the effects on the
marriage and children, to the change in the
supporters' social position or life? These issues are
only beginning to be confronted, but an attempt will
be made here to describe what is known about the
effects on the supporter and which features of care
are most stressful.

The Daily Grind

Wilkin (1979) discusses some of his findings of a study of caring for the mentally handicapped child under the heading 'The Daily Routine'. Bayley (1973) does a similar thing under the heading 'The Daily Grind'. In many ways Bayley's heading seems more appropriate for those supporting the dementing elderly and it is certainly worth while examining what life is like for the average supporter.

No one would, of course, claim that life is identical for everyone giving care to a dementing old person. Both supporters and dependants have their own personalities and histories, and the symptoms vary widely from one old person to another. However, there are similarities in the life situations of those who take on care, and all those who work with the elderly and their supporters should be aware of what it is like to give support. For many professionals encounters with the dementing old person will be brief and often not in the home. It is all too easy to see the dementing elder as 'a nice old lady' and hence to feel unsympathetic to the worries or complaints of supporters.

Supporters fall broadly into two groups – those who are residing in the same household with the dementing person and those who are not co-residents. Care for these two groups is quite different, although it is possible that the effects of continuing care on the supporter are the same. To give an idea of what the daily grind is like, two cases from my study have been selected which best represent the co-resident and non-resident supporters in my study.

Miss MacDonald, aged 46, lived with her mother in a high rise flat. She gave up her job because of a slight health problem and because of the necessity of keeping a constant watch on her mother. Mrs MacDonald only went to the day hospital two days a week, Tuesdays and Thursdays. On Tuesdays Miss MacDonald went into town to do her 'messages' and met her sister at lunch time. On Thursdays she went to the hairdresser and again had lunch with her sister.

Miss MacDonald's social life was extremely restricted. Besides seeing her sister on Tuesdays and Thursdays, her sister and husband visited, sometimes with their grandchildren, on Saturdays.

Mrs MacDonald had a living brother and sister, but their own poor health meant that they rarely visited.

There was a neighbour who was quite friendly but this did not extend to visiting in 'each other's house' and consisted mainly in talking over the balconies.

No practical help was received from this neighbour or from any of the relatives. However, Miss MacDonald expressed no resentment at this and her housework seemed to provide something to do. The flat was spotless and a high proportion of time was spent cleaning. For example, the windows were cleaned at least once a week.

Miss MacDonald busied herself tidying the flat, watching television and, of course, looking after her mother. On the whole Mrs MacDonald was not very disabled. She could not cook, clean, prepare a meal or generally participate in housekeeping activities. Mrs MacDonald needed some help getting dressed, but did not have to be dressed completely. However, she could not bathe and required extensive help when having a bath. Her hair and general grooming had to be done by her daughter. Mrs MacDonald was occasionally incontinent of urine. The problem might have been worse if Miss MacDonald did not frequently take her to the toilet and supervise.

Helping with dressing, grooming and toileting took up a fair amount of time, but certainly did not fill the day. Miss MacDonald could not pursue hobbies or read quietly because her mother followed her around and repeatedly asked questions. Miss MacDonald rarely took her mother out. This was for a number of reasons — the embarrassment of unpredictable behaviour, difficulty of getting her ready to go out in bad weather, and the fact that as soon as they got out Mrs MacDonald began talking about 'going home'. Thus, life for Miss MacDonald was an endless round of housekeeping chores and television, interspersed by only 2½ days of 'relief'. She described how often she wondered if she would make it through the weekend ... a weekend which started on Thursday at 4.00 and ended Tuesday morning at 10.00am when the ambulance came again to collect her mother for the day hospital.

For nearly all the supporters in my sample who were co-resident with the dementing old person, the daily routine consisted of an endless round of housekeeping tasks, e.g. helping the elder with dressing and toileting, etc., and then attempts to fill the time that was left.

Day hospital care provided a welcome break and an opportunity to get out of the house, usually to do the shopping. The tasks required to maintain the old person at home were rarely physically demanding, but often difficult because the dement would not co-operate.

Life for supporters not residing in the same household was richer and more complicated, and it was difficult to select a case which was representative of the daily routine for most supporters. The one selected was a daughter working part-time who was married and had an adult child still living at home.

Mrs McNeil was a 55-year-old married daughter. Mrs McNeil's mother was 81 and lived across town in a tenement flat. Mr and Mrs McNeil's son, aged 20, still lived at home. Mrs McNeil worked part-time.

Before Mrs Ford started attending the day hospital Mrs NcNeil visited her mother every day; the visits were to check on her mother, make sure she was taking her medicines, and to generally give her a little company. The schedule at the time of the interview had changed to the following: Sunday the mother was taken to Mrs McNeil's house for the afternoon and evening. Monday Mrs McNeil did not visit because Mrs Ford had a home help; but Mrs McNeil phoned. Tuesday Mrs McNeil went from work to her mother's house and fixed herself and her mother lunch. She then took her mother out for shopping or a general look around town. Because Mrs Ford was only mildly confused Mrs McNeil felt it was safe to put her on the bus to go home. Wednesday, Mrs Ford went to the day hospital, so her daughter did not visit, but phoned in the evening. Thursday Mrs McNeil repeated the procedure for Tuesday except she took her mother home and stayed later in the evening, waiting until her husband finished work. Friday Mrs Ford went to the day hospital and Mrs McNeil phoned in the evening. Saturday, Mrs McNeil did not work so collected her mother about noon, took her shopping in the afternoon and then took her home.

It had only been a week from the start of this routine until the interview. Before Mrs McNeil visited her mother every day, and had been visiting every day for 6 months. She said this was a terrible strain and had affected relations within the nuclear family.

As can be seen from this case, the daily routine for the non-resident supporter is different and consists largely of demands made on time resulting from the need for constant visiting. A much higher proportion of the dementing old people in the non-resident group had home-helps and meals-on-wheels, relieving supporters of these tasks. The dependants in the non-resident group were also less impaired and thus somewhat less in need of help from supporters in the instrumental activities of daily living or help with physical self-maintenance. Nevertheless, the level of dependency in each group was sufficient to dislocate the everyday routines of the supporters. This is not, of course, to say that the dislocation came on suddenly. Dependency with dementia develops slowly and insidiously in most cases and supporters gradually accommodate the impairment by adjusting daily routines.

Accounts of daily routine by supporters in my sample often focused on one or two particular problems. For example, the practical difficulties of getting an obese and uncooperative 80-year-old parent into the bath; or how to get an old man, disoriented for time with a very poor short-term memory, to take medications at the right times and in the right quantity. Supporters demonstrated considerable ingenuity in managing an old person with dementia at home, although it was usually a matter of preventing the occurrence of certain behaviours rather than getting the dependant to do certain things.

Because it is with ordinary tasks that services can provide the most effective help, it is important to know about the features of dementia and caregiving which cause supporters most difficulty. It may, of course, turn out that the features which cause most distress do not revolve around practical difficulties and may, therefore, be less open to intervention. Recent research, much of which is yet unpublished, has addressed itself to finding out which aspects of caregiving cause most strain and are least 'tolerable'. The findings of these studies, plus those of my own, will now be considered.

Intolerable problems
Sanford's (1975) paper on alleviation factors and tolerable versus intolerable difficulties in care

was the first to examine the 'problems' of home care systematically. Because his paper has been very influential and his terminology widely used, it is worth while considering the findings in some detail.

Sanford drew his sample from admissions to a hospital for non-medical reasons. Supporters were asked about the frequency of behaviour problems, plus which problems would have to be alleviated to restore a tolerable situation at home. Although this study was not concerned primarily with dementia, 31 of the 50 cases had a diagnosis of senile dementia. As can be seen in Table 5.3, Sanford found that sleep disturbance, faecal incontinence, night wandering, shouting, micturition - all features of dementia - were poorly tolerated.

Incontinence. Subsequent studies (Hirschfeld, 1978; Machin, 1980) and writings (Gray and Isaacs, 1979) have all noted that incontinence is very distressing for those caring for the dementing elderly. Isaacs et al. (1972) devote a whole chapter to it. It is not just the fact that the old person cannot control micturition or bowel movements that upsets the supporters, it is the problems that result from the cognitively impaired person's inability and lack of awareness as to what he or she is doing, or even when there is some awareness, the attempts by the dementing old person to cover up the accidents. Gray and Isaacs give the following example:

> The patient, who has always been clean and fastidious, soils her underwear with urine and faeces. Instead of rinsing and laundering them, she wraps them in newspaper and hides them in the cutlery drawer, where they are subsequently found by a horrified daughter. The patient indignantly denies having put them there.
>
> (p.20)

One of the old ladies in my sample had taken to defecating in the corners of the living-room. Her daughter-in-law, who was the principal supporter, found she could not cope with the mess and the smell and was told by her husband to leave it and he would clean it up when he got home from work, which meant, of course, that the old lady was left in the house with her faeces for many hours at a time. Another supporter, a daughter, had moved her incontinent father out of her house and back to his tenement flat because she did not want her new home ruined by faeces. She said she had always had a hard time keeping herself from being sick when she went to her father's flat and found him lying in bed with faeces on his face.

Night wandering and sleep disturbance. Both Machin (1980) and Hirschfeld (1978) found that night wandering and the consequent disturbance of sleep were very difficult to cope with. The supporters in my group also found that night wandering was virtually intolerable. Wandering at night has, of course, a different impact on supporters not residing in the same household. The non-resident supporters do not experience the sleep disturbance and sleep deprivation that co-resident supporters often experience. Prolonged periods of broken nights makes it very difficult to cope with other problems during the day, as anyone who has had a wakeful baby knows. However, for the non-resident supporter, night wandering means constant worry about the old person going out in the middle of the night. Many of the dementing old people in my sample had come into contact with the psychiatric services because of an episode or crisis of wandering about the city in the middle of the night, sometimes clad only in a nightdress.

Unaesthetic behaviour. Machin (1980) found that refusal to bathe or wash, or to be helped to, was a very serious problem which was not well tolerated in her study. Other behaviours which fell into her category of 'Lapses of Personal Hygiene' were also poorly tolerated.

Hirschfeld (1978) categorised refusal to bath as unaesthetic behaviour and found such behaviour particularly intolerable for the supporters in her study. She quotes one as saying, 'My mother-in-law used to be so particular. Her underwear was white and now I cannot get her brassiere off to put it into the washing machine. She will wear it and wear it, so I just sneak her clothes while she is asleep, wash them, and put them exactly back into place.' Another supporter in Hirschfeld's study was quoted as saying, 'My father's habit of spitting really bothers me. I have to wash the dishes in the sink, but I am wasting my breath telling him not to spit in there.'

Strange or bizarre behaviour. Behaviours which are unaesthetic, and some of the unpleasant aspects of incontinence, may be viewed as strange or bizarre. But whether or not such behaviours are categorised here, or under another heading, if they are viewed as strange by supporters they upset supporters and are poorly tolerated. Machin (1980) found that bizarre behaviours were especially upsetting when they first occurred. Hirschfeld (1978) noted that strange behaviour often came to be tolerated with simple acceptance. She cites one supporter talking of her husband: 'The other night he ate ten bananas with the peels: I forgot to cover them.' Hirschfeld reported that the family resorted to bitter, cynical humour when talking about the man's bizarre behaviours.

Dangerous behaviours. Dangerous behaviours are a worry for both co-resident and non-resident supporters. When dementing old people live alone dangerous behaviours often lead to permanent institutional care. One man in my sample set his clothing on fire attempting to throw a curtain out of the window that had caught on fire. Another burnt the living-room couch by pushing it against an electric fire. Gray and Isaacs (1979) even describe the 'burnt-out kettle' as a sign of brain failure (a sign of diminished vigilance).

Mood disturbance. Apathy, bouts of crying and a general lack of interest in anything are frequently mentioned by supporters as upsetting. Green et al. (1982), in a factor analytic study of scales administered to supporters of day hospital patients in Glasgow, found that supporters' distress was mainly a response to the patient's (diagnosed as suffering from senile dementia) withdrawn behaviour. Green and his colleagues did not find that 'active' disturbed behaviour was associated with any of the measures of supporters' stress.

Demands for attention and interpersonal conflict. Constant demands for attention and the presence of the supporter distress and annoy supporters. Machin (1980) included demands for attention, tantrums, cantankerous behaviour, abusive language, etc. under 'personality difficulties' and reported that this general category of 'problems' contained the majority of the citations for poorly-tolerated behaviours. Gilleard and his colleagues in Edinburgh have been studying the problems supporters of the mentally infirm elderly face, and have found that problems reflecting attentional and emotional demand on the supporter are mostly responsible for the reported level of strain (Gilleard et al. (1980).
The problems outlined above are those supporters rarely find unproblematic. They have been

found to cause burden and distress in the studies by Sanford, Machin, Hirschfeld, Green et al., Gilleard et al., and in my own study. Of course, problems which emerge as intolerable depend on the questions asked by the researcher. Compared to Sanford, Machin enquired more into interpersonal difficulties and also used a broader definition of what counted as an intolerable problem. Therefore, it is not surprising that she found interpersonal difficulties to be cited more frequently. Hirschfeld found slightly different intolerable problems, but again asked slightly different questions and used a more open-ended approach than either Sanford or Machin. Because of the open-ended nature of her interviews, Hirschfeld was able to examine in more detail the impact of problems on the supporter and was able to conclude, 'But the mere fact of a problem's existence did not determine its impact upon a given family's life. While some family members considered a certain behaviour the prime problem in handling the IM (impaired member), other family members hardly acknowledged the behaviour's existence.' Gilleard et al. (1980) also note that the level of strain experienced by supporters of the dementing elderly is only partly accounted for by the incidence of problems.

Supporter Feelings and Attitudes as a Source of Strain

The supporters' own feelings about the dementing relative, the dementing disorder and giving care can also contribute to the strains experienced. When the past relationship between supporter and dependant has been poor, supporters may give care 'because no one else will do it', i.e. out of a sense of (residual) moral obligation, and not because they feel that home care is what the dementing relative prefers or is better for the old person. A preliminary analysis of my data has indicated that the better the relationship prior to the development of dependency the less willing the supporter is to consider institutional care. Giving care 'because no one else will do it' leads to considerable resentment and even hostility to the dependant. Isaacs et al. (1972) found that in cases where old people had not received care from available relatives, there had usually been a long history of conflict or rejections of help and love by the dependant.

Interestingly, in my sample, supporters - and here I refer to daughters mainly - who had a very close relationship with the dependant prior to the development of dementia were most distressed and experienced most strain. Those who had poor relationships were less willing to give care, gave less care, and experienced, usually, less strain. However, some experienced guilt about not doing more for the dementing parent, e.g. visiting more often. Guilt about not taking the dependant into the supporters' home also contributed to the strain experienced by some supporters. This will be discussed again when the supporters' marriage and children are considered. Supporters also experience anxiety about how to deal with the dementing relative, and this appears to be related to how knowledgeable the supporter is about the disorder. Those who know almost nothing about senile dementia do not know to what to attribute the symptoms. In my sample, 10 of the first 37 supporters interviewed, when asked about the cause of the problems or symptoms, said they did not know. Only nine supporters said 'senile' or 'arteriosclerotic dementia' or 'going senile' when asked what about the source of the symptoms; eight said the problems were due to hardening of the arteries; five gave brain deterioration or 'brain gone' as a response to questioning, and another five said the dependant had had a 'shock' (stroke); 13 supporters said 'old age'; six gave an emotional event as a causal element in dementia. It was quite surprising to find that the supporters in my sample knew so little about dementia, about its causes, and, more importantly, its prognosis.

Knowledge about dementia influences supporters' perceptions of how to behave with the dementing relative. Like other types of mental illness, dementia is stigmatised and surrounded with uncertainties. Hence, there are few, if any, accepted ways of dealing with it. Many supporters in my sample felt they should not encourage dependence, but found it less stressful to do everything for the dependant and ignore mistaken perceptions, and mistakes in memory and orientation, etc. Because dementia is stigmatised, advice is not sought from other relatives or friends, and often not even from professionals. The first lady I interviewed kept her husband's incontinence and problem behaviour a secret from her daughers for 1½ years; she did not tell her doctor either. It wasn't until a daughter became aware that her mother was on the verge of mental and physical collapse and enquired as to what was bothering her that help was sought. It was not unusual to find that I was the only person that the supporter had ever confided in about the disorder. Although supporters appeared reluctant in many cases to speak to the GP about the dementing old person's behaviour, this does not mean that they did not want information or advice. Supporters expected the GP to volunteer information which, it seems, at least from my study, they rarely do.

Furthermore, as Wilkin (1979) noted, the behaviour of the supporters is open to criticism no matter what is done. If the supporter tries to hide the problem and contain it within the home she will be seen as being over-protective. If she tries to continue as normal she will be accused of denying the existence of a problem. If she seeks institutional care she will encounter social disapproval for 'rejecting' the dementing relative or lacking a proper moral obligation.

Effects on Marriage
In the emotional climate which caring for the demented elderly often creates, relationships between husbands and wives are likely to become strained. Although there is quite a lot of research on the effects on family relations of caring for the mentally ill, to date there has been little research on the effects of caring for a dependent parent on the family, especially on the supporter's marriage. Isaacs et al. (1972) touch on the strain put on marriages via a case-study approach, pointing out that the effects on the marriage depend to a large extent on relations between the married couple and the dependent old person before dementia. Where relations have been poor the spouse (usually the husband) may be not only unwilling to help, but positively obstructive. Married daughters in my study only rarely received help from their husbands when caring for a parent even when the couple lived in the same household. Husbands didn't even take over additional chores to relieve the burden on their wives. When the principal supporter was a son, their wives always helped a great deal, and often the daughter-in-law gave as much, if not more, help in those cases of 'shared caring'. (There were no cases of shared caring where the dependant was a woman's parent in my sample.) Sometimes married women supporters even suggested that giving care would be easier if they were not married, indicating considerable strain when attempting to fill two roles. Here are some extracts of a transcript with a supporter (R) about the subject of her marriage and the roles of caregiver and housewife:

MG   Has the care of your mother created any difficulties at all in your marriage?

R   Oh now yes, yes, quite a lot sometimes, oh yes there's lots of rows. Not so much rows about that, but ... about other things ... awful lot of jobs to be done which I've neglected to do. Ah eh ... of yes, it must cause a lot of discomfort. But not as such. Do you understand what I'm saying?

MG   I think what you are trying to say is that you have more arguments, perhaps more disagreements, but they're not directly about your mother. And am I correct in thinking that what has happened is that it's just created more tension in the household?

R   A great deal of tension. Sometimes there is direct rows about it.

MG   But your husband doesn't ever say anything like 'You must stop doing this'? Or does he sometimes suggest that you should stop giving so much care?

R   Well, I think he has said 'It's about high time this place was being looked at and other people, other things were ... matters were attended to.'

MG   How does this make you feel, does this ...

R   Oh yes. Well, it just means that I sneak about doing things. It makes you less open.

Machin (1960) has also found that marriages can be adversely affected. She found that husbands sometimes did not get on very well with the elderly dependant and that there was often jealousy between the couple which increased the tension. Furthermore, Machin also did not get support for her hypothesis that the vicissitudes of the caring role would have different effects on single supporters who were coping alone and supporters with husbands alone. As she says, 'Thus, when caring for an elderly person, it is not always an advantage to be married' (p.140). It would, of course, be unfair to leave the reader with the idea that supporters never found having a husband to be advantageous (and most of the men supporters found having a wife advantageous because they gave a great deal of practical help and emotional support). There were several supporters in my sample who felt that they would not have been able to carry on without their husband's emotional support. Mrs MacIntyre frequently said throughout the interviews that her husband was a wonderful source of emotional support. She did, however, acknowledge that caring for a dementing parent could be a source of considerable strain:

> I couldn't have carried on if he hadn't been so helpful I just couldna have - in fact I couldn't understand any girl keeping a mother or a father it's eh ... beginning to go like that in their old age if eh ... the husband was going to eh ... was really terrible. It would be terrible for the girl because I mean to say it's not his mother and you would be actually torn between the two, you know. Eh ... on, no, I couldn't have coped if I hadn't had my husband, definitely not.

> MG   But even so, it must be difficult for him ... does he ever express any kind of resentment?

> No he would just say, eh, eh, if I say 'She's not feeling too well' I won't ... I've seen him saying to me 'But you've yourself to think about', he says, 'If you crack up' he says 'What's going to happen then' he says, 'She's going to have to go some place' he says and he says 'It's not going to help'. You know he tries to, he tries to keep me, he tries to keep me right, eh ... oh he's wonderful with her you know, he's wonderful with her. Eh, he seems to have a different approach tae things. Of course, you see, it's not his mother and it doesn't affect him the same as it does me. Certainly there's lots of men I know wouldn't put up with the life that he's put up with. In fact nine out of ten wouldn't do it, you know. But, eh ... Oh, I just couldn't have carried on if it, if he hadn't been like that, you know.

Effects on Children

Because dementia only rarely occurs before the age of 65 it is uncommon for there to be very young children in the household of a dementing person. However, when there are young children or adolescents in the household there can be greater conflict, more difficulties and greater strain for the principal supporter, as can be illustrated by this case from my study.

Mrs McKay's mother had died two years before the interview. Her father had been showing signs of dementia for a number of years, but as he lived in a small town many miles away from the city, his behaviour and dependency had no direct impact on Mrs McKay, his youngest daughter. When her mother died unexpectedly, all of the children got together to discuss what should be done about Mr Craig. It seems that considerable pressure was put on Mrs McKay to give up her house and move into the family home and look after Mr Craig. Mrs McKay was annoyed and upset by the suggestion that she, just because she was divorced, should be the one to have to give care. However, she said it was clear that her brothers and sisters were unprepared to take Mr Craig into their homes so she decided she would take her father, but that she would move him to her home, a small 2-bedroomed council flat. One of the main reasons for not moving into the family's home was that her son, aged 11 at the time, did not want to move. A row developed, however, about moving the father to the city, and hence, only one of her six siblings gave any help.

Although Mrs McKay sometimes worried about the effects on her son (aged 13 at the time of the interview) of having a very demented and disruptive grandfather in the home, she was also very determined to keep her father at home and not 'put' him in an institution. When Mr Craig was first moved into the house the son gave up his bedroom and slept in the living-room in a sleeping bag on the settee. However, this did not work very well as Mr Craig wandered a great deal at night and disturbed him. So, Mrs McKay decided that her son should sleep in her room. However, they only had one bed and at the time of the interview the boy was still sleeping with her, even though she acknowledged that at his age this was definitely not a good idea. When asked if it was possible to move to a bigger flat Mrs McKay said she she had not asked because she couldn't afford the rent, her son didn't want to move, etc. But, the presence of her one and only friend and confidant across the street may have been the main reason for not attempting to find more suitable and bigger accommodation.

The boy's schoolwork had suffered, no doubt because of the many disturbed nights. Mr Craig was very restless at night and Mrs McKay and her son often had a hard time getting Mr Craig back to bed. Sometimes during these night wanderings he had become aggressive and the two of them ended up awake most of the night. According to Mrs McKay the teachers at her son's school were not at all sympathetic, seeing her son as lazy. When he described his grandfather's bizarre night behaviours to one of the teachers he was accused of telling 'lies' and making up quite unbelievable stories.

There was a great deal of conflict between the son and his grandfather and on one occasion the son had asked or suggested that his grandfather be put into a home or hospital. Mrs McKay reported that she replied 'Would you put me in a Home?' The boy burst into tears at the thought and never again said anything about his grandfather going into a home or institution.

One doesn't like to pass judgements on people in this sort of situation, but this was certainly one case in which one couldn't help but think that this supporter was allowing her son to suffer unnecessarily. Mrs McKay's father was so demented that obtaining a place in hospital would have been relatively easy. But each person's situation is complex, and Mrs McKay had reached the stage where caring for her father had become one of her few roles – she was unemployed and was living on supplementary benefits; over the two years of caregiving she had become more or less totally socially isolated.

Mrs McKay did not use the negative effects on her son as a way to get help and services, but another supporter in my sample was, to a certain extent, exploiting the general belief in our culture that children must come first.

Mrs McEwan was supporting her sister in her home on what she regarded as a 'temporary' basis. The sister had a son living in Aberdeen and Mrs McEwan regarded it as his duty to take responsibility for his mother. However, the son and his new wife lived in a small cottage with an upstairs toilet. As the dependant, Mrs McGill, was incontinent, the son felt that he could not take his mother in with him; both he and his wife worked and hence were out all day;

and anyway, his wife could hardly be expected to take care of his mother, and so on. Mrs McEwan's husband had chronic bronchitis and had had to retire early and rarely left the house, so it was thought that perhaps the McEwans could care for Mrs McGill during her illness. Mrs McEwan, however, worked full-time, and her grand-daughter of 16 lived with them.

The grand-daughter and Mrs McGill slept, not only in the same room, but in the same bed – even though Mrs McGill was incontinent. Asked if she had considered getting separate beds, Mrs McEwan replied that she had no intention of getting separate beds as Mrs McGill's son might then regard this arrangement of temporary care as permanent.

The grand-daughter did not like sleeping with her aunt and there were frequent arguments with the aunt and quite considerable conflict in the family since the arrival of the sister. Mrs McEwan acknowledged that her grand-daughter was distressed by the arrangement and 'suffering' because of it.

Mrs McEwan refused to answer or avoided all questions about whether or not she would like it if her sister was to move into an OPH or institution of some kind, saying only that it was her nephew's responsibility.

For grandchildren not living in the same household the impact of the dementing illness is naturally less. Grandchildren are, of course, often married with young children of their own and the requirements of young children certainly gives them a good reason for not becoming involved in the care of their dementing grandparents. Adolescent grand-children not living in the same house were reported by supporters as rather intolerant of the dementing grandparent. Younger grandchildren seemed to be more tolerant, but were reported as being afraid of granny or grandad if he or she exhibited unusual behaviour. One supporter felt saddened by the fact that her father had become so dirty and horrid that her 8-year-old child would not visit without becoming tearful, so she rarely visited with her daughter. As this man was the child's only living grandparent the daughter felt that the child would never have the opportunity to know or have a 'real' grandparent.

The supporters in the sample who did not reside in the same house and who had young children were greatly influenced by what they thought would be the effects on their children if they took the dementing relative into their own home. As would be expected, supporters assumed that the effects would be negative and thus were unwilling to consider home care.

Effects on External Family Relationships

So far no systematic research has been conducted on changes in relationships among relatives of dementing old people. What literature there is does not indicate that relatives always rally round, helping each other and the dementing old person - that is, sharing the burden. As noted earlier, women rather than men are principal supporters and even where the dementing person is the parent of a male, it is often the son's wife who does more than half the caregiving. It seems that once one person has taken on the responsibility the rest give even less help. One might, in such circumstances, expect the principal supporter to feel resentful and family relationships to become characterised by hostility, argument, criticism and dissension about care.

Sometimes supporters are evasive about whether or not they think other relatives ought to give more help. In other cases, supporters speak openly about their feelings of resentment that develop when siblings, especially, do not fully share the burden. Both supporters' morale and willingness to consider institutionalisation were significantly correlated with satisfaction with help from relatives in my preliminary analysis.

The Social Life of Supporters

For many of the supporters in my study, all social life revolved around the family, and so conflict within the marriage and between relatives affected the whole of the supporter's social life. Conflict reduced visits leaving the co-resident supporter more isolated.

As might be expected, the co-resident supporters in the sample were more socially isolated than the non-resident supporters. Relationships with neighbours were always rather superficial and the stigmatising nature of dementia frequently reduced contact even more. There were many instances of what Goffman calls 'disassociating'.

Few supporters in the co-resident sample said they had given up hobbies to give care, but as the disorder has such an insidious onset it is very likely that over time they had not only gradually given up social activities and hobbies, but had lowered their expectations too.

Non-resident supporters' social lives were less affected, and only a few said they had given up activities to give care. Working, for many of the women supporters in this group, was a much valued social outlet and none said she was willing to give this up.

Where the social life of the supporter had for many years been based on 'couple' activities, the loss of the dependant's cognitive capacities and increased dependency had a big impact on the supporter's social life. Male spouses tended to suffer less because they got more help, and hence more social contacts, from relatives, and seemed less reluctant than women supporters to go out and leave the impaired spouse alone.

Help from the Services

Conflict in marriage, negative effects on children, conflict in external relations and a reduction in social life no doubt add to the strain of coping with a dementing old person. The services available to the old person and her supporter should, however, mediate the effect of caregiving.

The services available in Britain include home-helps, meals-on-wheels and day centre care provided by the local authorities or voluntary associations. Incontinence and the inability to bathe usually means help from the community or district nursing services. In a few areas there are incontinence laundry services. Relief from the burden of constant attendance is provided to supporters by the health service via day hospitals. Relief from the task of care can also be obtained by using the 'holiday' or 'relief' bed in geriatric and psychogeriatric wards of hospitals and in some local authority residential homes. The general practitioner is usually the 'gatekeeper' to these services.

It is common to talk about 'packages' of service provision (DHSS, 1981), but there is little evidence that the amount and type of service provided (packaged) exactly matches need. In the area I researched the availability of day hospital care places meant that most supporters got only two days relief a week, rather than the amount needed or wanted. Goldberg and Connelly (1982) also note that patterns of attendance at day centres are often not related to individual need.

Surprisingly, analysis of my data revealed that none of the services (frequency of day hospital care, home-helps, meals-on-wheels, community nurse) influenced supporters' willingness to continue care.

However, the services were associated with supporters' psychological well-being, with greater service provision associated with higher morale and better mental health. Thus, the findings of my study indicate that while services may not reduce the demand for institutional care for the dementing elderly, they do influence caregivers' morale and psychological well-being.

Of course, service provision in my sample was relatively low and, more importantly from the point of view of statistical analysis, uniform. Uniformity of service provision may, at least partly, explain the lack of statistically significant correlations between service provision and supporters' attitudes to continued caregiving. Day hospital care for the dementing old person was regarded as essential to continued home care in my sample. Thus, while many preferred, given a free choice, institutional care, they would not have been <u>able</u> to give home care without the break that day care provided.

While day hospital care was crucial to home care, supporters viewed home-helps and meals-on-wheels with some ambivalence. Home-helps changed frequently and come on different days, confusing the confused elderly person even more. Meals-on-wheels, like home-helps, were only used by those living alone. Non-resident supporters worried about meals because the confused elderly often did not eat immediately and was thus at risk of food poisoning.

The services available to dementing old people have only been briefly outlined here, and the objective in mentioning them is to examine them as mediators of the effect on supporters of caregiving, rather than to discuss the effect on the dementing old person. I have not, therefore, discussed the role of day hospitals as therapy or rehabilitation. Therapy for dementing old people takes limited forms and takes place in only a limited number of hospitals. While the aim of therapies such as reality orientation (RO) is to improve orientation for the dementing old person, it might be expected that such improvement might be of benefit to their supporters too. There have been very few studies of the generalisation of improvements in cognitive functioning associated with RO to behavioural functioning, especially functioning outside the day hospital or treatment centre. Greene <u>et al</u>. (1982), have however reported that 'individualised' RO in a day hospital sample led to improvements in cognitive function as measured by psychometric tests and that as orientation improved there was a paralleled tendency for disturbed behaviour, as rated by relatives, to decrease. Furthermore, and most importantly for our purposes here, this was accompanied by an alleviation of self-reported stress on the part of the relative during the RO period.

Conclusions

Three ways of looking at the social dimensions of senile dementia are considered in this chapter: (1) socio-psychological factors playing a role in the aetiology of dementia; (2) the socio-psychological consequences for the sufferer; and (3) the social and psychological consequences of dementia for those who give care in the community. Although it was generally concluded that there is, to date, little evidence that social or psychological factors cause dementia, such factors do seem to have an influence on symptom formation and the course of dementia.

While social factors do not seem to be causal, there are social consequences of dementia for both sufferers and their supporters; social factors also mediate in the consequences for both the sufferer and the supporter. Some of the consequences considered used both published and unpublished research and findings and the author's own study. A case-study approach was also utilised to illustrate points raised.

It is customary when discussing research findings to mention the implications for future research and for policy and services. It would certainly not be exaggerating to say that more research should be done in the area of family care of the dementing or mentally-disordered elderly. If more and more old people live to an advanced age, and if the proportion of younger relatives available to care continues to decrease, and this is combined with a continuing policy of deinstitutionalisation, then it becomes imperative that policy-makers and service-providers have facts upon which they can base their decisions.

What are the facts? The findings from my own research and that of others indicates that the symptoms of dementia which are most stressful for supporters are incontinence, night wandering and sleep disturbance, unaesthetic, strange or bizarre behaviours, dangerous behaviours, mood disturbance and demands for attention. In many cases night wandering can be controlled with drugs, as can restless behaviour. There are aids to incontinence (incontinence pads, plastic pants, etc.) but often it is not the incontinence <u>per se</u> that upsets the supporters, but the behaviours associated with it. It is, in fact, tempting to conclude that nothing can be done about the symptoms of dementia which cause most burden or distress. However, more research is going into behaviour modification with the elderly and it may be that such techniques can be taught to supporters and used successfully in the home to control disturbing behaviours.

The symptoms of dementia interact with the supporters' feelings and attitudes to giving care, which are, in turn, influenced by the perceived effects on the supporters' marriage, children, relations with other relatives and social position. For some supporters the combination of all these variables has little impact, while for others the impact is such that the supporters' physical and mental health suffer.

The findings from the studies by Machin and Hirschfeld, plus my own results, indicate that help from other family members and from the services is often at a very low level. It is not perhaps surprising that help from services and family has not been found to be 'statistically significant' when associated with supporters' willingness to continue with home care or consider institutionalisation. Day hospital care was certainly essential to continued home care for the supporters in my sample, but, as noted by Carter (1981), the day hospital provides a break rather than the possibility for the supporter to lead an individual life.

The dislocation to normal life and the distress experienced when confronted with the disintegration of a loved one's personality and intellect mean that supporters, as much as sufferers, are the victims of senile dementia. While the dementing old person may benefit by the trend to deinstitutionalisation, the supporter may not. There is little evidence that deinstitutionalisation has been followed by a dramatic, let alone sufficient, increase in community services. Because of the shortage of community services, they tend to go to the elderly who live alone, those with worst prognosis for successful long-term maintenance in the community.

TABLE 5.1: Prevalence Rates for Dementia from
Kay et al. (1970)

Age	Prevalence (%)
65-9	2.3
70-4	2.8
75-9	5.5
80+	22.0

TABLE 5.2: Prevalence Rates for Dementia from
Gurland et al. (1980)

Age	Pervasively (1) Demented		Latent class (2) demented		Rational (3) score +6	
	Males	Females (%)	Males	Females (%)	Males	Females (%)
65-9	2	4	2	7	0	3
70-4	0	3	6	5	2	4
75-9	6	7	6	17	6	8
80+	6	16	15	32	9	16

Notes:

(1)   Cases at a clinical level of severity, i.e. which require the
       attention of a health care professional.

(2)   Latent class assignments derived from Lazarfeld's methods for
       detecting taxonic structures.

(3)   See Gurland et al. (1980) for further discussion of the rational
       scales. Items in the rational and latent class scales can be seen
       in the Appendix.

129

TABLE 5.3: Data from Sanford's (1975) Study of the Tolerance of Debility in Elderly Dependants

	Tolerance (1)	Frequency (2)
Blindness	0	2
Inability to walk at all	13	16
Sleep disturbance	16	62
Micturition	17	24
Shouting	20	10
Inability to get off commode unaided	21	38
Inability to get on commode unaided	22	36
Night wandering	24	24
Day wandering	33	12
Inability to walk unaided	33	18
Inability to get out of bed unaided	35	52
Dangerous and irresponsible behaviours	38	32
Inability to get in bed unaided	40	50
Incontinence of faeces	43	56
Physically aggressive behaviour	44	18
Inability to communicate	50	16
Falls	52	58
Personality conflicts	54	26
Inability to manage stairs unaided	60	10
Inability to feed unaided	67	12
Inability to dress unaided	77	44
Incontinence of urine	81	54
Inability to wash/shave unaided	93	54

Notes:

(1)   Tolerance was calculated in the following way:

$$\frac{\text{Problem frequency - alleviation factor frequency}}{\text{Problem frequency}} \times 100$$

The alleviation factor refers to problems which would need to be alleviated to restore a tolerable situation at home. Tolerance refers to the percentage of supporters able to tolerate problems.

(2)   Frequency refers to percentage of cases/supporters reporting the problem.

Notes

1.   Until fairly recently Alzheimer's disease was, by definition, a dementia of the pre-senile group. However, as noted by Miller (1977), in the clinical situation Alzheimer's disease can only be distinguished from senile dementia on the grounds of the arbitrarily fixed age of 65. Nevertheless, the distinction between Alzheimer's disease and senile dementia is possible in theory and on pathological grounds (Pearce and Miller, 1973). Although the debate about the distinction between Alzheimer's disease and senile dementia is an interesting one, what is more interesting from a sociological point of view is the use by self-help groups of the name Alzheimer's disease/Association rather than Senile Dementia Society/Association, i.e. the replacement in lay language of senile dementia or 'senility' with a named disease.

2.   Kay (1972), referring to American statistics, notes that in the age group 65-74 about 75 per cent of first admissions to state and county mental hospitals are due to brain syndromes. At ages over 75 years about 90 per cent of first admissions are due to organic brain syndromes. The figures for admissions to Scottish mental hospitals and psychiatric units are lower, but still indicate that in the age group 75+ the highest proportion of admissions are for dementia. Of admissions in the over 75 age group in 1979, 43 per cent had a diagnosis of senile dementia. Adding the category of 'psychosis with cerebral arteriolsclerosis' increases that figure to 52 per cent (Information Services Division, Common Services Agency, 1982).

References

Adelstein, A.M., Downham, D.Y., Stein, Z. and Susser, M.W. (1968) 'The Epidemiology of Mental Illness in an English City', Journal of Social Psychiatry, 3, 47-59.

Amster L.E. and Krauss, H.H. (1974) 'The Relationship between Life Crises and Mental Deterioration in Old Age', International Journal of Aging and Human Development, 5, 51-5.

Bayley, M. (1973) Mental Handicap and Community Care: A Study of Mentally Handicapped People in Sheffield, Routledge & Kegan Paul, London.

Bergmann, K., Foster, E.M., Justice, A.W. and Matthews, V. (1978) 'Management of the Demented Elderly Patient in the Community', British Journal of Psychiatry, 132, 441-9.

Berkman, P. 'Correlates of Psychiatric Disability among Community Aged', cited in Lowenthal (1965).

Bree, M.H. (1960) The Dement in the Community, Horton Group, HMC, Oxford.

Brody, E.M., Kleban, M.H., Lawton, M.P. and Silverman, H.A. (1971) 'Excess Disabilities of Mentally Impaired Aged: Impact of Individualized Treatment', The Gerontologist, 11, 124-33.

Carter, J. (1981) Day Services for Adults: Somewhere to Go, George Allen & Unwin, London.

Central Statistical Office (1981) Social Trends, HMSO, London.
Central Statistical Office (1981) Annual Abstract of Statistics (1981 edn.) HMSO, London.
Corsellis, J.A.N. (1962) Mental Illness and the Ageing Brain, Oxford University Press, London.
Department of Health and Social Security (1981) Report of a Study on Community Care, DHSS, London.
Equal Opportunities Commission (1980) The Experience of Caring for Elderly and Handicapped Dependants: Survey Report, Fieldwork by MAS Survey Research Ltd.
Faris, R.E.L. and Dunham, H.W. (1939) Mental Disorders in Urban Areas, Chicago University Press, Chicago.
Fisch, M., Goldfarb, A.I., Shahinian, S.P. and Turner, H. (1968) 'Chronic Brain Syndrome in the Community Aged', Archives of General Psychiatry, 18, 739-45.
Folsom, J.C. (1967) 'Intensive Hospital Therapy for Geriatric Patients', Current Psychiatric Therapy, 7, 209-15.
Folsom, J.C. (1968) 'Reality Orientation for the Elderly Patient', Journal of Geriatric Psychiatry, 1, 291-307.
Garside, R.F., Kay, D.W.K. and Roth, M. (1965) 'Old Age Mental Disorders in Newcastle upon Tyne. Part III. A Factorial Study of Medical, Psychiatric and Social Characteristics', British Journal of Psychiatry, 111, 939-46.
Gianotti, G. (1975) Psychiatr. Clin., 8, 99-108. cited in Gurland (1981).
Gianturco, D.T., Breslin, M.S., Heyman, A., Gentry, W.K., Jenkins, C.D. and Kaplan, B. (1974) 'Personality Patterns and Life Stress in Ischaemic Cerebrovascular Disease', Stroke, 5, 453-60. cited in Verwoerdt (1981).
Gilleard, C. (1982) 'Stresses and Strains amongst Supporters of the Elderly Infirm Day Hospital Attenders', unpublished interim report, Psychogeriatric Day Centre Research Project, Department of Psychiatry, University of Edinburgh.
Gilleard, C.J., Watt, G. and Boyd, W.D. (1981) 'Problems of Caring for the Elderly Mentally Infirm at Home', paper presented at the 12th International Congress of Gerontology, July, Hamburg.
Goldberg, E.M. and Connelly, N. (1982) The Effectiveness of Social Care for the Elderly: An Overview of Recent and Current Evaluative Research. Heinemann Educational Books, London.
Goldstein, K. (1959) 'Functional Disturbances in Brain Damage', in S. Arieti (ed.), American Handbook of Psychiatry, Basic Books, New York, pp. 770-93.
Gottesman, L. and Brody, E. (1975) 'Psycho-social Intervention Programs within the Institutional Setting', in S. Sherwood (ed.), Long-term Care: A Handbook for Researchers, Planners, and Providers, Spectrum, New York, pp. 455-509.
Grad de Alarcon, J. (1971) 'Social Causes and Social Consequences of Mental Illness in Old Age', in D.W.K. Kay and A. Walk (eds.), Recent Developments in Psychogeriatrics: A Symposium, British Journal of Psychiatry Special Publication, No. 6, pp.75-86.
Gray, B. and Isaacs, B. (1979) Care of the Elderly Mentally Infirm, Tavistock, London.

Greene, J.G., Smith, R., Gardiner, M. and Timbury, G.C. (1982a) 'Measuring Behavioural Disturbance of Elderly Demented Patients in the Community and its Effects on Relatives: A Factor Analytic Study', Age and Ageing, 11, 121-6.

Greene, J., Smith, R. and Gardiner, M. (1982b) 'Evaluating Reality Orientation with Psychogeriatric Patients', in R. Taylor and A. Gilmore (eds.), Current Trends in British Gerontology, Gower, Aldershot, pp. 104-7.

Gruenberg, E.M. (1953) 'Community Conditions and Psychoses of the Elderly', American Journal of Psychiatry, 110, 888-96.

Gruenthal, E. (1927) 'Klinisch-anatomisch Vergleichende Untersuchungen ueger den Greisenblodesinn', Z. Ges. Neurol Psychiatr., 111, 763. cited in Post (1965).

Gurland, B.J. (1981) 'The Borderlands of Dementia: The Influence of Sociocultural Characteristics on Rates of Dementia Occurring in the Senium', in N.E. Miller and G.D. Cohen (eds.), Clincial Aspects of Alzheimer's Disease and Senile Dementia, Aging, Vol. 15, Raven Press, New York, pp. 61-80.

Gurland, B.J., Copeland, J.R.M., Kelleher, M.J., Sharpe, L. and Kuriansky, J.B. (1978) A Preliminary Report on the US-UK Geriatric Community Study, Department of Geriatrics Research, New York State Psychiatric Institute, New York (mimeograph). Cited in Gurland (1981) and in Gurland et al. (1983) The Mind and Mood of Ageing: Mental Health Problems of the Community Elderly in New York and London, Croom Helm, London; Haworth, New York.

Gurland, B.J., Dean, L., Cross, P. and Golden, R. (1980) 'The Epidemiology of Depression and Dementia in the Elderly: The Use of Multiple Indicators of these Conditions', in J.O. Cole and J.E. Barrett (eds.), Psychopathology in the Aged, Raven Press, New York.

Hardt, R.H. (1959) 'The Ecological Distribution of Patients Admitted to Mental Hospitals from an Urban Area,' Psychiatric Quarterly, 33, 126-44. Cited in Grad de Alarcon (1971).

Hare, E.H. (1956) 'Mental Illness and Social Conditions in Bristol', Journal of Mental Science, 39, 349-57.

Hirschfeld, M.J. (1978) Families Living with Senile Brain Disease, dissertation submitted in partial satisfaction of the requirements for the degree of Doctor of Nursing Science, University of California, San Francisco.

Hunt, A. (1978) The Elderly at Home: A Survey Carried out on Behalf of the Department of Health and Social Security, HMSO, London.

Information Services Division, Common Services Agency (1982) Scottish Health Statistics 1980, HMSO, Edinburgh.

Isaacs, B., Livingstone, M. and Neville, Y. (1972) Survival of the Unfittest: A study of Geriatric Patients in Glasgow, Routledge & Kegan Paul, London.

Jenkins, J., Felce, D., Lunt, B. and Powell, L. (1977) 'Increasing Engagement in Activity of Residents in Old People's Homes by Providing Recreational Materials', Behaviour, Research and Therapy, 15, 429-34.

Jolley, D.J. and Arie, T. (1978) 'Organization of Psychogeriatric Services, British Journal of Psychiatry, 132, 1-11.

Kahn, R.L., Pollack, M. and Goldfarb, A.I. (1961) in P. Hoch and J. Zubin (eds.) Psychopathology of Aging, Gruen & Stratton, New York, pp. 104-13. Cited in Gurland (1981).

Kay, D.W.K. (1972) 'Epidemiological Aspects of Organic Brain Disease in the Aged', in C.M. Gates (ed.), Ageing and the Brain, Plenum Press, London, pp. 15-27.

Kay, D.W.K., Beamish, P. and Roth, M. (1964) 'Old Age Mental Disorders in Newcastle upon Tyne, British Journal of Psychiatry, 110, 146-58.

Kay, D.W.K., Bergmann, K., Foster, E.M., McKechnie, A.A. and Roth, M. (1970) 'Mental Illness and Hospital Usage in the Elderly: A Random Sample Followed Up', Comprehensive Psychiatry, 11, 26-35.

Kutner, B., Fanshel, D., Togo, A.M. and Langner, T.S. (1956) Five Hundred over Sixty, Russell Sage Foundation, New York.

Larsson, T., Sjorgren, T., and Jacobsen, G. (1963) 'Senile Dementia', Acta. Psychiatr. Scand., Suppl. No. 167. Cited in Miller (1967).

Locke, B.Z., Kramer, M. and Pasamanick, B. (1960) 'Mental Diseases of the Senium at Mid-century: First Admissions to Ohio State Public Mental Hospitals', American Journal of Public Health, 50, 998-1012. Cited in Grad de Alarcon (1971).

Lowenthal, M.F. (1965) 'Antecedents of Isolation and Mental Illness in Old Age', Archives of General Psychiatry, 12, 245-54.

Machin, E. (1980) A Survey of the Behaviour of the Elderly and their Supporters at Home, thesis presented for the degree of Master of Science, University of Birmingham.

Meacher, M. (1972) Taken for a Ride: Special Residential Homes for Confused Old People: A Study of Separatism in Social Policy, Longman, Bristol.

Medical Research Council (1983) 'Senile Dementia', MRC News, 18, 6-7.

Miller, E. (1977) Abnormal Ageing: The Psychology of Senile and Presenile Dementia, John Wiley, London.

Morgan, R.F. (1965) 'Note on the Psychopathology of Senility: Senescent Defence against the Threat of Death', Psychological Reports, 17, 305-6.

Newroth, A. and Newroth, S. (1980) Coping with Alzheimer's Disease: A Growing Concern, National Institute on Mental Retardation, Downsview, Ontario.

Noyes, A.P. and Kolb, L.C. (1958) Modern Clinical Psychiatry, W.B. Saunders, New York, Cited in Amster and Krauss (1974).

Oakley, D.P. (1965) 'Senile Dementia: Some Aetiological Factors', British Journal of Psychiatry, 111, 414-9.

Office of Health Economics (1979) Dementia in Old Age, Office of Health Economics, London.

Office of Population Censuses and Surveys (1980) Population Projections, HMSO, London.

Parsons, P.L. (1965) 'Mental Health of Swansea's Old Folk', British Journal of Preventive Social Medicine, 19, 43-7.

Pearce, J. and Miller, E. (1973) Clinical Aspects of Dementia, Bailliere Tindall, London.

Pfeiffer, E. (1975) J. Am. Geriatri. Soc., 23, 433-9. Cited in Gurland (1981).

Post, F. (1944) 'Some Problems Arising from a Study of Mental Patients over the Age of Sixty Years', Journal of Mental Science, 90, 554. Cited in Post (1965).

Post, F. (1965) The Clinical Psychiatry of Late Life, Pergamon, Oxford.

Roth, M. and Bergmann, K. (1981) 'Comments Made on Gurland's (1981) Paper', in N.E. Miller and G.D. Cohen (eds.), Clinical Aspects of Alzheimer's Disease and Senile Dementia, Raven Press, New York, pp. 80-4.

Rothschild, D. (1937) 'Pathologic Changes in Senile Psychoses and their Psychobiologic Significance', American Journal of Psychiatry, 93, 757. Cited in Post (1965).

Rothschild, D. (1942) 'Neuropathological Changes in Arteriosclerotic Psychoses and their Psychiatric Significance', Arch. Neurol. Psychiat. (Chicago), 48, 417. Cited in Post (1965).

Sainsbury, P., Costain, W.R. and Grad, J. (1965) 'The Effects of a Community Service on the Referral and Admission Rates of Elderly Psychiatric Patients', in Psychiatric Disorders in the Aged, Geigy, Manchester, pp. 23-37.

Sanford, J.R.A. (1975) 'Tolerance of Debility in Elderly Dependants by Supporters at Home: Its Significance for Hospital Practice', British Medical Journal, 3, 471-3.

Sinnott, J.D. (1977) Gerontologist, 17, 459-63. Cited in Gurland, (1981).

Tobin, S.S. and Lieberman, M.A. (1976) Last Home for the Aged: Critical Implication of Institutionalization, Jossey-Bass, London.

Tomlinson, B.E. and Kitchener, D. (1972) J. Pathology, 106, 165-85. Cited in Office of Health Economics (1979).

Verwoerdt, A. Clinical Geropsychiatry, Williams & Wilkins, London.

Wheatley, V. (1979) Supporters of Elderly Persons with a Dementing Illness Living in the Same Household, thesis submitted for the degree of Master of Science, University of Surrey.

Wilkin, D. (1979) Caring for the Mentally Handicapped Child, Croom Helm, London.

Williams, H.W., Quesnel, E., Fish, V.W. and Goodman, L. (1942) 'Studies in Senile and Arteriosclerotic Psychoses: Relative Significance of Extrinsic Factors in their Development', American Journal of Psychiatry, 98, 712-15. Cited in Miller (1977).

Wilson, D.C. (1955) 'The Pathology of Senility', American Journal of Psychiatry, 111, 902-6. Cited in Miller (1977).

Chapter Six

THE MEASUREMENT OF ENGAGEMENT IN THE INSTITUTIONALISED ELDERLY

Malcolm McFadyen

The lack of activity among residents, and the lack of opportunity for participation in activity, have long been considered to be the most distinctive features of institutions caring for the elderly infirm (Townsend, 1962). In a recent review of the literature on the quality of life of residents in institutions caring for the elderly, Hughes and Wilkin (1980) state that 'the traditional picture of lounges in residential houses with residents sitting around the walls, not communicating and not engaged in any activity, is apparently still as accurate today as it was when Townsend first described it'. If we are to change this situation we need to improve our understanding of the relation between activity and 'quality of life'. A prerequisite of this is to be able to measure objectively engagement in activity (hereafter referred to as 'engagement').

The concept of engagement derives from two related but separate sources. At a theoretical level it has been central to attempts to conceptualise development in later life (Cumming and Henry, 1961; Havighurst, 1968; Knapp, 1977). At a practical level it derives from attempts by those who believe that the quality of care/quality of life of the institutionalised elderly is less than optimal (Townsend, 1962; Robb, 1967; Meacher, 1972), to improve this situation (Blunden and Kushlick, 1975).

While there is an overlap in the meaning of the term in these two different contexts, it is not used identically. The developmental theorists have tended to emphasise social activity, and associated experimental work has generally used reported participation in social activities as its operational measure. In the 'quality of life' literature, engagement usually refers to any purposeful activity (including social interaction) and is measured by direct observation. While I shall briefly comment on its use within developmental theory, this chapter will be concerned mainly with engagement defined as any purposeful activity.

Engagement and Theories of Ageing

Cumming and Henry (1961) proposed that ageing involved a withdrawal by the elderly person from social activity and, reciprocally, decreased demand by society on the individual to participate. They further suggested that this mutual withdrawal may be of functional value to the ageing individual, and to society. By this view, the relation between quality of life and participation in social activity is different for the elderly from that of younger people. While there is some evidence of decreased social participation in the elderly (Abrams, 1978; Hunt, 1978), evidence that this reduction is of functional value is, at best, equivocal (Knapp, 1976, 1977).

Cumming and Henry's theory is commonly contrasted with the views of Havighurst (1968) who suggests that the needs of the elderly for social participation are no different from those of younger age groups. Havighurst implies that social activity is positively associated with life satisfaction at all ages, which has led to his views being called an activity theory of ageing (Lemon et al. 1972), and to studies which examine the relation between life satisfaction and level of social participation within an elderly population (e.g. Knapp, 1977). Such studies miss the main point of Havighurst's view, which is that there is no difference between elderly and other ages in their need for social participation. Only studies using different age groups can examine this issue, and these are lacking.

In the absence of better evidence on the functional value of reduction in social particip- ation to the elderly, it seems a more defensible position to consider that the elderly should not be treated differently from other age groups. This does not, however, mean an adoption of a 'social activity is good for you' position, simply that psychological/sociological theories of development in later life are not, at least as yet, a rich source of ideas for those concerned with the practical care of the elderly.

Policy on Care of The Institutionalised Elderly

There seems to be general agreement that the elderly in general, and particularly those in institutional care, have been provided with less than ideal living conditions, and that things should be improved (DHSS, 1978; British Geriatrics Society and Royal College of Nursing, 1975; British Medical Association, 1976).

For the institutionalised elderly this is conceived of in terms of encouraging a more domestic environment, encouraging greater independence of residents, not only in self-care etc., but in exercising control over more aspects of their life; more awareness of the needs of individuals, and encouraging a more stimulating physical and social environment. Such policy statements are, of necessity, based more on humanitarian values than on developmental theory, and on persuasive, though largely untested, accounts of the negative effects of institutions (Goffman, 1961). In practical terms, problems arise not only in establishing that such changes increase life satisfaction, but also in implementing the changes in the first place.

It is well recognised that a considerable gap exists between statements of policy and actual practice (Personal Social Services Council, 1975; DHSS, 1976; Evers, 1981). One of the reasons for the discrepancies is that such statements of philosophy, while readily acceptable as meaningful in broad terms, are imprecise in terms of the operations required for objectives to be achieved (Kushlick, 1975). Not only are we imprecise about the kind of care operations to be performed, and by whom, we have only vague notions about how we shall recognise when an improved or optimal quality of life is being attained (Davies and Knapp, 1981).

Engagement and Quality of Life in Institutions

If we are to make the proposed changes, then the first requirement is to be able to define operationally the various concepts embodied in policy statements to allow measurement, without which it cannot be known whether change has been achieved and if it has had the desired effect. Much work has already been done on the measurement of life satisfaction (Neugarten et al., 1961; Bradburn, 1969; Peace et al., 1979), aspects of the physical environment (e.g. Sommer and Ross, 1958) and ward milieu (Pincus, 1968, Moos et al., 1979). This work is reviewed by Hughes and Wilkin (1980), George and Bearon (1980) and Davies and Knapp (1981). As a further contribution to this aim of providing operational measures of concepts potentially related to quality of life, Kushlick and his colleagues introduced the concept of engagement (Blunden and Kushlick, 1975). At its simplest, engagement refers to doing something rather than doing nothing. To count as engagement, doing something is usually qualified to exclude 'deviant' or 'non-adaptive' behaviours. Blunden and Kushlick define it thus: 'A person may be said to be engaged ... if he is reacting with materials or with people <u>in a manner which is likely to maintain or develop his skills and abilities</u>' (emphasis added). 'Conversely, a person can be seen to be "non-engaged" when he is "doing nothing" ... The person can be seen to be "engaged" or not, and engagement can therefore be assessed by observation.'

The origins of Kushlick's concept of engagement can, in part, be traced to earlier American workers within the 'behaviour analysis' movement (the term used by those whose approach derives from Skinner's operant conditioning model) (Lindsley, 1964; McClannahan, 1973; Whatmore et al., 1975; Felce et al., 1980). However, the measurement of engagement stands independently of any particular theoretical approach.

Kushlick's Measure of Engagement
The current measure of engagement used by Kushlick and his colleagues is, essentially, to count the number of residents who are engaged in some (adaptive) activity at any one time, and express this as a proportion of the total number of residents present at that time (observer stationed in a particular location within the institution). The measure is well documented (Jenkins et al., 1978; Felce et al., 1980) and has been found to be highly reliable in terms of agreement between different observers. The measure has been used by Kushlick's colleagues in the Wessex Health Care Evaluation Research Team in a number of substantive studies of methods of increasing engagement in old peoples' homes (Jenkins et al., 1977; Lunt et al., 1977a; Powell et al., 1978; Felce and Jenkins, 1979), and in a study of the effect of different levels of staff input on engagement (Lunt et al., 1977b).

An Alternative Measure of Engagement
An alternative measure of engagement which was

developed in an attempt to overcome certain limitations of this particular measure will be described in detail.

The Wessex team's measure was seen as having two major limitations, both arising from the particular method of time sampling used in the observations. First, since engagement is recorded in terms of what proportion of the group of residents is engaged, it does not easily allow for a more detailed breakdown of the kinds of activity engaged in. Secondly, it does not allow the measurement of the amount or pattern of engagement. Thus one cannot easily relate engagement to personal variables, such as degree of functional impairment, or other variables related to quality of life (George and Bearon, 1980) or quality of care (Linn and Linn, 1980).

It is possible that these limitations result from the derivation of the concept from the work of the 'behaviour analysts', who tend to emphasise the effects of environmental (physical and social, particularly so-called 'reinforcement' and 'stimulus control' effects), and to give less weight to intra-personal variables. This same emphasis is apparent in the work of the Wessex team which leaves them open to being interpreted as suggesting that amount of activity is a direct index of quality of life. However, the concept of engagement need not be restricted in this way. The relationship between engagement and such factors as life satisfaction has to be established empirically.

A more flexible measure of engagement, which can be related to personal as well as environmental variables, can be achieved by a relatively simple variation on the Wessex team's sampling procedure. Rather than recording the proportion of residents engaged in each observation period, an observer records the activity being engaged in by each individual over a number of occasions. Not only does this allow individual as well as group measures of engagement, it allows a flexible categorisation of the activities.

Categories of Engagement

The particular technique I have used again derives from the behaviour analysis literature (Schaeffer and Martin, 1966). Each resident is observed once in each observation period. (In my own work the observation period has been approximately half an hour, but this could be varied to suit the purpose of particular studies.) The activity recorded is the activity being engaged in when observation starts. If necessary approximately 30 seconds is allowed for clarification of what the resident is doing, but any change in activity after observation has started is ignored. The observer records a brief written description of what the resident is doing and codes the behaviour according to a previously learned category system. The category system I have used is given in Figure 6.1, with brief definitions where necessary. (Again the category system used could vary to suit the purpose of any particular study.) The observer also records whether the resident is involved in any verbal interaction, using the codes in Figure 6.2. Location and general posture (sitting, standing, walking, lying down) can also be recorded where appropriate to the study. The instruction for the written description is that it should allow someone other than the observer to code the activity from the written description. An example of a completed coding sheet is given in Figure 6.3.

The data thus generated can be analysed in a variety of ways. First, they can be used to provide a description, in terms of categories used, of the pattern of activity either of the group or of individuals (obviously analysis in terms of individuals would require more observations than for groups). A 'score' similar to that used by the Wessex research team can be obtained by a simple calculation of the proportion of observations in which some activity was recorded. With the category system in Figure 6.1, it is probably simpler to calculate a 'non-engagement' score, for which I have combined the 'doing nothing' and 'asleep' categories. Likewise, the proportion of any particular category can be calculated, as can any meaningful combination of categories. I have combined the categories, as shown in Figure 6.1, to provide an alternative 'active engagement' score which reflects not only frequency but the quality of engagement.

Training of Observers

As with any coding or rating system, it is desirable that observers have some training prior to data collection (Hall, 1980). A standard brief training has been developed which consists of four stages:

Stage 1. Trainer (someone with prior experience of using the observation system) outlines the categories system, and discusses these with the trainee to ensure that the written descriptions are understood.

<u>Stage 2</u>. Trainer and trainee carry out a number (most commonly 20-30) observations simultaneously, recording a written description, and coding, of the observed activity and any verbal interaction. After each observation, the written description and the coding of activity and (if present) interaction are compared, and any differences are discussed. It is for the trainer to ensure that the observations made cover the whole range of categories to be used.

<u>Stage 3</u>. Trainee and trainer carry out a number of simultaneous observations, and make written descriptions and codings without discussion, and percentage agreement is calculated.

<u>Stage 4</u>. Trainer and trainee exchange record forms with the original codes obscured. Each codes the other's observations on the basis of the written descriptions, and again percentage agreement between the original and later coding is calculated.

<u>Inter-observer Agreement</u>. At end of training this is typically over 90 per cent using the category system in Figure 6.1. Consistency of use of the coding system during the data collection stage can be checked by having someone other than the observer code activities from a sample of the observer's written descriptions. Again, with the category system used here, agreement is typically greater than 90 per cent.

<u>Reliability</u>
Inter-observer agreement constitutes one aspect of reliability - whether descriptions and coding of activity is recorded consistently by different observers. As noted above, agreement is typically greater than 90 per cent between pairs of observers.

A further aspect of reliability concerns the number of observations required to provide an adequate sample of the residents' activities. In a psychiatric ward an analysis of the engagement pattern of 30 residents based on 20 ratings gave a very similar picture to an analysis based on 60 ratings (Table 6.1). Rank order correlations for the measures of non-engagement and active engagement were 0.88 and 0.92, respectively, and for the most commonly recorded sub-categories of leisure, watching, and doing nothing, the correlations obtained were 0.92, 0.80 and 0.86. The correlation for two-way interactions as 0.91. Very similar results were obtained in an old people's home when an analysis of the engagement pattern of 24 residents based on 20 observations per person (Table 6.2) was compared with an analysis based on 54 observations per person. Here the equivalent correlation values were: non-engagement, 0.94; active engagement, 0.96; leisure, 0.96; watching, 0.77; doing nothing, 0.92; two-way interactions, 0.76. It may be concluded that a sample of 20 or more observations provides a reliable picture of the engagement pattern of residents in an institution.

Finally, what of reliability from one occasion to another? A ward of 20 elderly psychiatric patients was studied on two occasions 6 months apart. Rank order correlations of 0.63 and 0.71 (both significant at $p < 0.01$) were obtained for the non-engagement and active engagement measures. Of course, it is always desirable that reliability is assessed within any particular study, but the above results indicate that engagement can be reliably measured using this technique.

Engagement and The Time Dimension
With this type of technique it is important to consider what effect sampling at different times of the day might have. If one is only concerned with measuring change of engagement, then it is obviously necessary to ensure that comparison is based on measures obtained from observation made at similar times. However, if one is interested in obtaining a reasonably authentic representation of the overall engagement pattern in an institution, or of individuals, it is necessary to arrange that observations are made at a variety of times throughout the normal day. Days when routine of the institution is disrupted, e.g. by outings, should be avoided (unless, of course, the object is to study the effect of such disruptions).

Analysis of the variation in engagement with time of day in three different populations (old people's home, psychogeriatric ward, elderly psychatric ward) shows that engagement does vary (Figures 6.4 and 6.5). Given that one would expect some differences because of differences in population and of institution, there is considerable similarity in the variation in engagement with time. It is reassuring to see that non-engagement consistently peaks after lunch! Correspondingly, active engagement is lowest at this time, with a consistent peak in late afternoon. The psycho-geriatric group shows the least variation in active engagement as one might expect.

Although sampling engagement at different times of day will, therefore, produce bias in the pattern of engagement, individuals were found to retain their relative position. In an analysis of two populations (old people's home and psychogeriatric ward) there were significant rank order correlations for non-engagement (0.80 and 0.83, respectively), and for active engagement (0.87 and 0.93) when morning and afternoon was compared. Sub-categories and two-way interactions also show consistency (e.g. leisure, 0.74 and 0.92; doing nothing, 0.65 and 0.74; two-way interaction, 0.77 and 0.88). For both populations the proportion of leisure observations was significantly greater in the afternoon.

Cost of Collecting Data on Engagement

Davies and Knapp (1981, pp. 26-7) question whether current techniques of measuring engagement may be too expensive to be practical for large-scale studies. Thirty observations per person (for many purposes 20 observations would be sufficient) would take on average 10-20 minutes per resident depending on how far the observer has to go between observations). A further 5-10 minutes per person would be required for analysis (depending on the complexity of the category system used). Thus, about 15-30 minutes per resident is required. Observers need not be highly qualified professionals. Training of observers is relatively simple, and requires probably less than half an hour per observer. Engagement measurement, therefore, compares very favourably with other psychological measures in terms of costs.

Relation of Engagement to Dementia

Most of the work of the Wessex team and the American behaviour analysts has been on residents of homes for the elderly, rather than psychogeriatric hospital wards where a much greater proportion of residents (at least in the UK) are likely to be suffering from some significant degree of dementia. To suggest that there is scope for increasing opportunity for activity with such patients implies that engagement is, at least to some extent, independent of degree of dementia. This assumption is certainly not shared by many nursing and medical staff who interpret the lack of activity to be simply another aspect of dementia. It is difficult to assess accurately the relationship between engagement and dementia from group data of the kind obtained from the Wessex measure. First, demented and non-demented old people are likely to be in different institutions. Even where, in old people's homes, there may be a mixture of demented and non-demented residents, the two groups are often either physically separated or otherwise subject to different regimes, so that any differences found might be attributable to factors other than dementia.

The technique described above allows individual measurement of engagement, which can then be related directly to individual measures of degree of dementia. McFadyen et al. (1982) report such a study in two populations, 30 patients in a geriatric psychiatry ward and 24 residents in an old people's home. Staff ratings of cognitive impairment (memory and orientation) showed low and non-significant correlations with non-engagement (r=0.14 for home, r=0.11 for ward), and with two-way social interactions (r=0.29 for home, r=0.23 for ward). Active engagement did not correlate significantly with rated cognitive impairment for the old people's home (r=0.24), but did at a low level for the ward population (r=0.34, p < 0.05). In the old people's home mental status questionnaire scores (Wilson and Brass, 1973) were also available. This is a brief interview measure of cognitive impairment, and is considered to be a sensitive measure of degree of dementia. MSQ scores and staff-rated cognitive impairment correlated highly (r=0.77 sig. at p < 0.001). However, MSQ scores did not correlate significantly with non-engagement, active engagement, or two-way interaction (r=0.30, 0.34 and 0.30, respectively, d.f.=22). It seems reasonable to conclude that lack of activity is not simply another aspect of dementia, although one might expect that the type of activity engaged in will be affected by degree of dementia.

Amount and Pattern of Engagement – Descriptive Data

To date, data on elderly patients or residents have been collected in four settings, an old people's home, a geriatric psychiatry ward, a ward caring for old (psychotic) psychiatric patients, and a geriatric ward in a general hospital.

The age ranges of residents in the different settings were roughly similar (mean ages: 'old' psychiatric ward, 72; geriatric psychiatry ward, 80; geriatric ward, 79; old people's home, 84). Residents in the geriatric psychiatry ward were mostly demented and considered to require continuing care. Most were mobile. The old people's home residents varied most widely in terms of cognitive impairment. Again, most were mobile. Very few of the residents in the 'old psychiatric' ward were considered to be demented, but all were mobile, long-stay psychotic patients. The residents in the geriatric ward of the general hospital were mostly short-stay patients admitted for investigation and treatment of specific illnesses. Most were mobile, some with the help of aids. Only one patient required to be in bed continuously. Very few were considered to be demented. Table 6.3 presents the data in terms of specific categories of activity. Table 6.4 presents a summary in terms of active, passive and non-engagement (deviant behaviour shown separately).

The old people's home residents spend about 70 per cent of their time in active engagement (about 50 per cent in leisure activities) and about 20 per cent of their time doing nothing or asleep. When they are engaged, this is generally active rather than passive. In contrast, the geriatric psychiatry ward residents spend only 30 per cent of their time actively engaged (only 15 per cent in leisure activities) and 35 per cent doing nothing or asleep. When they are engaged, this is as likely to be passive as active. The 'old psychiatric' ward residents and the geriatric ward residents spend even more of their time non-engaged than the residents on the geriatric psychiatry ward, but when they are engaged it is more likely to be active, with more time in leisure activities.

It is tempting to speculate what part of the variation in engagement is due to population and what part is due to setting, but this would be premature. Differences between settings may be due to many factors - population, physical environment, social milieu, number (and density) of residents, number and type of staff, admission/discharge policy, etc. It will take larger-scale studies than have been completed to date to establish whether these patterns are typical of the various settings. At present the data can only be considered to be descriptive, and indicative of the variation to be found.

Further Analysis of Categories of Engagement
It can be seen that most of the variation in active engagement is in terms of the leisure category, within passive engagement, in terms of the watching category, and within non-engagement, in terms of the doing nothing category.

Leisure activities. A breakdown of the leisure category is available for the old people's home, geriatric psychiatry ward and 'old psychiatric' ward. This shows further differences in the behaviour patterns (Table 6.5), with the old people's home showing the widest variety of activity, and the geriatric psychiatry ward showing the most restricted range of activities. I would suggest that for comparison purposes leisure is too broad a category, and that it would be useful to further subdivide it, either at the time of initial coding of observation, or subsequently.

Verbal interactions. The method of observation described is not ideal for the detailed analysis of verbal interactions (Lipman et al., 1979), but it does allow one to look at the frequency and pattern of such exchanges.

The relative frequency of interactions is similar for the old people's home (13 per cent) and the two geriatric wards, (12 and 11.7 per cent) with a much lower level being observed in the long-stay psychiatry ward (4.4 per cent). Table 6.6 shows the relative frequencies of the different categories of interactions. Since most one-way communications are either requests (from residents to staff) or instructions (staff to residents), it is perhaps more useful in terms of engagement analyses to look at two-way interactions. The relative frequency (as a proportion of all interactions) is surprisingly consistent (68-85 per cent), but there is wide variation in whether these conversations are with other residents, visitors or staff. It is perhaps interesting to note that McFadyen et al. (1982) found that, as for other engagement indices, there is little evidence that frequency of conversations is significantly related to lack of cognitive impairment. Indeed, further analysis of the leisure category (Table 6.5) reveals that the most confused group in the geriatric psychiatry ward, spends proportionately more time 'chatting' (65 per cent of leisure observations) than the least confused group in the old people's home (29 per cent of 'leisure' observations).

Prospects for Research

Faragher (1978) considers that a primary cause of the difficulty in assessing quality of life in residential institutions is the lack of a developmental theory of ageing. Is such a view - and it is widespread (Davies and Knapp, 1981) - not an expression of ageism (Hendricks and Hendricks, 1977, pp. 14-16), a stereotyping of elderly people? It is surely not reasonable to expect the same uniformity of stages in growing old as one finds in the developing child. Old age is much more a culturally-determined concept than childhood. What are we to make of the fact that, with increasing longevity, and a decreasing retirement age, people in western society are faced with the prospect of spending almost as long a period in old age as in middle age? What period is then to be defined as the later years? What of the role of retirement from work in a population where many face prolonged periods of unemployment at all ages?

There may be some value in considering adjustment to various situations which become more likely with age - e.g. bereavement of spouse, illness, loss of job status, elevation to the peerage, or to the Bench - but such information may tell us more about the situation than of ageing itself. This is, of course, to argue a position closer to Havighurst than Cumming and Henry, in so far as I am questioning the usefulness of any simple, comprehensive distinction between old age and any other mature adult age in terms of the necessary or sufficient conditions for an adequate quality of life (see also, McCulloch, 1981). This is not to deny the need for a better understanding of the conditions required for an adequate quality of life at any (adult) age (e.g. Maslow, 1954), a topic sadly neglected by psychologists.

I would hope that further work would be less concerned with attempting to identify a 'best buy' among potential indices of quality of life (Davies and Knapp, 1981). The concept is clearly multidimensional (Peace et al., 1979; George and Bearon, 1980) and there can be little doubt that we are a long way from understanding the complex relations between engagement, personality, institutional environments, life satisfaction and the other variables involved (Hughes and Wilkin, 1980, part II). There can equally be little doubt that we shall remain so until the variables can be operationally defined and measured, to allow more systematic study of their inter-relationship.

It also seems naive to consider the relation between quality of life and engagement in such simplistic terms as whether there is a direct correlation between the two, especially in institutional populations (Davies and Knapp, 1981). We might expect that there would be little to choose between enforced inactivity and enforced activity

(Kimble and Townsend, 1974; George, 1978; Briers, 1979). At a conceptual level, therefore, the studies of the Wessex group and others, showing increased engagement with the introduction of various materials or activities (Jenkins et al., 1977; Powell et al., 1978; McCormack and Whitehead, 1981) could be said to beg the question of the relationship between activity and quality of life. How then can we make use of measures of engagement within the context of improving quality of life?

The most immediate use is at an operational, rather than conceptual level. Psychologists may, rightly I think, be accused of becoming so concerned wth conceptual and methodological problems that they have little relevance in the practical world of those who have to make and implement policy for the present care of the elderly in institutional settings. As noted earlier, there is fairly general agreement about the changes wished for in care of the elderly in institutions (Evers, 1981). Most of these can be subsumed within the concept of de-institutional-isation (Linn and Linn, 1980). Being able to have operational measures, not only of engagement, but also of ward milieu, physical environment, life satisfaction, etc. (Hughes and Wilkin, 1980, part II), should allow not only better monitoring of whether intended changes have occurred, but also evaluation of the effect they have had on residents. An interesting extension of this would be to look at differences between actual and intended effects of changes in policy. Yet again, one might study the effect of different strategies of achieving change, e.g. changing the physical environment (Canter and Canter, 1979), changing nurses' attitudes (McFadyen, 1982; van Zwanberg, 1982), employing 'diversional therapists', etc.

Since we cannot assume that increased engagement means improved quality of life, it is perhaps a questionable strategy to study changes designed solely to increase activity. However, it would seem reasonable to study the effects on engagement of changes designed to de-institution-alise the physical and social environment. While there is no reason to expect that enforced increase in activity would improve quality of life, there is some evidence, as yet mainly descriptive rather than experimental, that decreasing institutional aspects of the environment, either planned (Hitch and Simpson, 1972; Gupta, 1979), or unplanned (Adams, et al., 1979), leads to a spontaneous increase in activities. In other words, while increased

149

engagement does not <u>ensure</u> a better quality of life, improved quality of life would normally involve increased engagement. It is in this context that engagement may be shown to be a useful index (among others) of quality of life/quality of care.

FIGURE 6.1: Definition of Engagement Categories

SHI = Self-Help Independent:

Any self-care activity
carried out without staff
assistance.

L = Leisure:

Any non-deviant active
behaviour judged by O
to be for the person's
amusement or occupation.
Watching television included
here.

Wk = Walking:

Walking.

O = Other non-deviant behaviour:

Active behaviours not
falling to the above categories.

SHD = Self-help dependent:

Any self-care activity
carried out with staff
assistance.

W = Watching:

Showing 'passive' interest
in some identifiable event
in the physical or social
environment.

DB = Deviant Behaviour:

Behaviour judged to show
delusional, hallucinatory,
or unwarranted aggressive
quality, e.g. physical aggression,
talking to self, undressing
inappropriately.

A = Asleep:

Asleep.

DN = Doing nothing:

Showing no involvement
or interest in the environment.

DN?W:

Observer unable to decide
between categories DN
and W.

FIGURE 6.2: Codes for Verbal Interactions

R ⟷ R:	Two-way interaction between residents.
R ⟷ S:	Two-way interaction between resident and staff.
R ⟷ V:	Two-way interaction between resident and visitor.
R ⟶ R) R ⟵ R)	One-way interaction between residents.
R ⟶ S) S ⟵ R)	One-way interaction between resident and staff.
R ⟶ V) V ⟵ R)	One-way interaction between resident and visitor.

FIGURE 6.3: Example of Completed Record Form

17th March 1983

RATER: .Jane.Green.......... PATIENT:..Ann.Brown........

Date/Time	Location	General Behaviour	Interaction	Brief description of specific behaviour and content of any interaction (if possible)	Engagement
8.30 am	DR	S		eating bacon and eggs	SHI
9.00 am	L	S		looking ahead (no obvious focus)	DN
9.30 am	L	S		reading paper	L
10.00 am	T	St		washing **her hands**	SHI
10.30 am	BR	L (on bed)		talking to self("I don't know who did it")	DB
11.00 am	L	S		watching me and passers by	W
11.30 am	L	S	R ←→ R	talking to other resident and watching TV	L
12.00 noon	L	S		watching other residents chatting	W
12.30 pm	DR	St		helping other resident sit down at table	O
1.00 pm	DR	S	R ←→ R	chatting to neighbour at table (lunch)	L
1.30 pm	L	St.		being assisted by other resident to put on cardigan	SHD
2.00 pm	L	S		sleeping	A
2.30 pm	L	S		sleeping	A
3.00 pm	BR	St		looking (for spectacles) in drawer	O
3.30 pm	L	S		watching TV	L
4.00 pm	L	S		drinking tea	SHI
4.30 pm	T	St.	R →S	being helped to toilet by staff ("Thank you")	SHD
5.00 pm	L	S		watching TV	L
5.30 pm	L	Wk		walking from lounge to dining room	Wk
6.00 pm	DR	S		eating macaroni cheese	SHI
6.30 pm	L	S		watching TV	L
7.00 pm	L	S		watching TV	L
7.30 pm	L	S		sleeping	A
8.00 pm	L	S		drinking cocoa	SHI
8.30 pm	L	S		watching TV	L
9.00 pm	L	S	R ←→ S	chatting with staff about TV programme	L

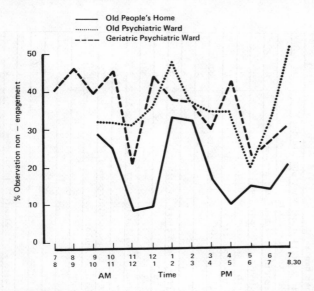

FIGURE 6.4: Variation in Non-Engagement with Time of Day

FIGURE 6.5: Variation in Active Engagement with Time of Day

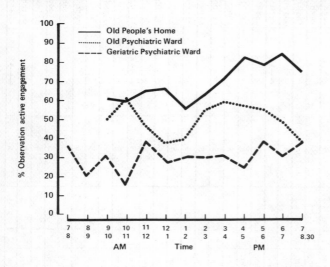

154

TABLE 6.1: Geriatric Psychiatry Ward

Specific Behaviours (% ages of Total Observations)

| | Active Engagement | | | | Passive Engagement | | Non-engagement | | | |
	SHI	L	WK	O	SHD	W	A	DN	W?DN	DB
60 Observations	10	15 (30%)	1	4	5 (29%)	24	12 (35%)	23	<1	6
20 Observations	7	17 (30%)	2	4	4 (29%)	25	14 (36%)	22	0	5

TABLE 6.2: Old People's Home

Specific Behaviours (% ages of Total Observations)

	Active Engagement				Passive Engagement		Non-Engagement			
	SHI	L	WK	O	SHD	W	A	DN	W?DN	DB
54 Observations	15	48	5	1	1	9	8	13	<1	0
		69%				10%		21%		
20 Observations	10	50	6	1	1	8	8	14	<1	1
		67%				9%		22%		

156

Specific Behaviours (% ages of Total Observations)

	SHI	L	WK	O	SHD	W	A	DN	DB
Old People's Home	15	48	5	1	1	9	8	13	0
Geriatric Psychiatry Ward	10	15	1	4	5	24	12	23	6
'Old Psychiatric' Ward	11	19	7	7	1	9	26	17	3
Geriatric Ward – General Hospital	8	23	3	5	5	17	13	26	0

TABLE 6.4:

Summary (% ages of Total Observations)

	Active engagement	Passive engagement	Non-engagement	Deviant behaviour
Old People's Home	69	10	21	0
Geriatric Psychiatry Ward	30	29	35	6
'Old Psychiatric' Ward	44	10	43	3
Geriatric Ward – General Hospital	39	22	39	0

TABLE 6.5: Analysis of Leisure Category

(% ages of Total Number of Leisure Observations)

	Watching Television	Reading	Speaking	Knitting and Sewing	Other
Old People's Home	20	21	29	-	29
Geriatric Psychiatry Ward	5	11	65	-	19
'Old Psychiatric' Ward	26	26	16	21	11

TABLE 6.6: Specific Behaviour: Social Interactions

(% ages of Total Number of Social Interactions)

	R↔R	R→R	R←R	R↔S	R→S	S→R	R↔V	R→V	V→R
Old People's Home	67	11	0	11	4	0	7	0	0
Geriatric psychiatry ward	58	11	3	6	4	14	4	0	0
'Old psychiatric' ward	34	5	0	13	10	8	26	3	0
Geriatric ward – general hospital	18	6	0	34	6	7	19	4	6

References

Abrams, M. (1978) Beyond Three-score and Ten, Age Concern, Mitcham.

Adams, J., Davies, J.E. and Northwood, J.N. (1979) Nursing Times, 27 September, 4 and 11 October.

Blunden, R. and Kushlick, A. (1975) 'Looking for Practical Solutions', Age Concern Today, 13, 2-5.

Bradburn, N. (1969) The Structure of Psychological Well-being, Maine Publishing Co., Chicago.

Briers, J.M. (1979) Residential Care for the Elderly in London, study by DHSS Social Work Service, London Region, DHSS, London.

British Geriatrics Society and Royal College of Nursing (1975) Improving Geriatric Care in Hospital, Royal College of Nursing, London.

British Medical Association (1976) Care of the Elderly: Report of the Working Party on Services for the Elderly, British Medical Association, London.

Canter, D. and Carter, S. (1979) Designing for Therapeutic Environments: A Review of Research, John Wiley, Chichester.

Cumming, E. and Henry, W.E. (1961) Growing Old: The Process of Disengagement, Basic Books, New York.

Davies, B. and Knapp, M. (1981) Old People's Homes and the Production of Welfare, Routledge & Kegan Paul, London.

DHSS (1976) Priorities for Health and Personal Social Services in England, consultative document, HMSO, London.

DHSS (1978) A Happier Old Age, HMSO, London.

Evers, H.K. (1981) 'Tender Loving Care - Patients and Nurses in Geriatric Wards', in L. Archer Copp (ed.) Recent Advances in Nursing 2: Care of the Aging, Churchill Livingstone, Edinburgh.

Faragher, T. (1978) Notes on the Evaluation of Residential Settings, Clearing House, LASS Research, No. 2, 59-85.

Felce, D. and Jenkins, J. (1979) 'Engagement in Activities by Old People in Residential Care', Health and Social Services J., 2 November, (pp. E23-E8).

Felce, D., Powell, L., Lunt, B., Jenkins, J. and Mansell, J. (1980) 'Measuring Activity of Old People in Residential Care', Evaluation Review, Vol. 4, No. 3, 371-87.

George, L.K. (1978) 'The Impact of Personality and Social Status Factors upon Levels of Activity and Psychological Well-being', Journal of Gerontology, 33, 840-7.

George, L.K. and Bearon, L.B. (1980) Quality of Life in Older Persons, Human Sciences Press, New York/London.

Goffman, E. (1961) Asylums: Essays on the Social Situation of Mental Patients and Other Inmates, Doubleday, New York.

Gupta, H. (1979) 'Can we De-Institutionalise an Institution? Part II', Concord, 23, 47-57.

Hall, J.N. (1980) 'Ward Rating Scales for Long-stay Patients: a Review', Psychological Medicine, 10, 277-88.

Havighurst, R.G. (1968) 'Personality and Patterns of Ageing', The Gerontologist, 8, 20-3.

Hendricks, J. and Hendricks, C.D. (1977) Aging in a Mass Society,

Winthrop, Cambridge, Mass., pp. 14-16. Reprinted as 'Ageism and Common Stereotypes', in V. Carver and P. Liddiard (eds.), An Ageing Population, (1978) Hodder & Stoughton, Sevenoaks.

Hitch, D. and Simpson, A. (1972) 'An Attempt to Assess a New Design in Residential Homes for the Elderly', British Journal of Social Work, 2, 481-501.

Hughes, B. and Wilkin, D. (1980) Residential Care of the Elderly: A Review of the Literature, University of Manchester, unpublished report.

Hunt, A. (1978) The Elderly at Home, HMSO, London.

Jenkins, J., Felce, D., Lunt, B. and Powell, L. (1977) 'Increasing Engagement in Activity of Residents in Old People's Homes by Providing Recreational Materials', Behaviour Research and Therapy, 15, 429-34.

Jenkins, J., Felce, D., Powell, E. and Lunt, B. (1978) Measuring Client Engagement in Residential Settings for the Elderly, Research Report No. 120, Health Care Evaluation Research Team, Winchester.

Kimbell, A. and Townsend, J. (1974) Residents in Elderly Persons' Homes, Cheshire County Council Social Services Department.

Knapp, M.R.J. (1976) 'Predicting the Dimensions of Life Satisfaction', Journal of Gerontology, 31, 595-604.

Knapp, M.R.J. (1977) 'The Activity Theory of Ageing: an Examination in the English Context', Gerontologist, 17, 553-9.

Kushlick, A. (1975) 'Improving Services for the Mentally Handicapped', in Kiernon, C.C. and Woodford, F.P. (eds.), Behaviour Modification with the Severely Retarded, Associated Scientific Publishers, Elsevier.

Lemon, B.W., Bengtson, V.L. and Petersen, J.A. (1972) 'An Exploration of the Activity Theory of Ageing: Activity Types and Life Expectation Amongst In-movers to a Retirement Community', Journal of Gerontology, Vol. 27, 511-23.

Lindsley, O.R. (1964) 'Geriatric Behavioural Prosthetics', in R. Kasternbaum (ed.), New Thoughts on Old Age, Springer, New York.

Linn, M.W. and Linn, B.S. (1980) 'Qualities of Institutional Care that Affect Outcome', Aged Care and Services Review, 2, No. 3, 1-14.

Lipman, A., Slater, R. and Harris, H. (1979) 'The Quality of Verbal Interaction in Homes for Old People', Gerontology, 25, 275-84.

Lunt, B., Felce, D., Jenkins, J. and Powell, L. (1977a) Staff Use of Written Procedures for Organising a Recreational Activities Session in a Home for the Elderly Mentally Infirm', Health Care Evaluation Research Team Report, No. 131, University of Southampton, Winchester.

Lunt, B., Felce, D., Jenkins, J. and Powell, L. (1977b) 'Organising Recreational Activity Sessions in a Home for the Elderly Mentally Infirm: The Effect of Different Levels of Staff Input on Resident Participation', Health Care Evaluation Research Team Report, No. 130, University of Southampton, Winchester.

McClannahan, L.E. (1973) 'Therapeutic and Prosthetic Living Environments for Nursing Home Residents', The Gerontologist, 424-9.

McCormack, D., and Whitehead, A. (1981) 'Effect of Providing
162

Recreational Activities on Engagement Level of Long-Stay Geriatric Patients', Age and Ageing, Vol. 10, No. 4, 287-91.

McCulloch, A.W. (1981) 'What Do We Mean by "Development" in Old Age?', Ageing and Society, Vol. 1, No. 2, July, 229-45.

McFadyen, M. (1982) Workshops on Staff Attitudes (in Care of Elderly), Teaching Notes, unpublished MSc, available from author.

McFadyen, M., Prior, T. and Kindness, K. (1982) 'Engagement: An Important Variable in the Institutional Care of the Elderly', in R. Taylor and A. Gilmore, (eds.), Current Trends in British Gerontology, Proceedings of the 1980 Conference of the British Society of Gerontology, Gower, Aldershot.

Maslow, A.H. (1954) Motivation and Personality, Van Nostrand, Princeton, New Jersey.

Meacher, M. (1972) Taken for a Ride, Longman, London.

Moos, R.H., Gauvain, M., Lemke, S., Max, W. and Mehren, B. (1979) 'Assessing the Social Environments of Sheltered Care Settings', The Gerontologist, 19, 1, 74-82.

Neugarten, D.L., Havighurst, R.J. and Mobin, S.S. (1961) 'The Measurement of Life Satisfaction', Journal of Gerontology, 16, 134-43.

Peace, S.M., Hall, J.F. and Hamblin, G. (1979) The Quality of Life of the Elderly in Residential Care: A Feasibility Study of the Development of Survey Methods, Polytechnic of North London, Survey Research Unit.

Pincus, A. (1968) 'The Definition and Measurement of the Living Environment in Homes for the Aged', The Gerontologist, 8, 3, 207-10.

Powell, L., Felce, D., Jenkins, J. and Lunt, B. (1978) 'Increasing Engagement in a Home for the Elderly by Providing an Indoor Gardening Activity', Health Care Research Team, Report No. 128, University of Southampton, Winchester.

Personal Social Services Council (1975) Living and Working in Residential Homes, PSSC, London.

Robb, B. (1967) Sans Everything, Nelson, London.

Schaeffer, H.H. and Martin, P.L. (1966) 'Behavioural Therapy for "Apathy" of Hospitalised Schizophrenics', Psychol. Rep., 19, 1147-58.

Sommer, R. and Ross, H. (1958) 'Social Interaction on a Geriatric Ward', Int. J. Soc. Psychiatry, 4, 128-33.

Townsend, P. (1962) The Last Refuge. A Survey of Residential Institutions and Homes for the Aged in England and Wales, Routledge & Kegan Paul, London.

van Zwanenberg, F. (1982) Nursing Auxiliaries Training Workshop 1, Help the Aged, London.

Whatmore, R., Durward, L. and Kushlick, A. (1975) 'Measuring the Quality of Residential Care', Behaviour Research and Therapy, 13, 4, 227-36.

Wilson, L.A. and Brass, W., (1973) 'The Usefulness of the Mental Status Questionnaire', Age and Ageing, 2, 92.

Chapter Seven

THEORETICAL AND PRACTICAL CONSIDERATIONS IN REALITY ORIENTATION THERAPY WITH THE ELDERLY

Ian Hanley

Introduction

Does reality orientation therapy (RO) as first designed some 20 years ago have credibility in the care of the elderly today? What is the conceptual basis for RO and how strong are its theoretical foundations? In the light of research that indicates generally only marginal (if any) improvement in patient functioning as a result of RO programmes, what justification is there for a situation where 'reality orientation in some form is currently the most typical treatment for elderly mentally impaired nursing home residents' (Carroll and Gray, 1981)? These are some of the issues that run as a general theme through this chapter. Readers interested in assessing the empirical evidence for the effectiveness of RO are referred to Chapter 8, and to two recent reviews (Holden and Woods, 1982; Powell-Proctor and Miller, 1982). Before doing so however they may wish to consider the issues raised below.

It appears that reality orientation is in a conceptual dilemma. The quote from Carroll and Gray (1981) indicates that RO 'in some form' is widely applied. But this does not imply general acceptance of RO and a consensus as to what is involved in RO procedures. There is considerable variation in what passes for RO in different settings. In some, for example, all that constitutes RO is a board clearly displaying day, date and time (often out of date)! Ask any two people what RO is and you will get two different responses. Some see it as nothing more than the forced indoctrination of elderly people with items of information of dubious importance (Gubrium and Ksander, 1975). Others criticise it for apparently advocating confrontation with the elderly confused patient (Carroll and Gray, 1981) while others applaud its humanitarian aspects (Arie, 1978; Hanley, 1980). Some see it as having great potential in the management of dementia (Miller, 1977) while others treat such a suggestion with disdain (Wershaw, 1977). Viewed by many as low-key and common sense, others have attested to RO having roots in the principles of learning (Arie, 1978). In contrast to the disappointing results from controlled trials, many practitioners in the field are convinced none the less that RO works (Drummond et al., 1978). It seems then that RO can be all things to all people.

If RO is to develop into a coherent treatment package an effort must be made to proceed beyond the general first principles that have been interpreted so variously and reach a clearer description of the actual techniques involved. Clear definition of procedures should lead to greater consensus and understanding, and less variability in practice. One of the virtues of RO is undoubtedly the fact that it was conceived and developed initially by nurses, practitioners and others at the grass roots of care provision. This has presumably accounted for RO having a flavour of practicality and common sense. One drawback, however, has been the failure to develop RO in the scientific tradition over the past 20 years. The time is ripe to 'beef up' RO in both theory and practice. One way to achieve this is to draw on the findings from empirical studies of memory, learning and behavioural functioning in the elderly, incorporate these into RO procedures, and as an end result give RO greater scientific credibility and a stronger base for further evaluation and development. This writer believes firmly that RO has the potential of being developed into a comprehensive strategy for the management of mental impairment, much in the same way as cognitive therapy, for example, can address the general psychological and behavioural impact of reactive depression in younger adults.

Let us start then by examining who might benefit from RO, what those benefits (aims) of RO might be and what the general methods are. We shall then go on to identify those findings from the experimental psychology of learning, memory and behavioural change that can be usefully incorporated into the methods to make them both more explicit and more effective.

Target Populations for RO

Reality orientation was originally described as a rehabilitation technique for elderly psychiatric patients. Folsom (1968) reports on the phases of development of RO in veterans' psychiatric units from 1959 to 1965. The goal of the programme he described was to address the unmet emotional needs of individual patients by encouraging nursing assistants to spend more time in one-to-one, personal contact with patients, attend to the 'attitude' they displayed, and place an overall emphasis on stimulating patient activity. A set of nine simple guidelines to RO emerged in 1962, two further points were added in 1963, and four more were included in the Training Manual that emerged later (American Hospitals Association, 1976). It is apparent from Folsom's description of RO in its early stages that the key concern was to address the general sensory and emotional deprivation experienced by long-stay psychiatric patients (Table 7.1).

Reality orientation then evolved considerably between 1965-1970 at the Tuscaloosa Veterans' Association Hospital. Letcher et al. (1974) retrospectively reviewed the progress of 125 male patients who had received RO over those years. This population was not a psychiatric group with a long history of hospitalisation, but rather averaged over 80 years of age at admission and had diagnoses of dementia (80 per cent) and cerebral vascular accidents (15 per cent). Letcher et al. define RO as 'one phase of a total rehabilitation program for the confused and disoriented patient'. Thus RO came to be associated in this period with the management of the mentally-impaired elderly. This has remained the case since, although it should be noted that RO has never been described as suitable for one type of patient exclusively.

Descriptions of RO rarely mention diagnosis. Drummond et al. (1978), for example, describe RO as a 'basic technique used in the rehabilitation of persons having memory loss, confusion and time-place-person disorientation'. Although a variety of diagnoses can be associated with such symptoms, the most prevalent are senile dementia Alzheimer's type (SDAT) and multi-infarct or arteriosclerotic dementia. The massive challenge to the health services posed by these diseases has been extensively documented elsewhere (Lishman, 1977). Within psychogeriatric hospital settings the majority of patients have dementia of one form or other and

166

within social service run residential homes estimates of organic mental impairment range from 30-65 per cent (Masterton et al., 1979; Gilleard et al., 1980). When the even greater numbers of mentally-impaired elderly living in the community are included the British Medical Journal's editorial of 1978 was obviously not exaggerating when it referred to dementia as 'the quiet epidemic'.

One of the recommendations of a report published by the Medical Research Council (Lishman, 1977) was for more work on psychological management and on finding improved ways to care for demented patients and attempt to improve their level of functioning. As the Medical Research Council report points out, 'many demented patients deteriorate slowly and survive for many years, and the disabilities they present at various stages seem often greater than they need be'.

Reality orientation, then, although potentially useful in the management of the elderly psychiatric patient, has most to offer if proven effective with those suffering dementia for which there is no known cure. Although results of evaluative trials to date are not particularly encouraging it will be argued later in this chapter that no study of RO to date has demonstrated that RO was actually implemented, i.e. that staff changed their behaviour towards patients along the lines of the general RO guidelines shown in Table 7.1

Before considering the effectiveness of RO, however, the goals we seek to achieve through its application must first be established.

Objectives of RO

It appears from the evaluative trials of RO, many of which are referred to in this chapter, that RO has but one objective, namely, to improve cognitive and behavioural functioning. Given the devastating impact of the dementias this is a laudable aim and one that will receive consideration later. It is, however, one that is not immediately evident from the RO guidelines in Table 7.1. It is clear from these that the first concern of RO must be a basically humanitarian interest in the way care is delivered to such patients.

Quality of life in dementia. Dementia is a progressive condition characterised by increasing general mental impairment and behavioural dis-ability. There is no known cure and although the end-point of the process is death, survival can be protracted with the patient maintained at increasing

167

levels of dependence and personal indignity. There is some evidence that patients with dementia in institutional care are surviving longer than previously (Christie, 1982). Although it is well established that dementia victims lack both insight into their condition, especially in the late stages, and frequently display labile mood swings, it is generally accepted that they are still capable of responding to their environment.

The environment that RO provides emphasises respect, dignity, interaction and success and is an improvement - psychologically - over many current settings. Holden and Woods (1982) suggest that even if RO produces only changes of minor clinical significance it should still be used as a communication method to increase the person's quality of life by improving interaction with the staff. One problem in this regard is finding a means of measuring quality of life that can be used with the mentally impaired. Until this can be accomplished we are left essentially with value-judgements as to what constitutes improved quality of life in dementia.

Some no doubt may argue that bland institutional environments, purely custodial regimes, and negligible amounts of personal communication between staff and patients, reflect the most humanitarian means of caring. The alert elderly in institutional care, who in many situations share accommodations with the mentally impaired, do not appear to hold this view, however. In an evaluation of their reaction to the implementation of an RO programme in a residential home they responded positively to the introduction of orientation aids such as signposts, notice boards, calendars, etc. Moreover the staff were convinced that the alert residents were 'jealous' of the increased attention paid to the confused (Hanley, 1981a). Although other data from this study suggested that in fact the number and quality of interactions between staff and confused residents did not increase significantly as a result of RO 'implementation', it is interesting to note that alert residents seemed to welcome orientation aids and increased contact with staff.

Quality of life is difficult to measure directly, but perhaps as Holden and Woods (1982) have suggested it is sufficient to apply the normalisation principle and assess the degree to which the person's life-style can continue despite dementia. Here RO and the attitudes underlying it can be seen as part of the attempt to help the dementing person function in as normal a manner as possible.

Anxiety and dementia. Arie (1978) has remarked on the
anxiety that can accompany memory loss and cognitive
impairment. Not to recognise person or place is
distressing whether or not dementia is present. It
has long been recognised that both organic and
functional conditions can co-exist. Reality
orientation, with its emphasis on providing the
mentally-impaired person with time-place-person
orientation and a running commentary on what is
happening around him, may well be reassuring and act,
as Arie poetically predicts, 'like a beam of light
across a murky fog'. Again there are problems with
testing this hypothesis empirically as anxiety, and
the agitation it generates, are difficult to measure
in the mentally-impaired elderly. Still it is one
that is worthy of further attention when considering
the possible aims of a RO programme. Whether or not
information provided in RO is retained is not the
sole concern. Simple comprehension at the moment of
presentation may be important in its own right as an
anxiety reducer, and may further enhance the quality
of life of those with dementia.

Depressive withdrawal. The incidence of depression
tends to increase with age. For the elderly patient
with dementia faced with repeated failure at tasks
that were once easily completed, depressive
withdrawal may be one way of coping. For others
without dementia, depression is a common reaction to
traumatic life events, illness and lack of confidants
(Murphy, 1982). Some have speculated that acceptance
of 'disengagement' theory has led depression in its
milder forms, e.g. that presenting as apathy, to be
under diagnosed in the elderly. The existence of
depressive pseudo-dementia has been long established
(Kiloh, 1961) together with the recognition that this
is often hard to distinguish diagnostically from
dementia proper.

As should become clearer later when procedures
are discussed, RO assists the elderly person to
function close to potential. Interactions are
structured so that the demands placed on the person's
memory and behaviour are such that success is
guaranteed, reviving confidence and self-esteem.
Every available opportunity is used to engage the
elderly person in a positive fashion. Whether or not
RO is effective in reducing mood disturbance has not
been tested empirically, although several writers
have reported that impression (Holden and Woods,

1982). If proven effective, RO would not only serve to reverse some impairments evident in patients suffering a depression co-existent with a dementia but might presumably also help identify the pseudo-dementia patient by sparking improvements in his condition.

Cognitive and behaviour changes. The search for such changes has marked most of the evaluative work to date. RO emphasises the repeated presentation of orientation-related information, the correction of confused speech and behaviour, and the encouragement of greater levels of behavioural independence. Not surprisingly, then, studies have looked for changes in orientation and behaviour. The former is typically measured by the verbal responses of the subject to a set of orientation questions. Changes in behaviour, on the other hand, have been monitored by behaviour rating scales.

Most work to date has looked at the effects of classroom RO, a procedure designed to supplement the main 24RO approach (see Chapter 8). Cognitive but rarely behavioural changes have been reported. The lack of work on 24RO reflects the difficulty in operationalising these procedures. As will be described later, there is as yet no evidence to suggest for 24RO that 'the patient gets the pill'. Therefore the effectiveness of 24RO has not been adequately tested, though there are some pointers that the procedures involved may be highly effective (Hanley, 1981b).

Evaluation of any procedures in the management of dementia is a difficult operation as slowing down rather than reversing the course of deterioration is the primary aim. Improvements in condition are the exception rather than the rule. Figure 7.1 illustrates the situation with line (a) represent-ative of what happens to self-care ability in dementia. More and more assistance is required until there is a need for almost total physical nursing care. Line (b) optimistically represents a stabilisation of self-care ability at a level where there is considerable independence. Line (c) represents what may be the realistic goal of RO in dementia - a slowing-down of deterioration with the patient taking longer to reach the area of greatest indignity.

It will be demonstrated later that RO may have sufficient flexibility to meet the assessed needs of a patient at any point on this notional deterioration curve, i.e. RO procedures can be fine-tuned to the needs of individual patients.

Effects on care-givers. Dementia victims are typically cared for in institutions or alternatively by family members at home. Researchers have found negative attitudes and stereotypic thinking with regard to the aged among personnel in nursing homes and other institutional settings (Kahana and Coe, 1969; Kosberg and Gorman, 1975). In the home setting there is evidence of considerable strain on care-givers (Sanford, 1975; Gilhooley, 1981). Arie (1981) has identified what he calls 'the staff factor' as the major limiting factor, other than cost, which affects quality of care. Styles of service must be identified which meet not only the needs of the old people themselves but also the needs of the caregivers. As RO is delivered through caregivers an aim must surely be to determine its impact on their attitudes and behaviour. This has been an almost totally neglected question in RO research to date. One study (Smith and Barker, 1972) assessed staff attitudes before and after a five-day RO training course. Trainees showed a marked increase in positive attitudes to the elderly which was maintained after six months. This is an encouraging result, but as trainees were not actually involved with practising RO over the six-month period it is not possible to gauge the impact of actual RO implementation on their attitudes.

In the practical sense attitudes become of real interest when they positively impact the diverse set of behaviours performed by staff in providing patient care. Attempts to determine specifically the effect of attitudes on patient care have been beset with methodological problems (Adelson et al., 1982). The converse condition may exist where a change in behaviour is the precursor to attitude change, and a change, then, in the caregivers' behaviour from non-RO behaviour to RO behaviour may be a desirable objective.

A few studies have examined the impact of RO on staff behaviour. Woods (1980) evaluated the behavioural effects of training care-staff to conduct classroom RO. Using a direct observational procedure they assessed the frequency of various operationally-defined verbal behaviours before and after training. A significant increase in RO behaviour occurred after training. Outside the RO classroom a similar exercise could not be conducted. A high proportion of the staff-resident interactions occurred in relation to bathing, dressing, toileting, etc., and not in the 'public' areas of the institution where interactions could be easily observed. Hanley (1981a) reports the results of such an investigation. He observed all interactions between staff and patients over an eight-hour sampling schedule that covered all time periods between 9am and 5pm. Staff were unaware of the exact purpose of these ratings, as direct observation of patient behaviour was a matter of routine in both the hospital and the old people's home involved. Each staff-patient interaction was coded for the presence or absence of six easily observable RO behaviours (Table 7.2). (Other RO behaviours considered more difficult to rate were excluded.)

The ratings were conducted once before and once after an RO training programme that marked the implementation of 24RO in these settings. No change was found in either the number of interactions staff had with patients (approximately one per hour) or in the quality of the interactions as measured by the mean number of RO behaviours present per interaction. In addition, when staff were asked to rate their own interactions with patients they indicated a belief that they were carrying out these procedures. This was clearly not the case (Table 7.3). In both hospital and home, both before and after the 'implementation' of 24RO, the typical interaction between staff and patient included only one or two of the six behaviours considered characteristic of 24RO! These results need to be replicated in other settings and with careful attention to the contents of the training programmes involved. The programme used by Hanley (1981a) included lectures, handouts, audiovisual presentations, group discussions and opportunities to observe high quality classroom RO. Little attention was given to having staff role-play 24RO interactions and herein perhaps lies a weakness of this training approach, which may account for the apparent lack of staff behaviour change.

Irrespective of the reason for this disappointing result, one thing is clear - changes in staff behaviour cannot be assumed to occur when RO is introduced, even when staff are favourable to the programme. Hanley et al. (1981) in describing the nature of their RO programme, as applied in the setting of an Edinburgh old people's home, pointed out how well it was received by the staff involved. In the absence of data to demonstrate changes in staff behaviour as a result of RO implementation, findings to date (e.g. Zepelin et al., 1981) that indicate little positive effect for 24RO on patient functioning, are what one would expect, and should not be taken as indicative of what <u>might</u> be achieved were RO demonstrably implemented.

RO has not yet been systematically applied in the home environment. Caregivers here are typically under considerable strain. Gilhooley (1981) has pointed out that many cope by ignoring the behaviour of their demented relative. It remains to be tested how effective RO is in such situations. Perhaps relatives ignore certain behaviours because they lack the knowledge and skills to cope with them directly. Any evaluation of RO in community care should, as a priority, examine the effects on the stress level and coping ability of caregivers.

24-Hour RO - General Methods

For a number of reasons this discussion is restricted to 24RO and does not cover the popular classroom RO procedure. First, 24RO is the main form that RO takes; classroom RO is considered secondary (Drummond <u>et al</u>., 1978); secondly, the methods of classroom RO have been described in detail elsewhere (Drummond <u>et al</u>., 1978; Hanley and Oates, 1980); and lastly the generality of the 24RO approach has made it difficult to implement effectively, as the data presented above bear witness.

Drummond <u>et al</u>. (1978) present a somewhat general account of 24RO that is nevertheless more explicit than the guidelines of Table 7.1. They specify that all staff are involved and that every contact with the patient is used: (a) to present information on who he or she is, where he or she is, what time of day it is, what is happening in the persons surroundings; (b) to correct confused speech and actions; and (c) to prompt and encourage appropriate behaviours. In addition, (d) the environment is reorganised to provide large, highly visible orientation aids such as calendars, notice-boards, directional arrows, colour-coded areas, etc. Thus 24RO has two general components, an interpersonal-interactional component and a pros-thetic environmental component. A study by Hanley (1981b) compared the effectiveness of these components applied to the correction of one specific problem, namely, disorientation to the ward environment. The procedures involved provide an illustration of RO interactional style.

The ability of patients with moderate-severe dementia to locate each of eight locations in a typical Nightingale ward was determined directly. As expected the results (base-line, Figure 7.2) reflected poor ward orientation. A prescribed treatment, emphasising the staff-patient interactional components of 24RO was then introduced. For two trials on each of seven occasions spread over a two-week period patients were asked to demonstrate ward orientation behaviours with relevant information and correction provided as required by the staff member involved. A typical training interaction was as follows:

> Staff Member: Mrs Smith show me the dining-room please. Show me where you have your meals. (Mrs Smith wanders past the dining-room door.)
> Staff Member: (pointing to dining-room). This is the dining-room. It is the last door on the corridor. Look. The tables are set for tea. What room is this Mrs Smith?
> Mrs Smith: Dining-room.
> Staff Member: That's good Mrs Smith, this is the dining-room. Now show me your bedroom. Show me where you sleep.

As a result of this training, ward orientation increased considerably to the five ward locations trained. However the improvements did not noticeably generalise to the locations that were left untrained. Ward orientation declined when training was withdrawn, increased when the treatment was reinstated, and finally returned to base line over an extended follow-up period after treatment was terminated. In this study the patient most definitely 'got the pill'. This was achieved by: (a) designating one staff member as responsible for the programme; (b) prescribing exact treatment schedules for selected patients; (c) clear identification of the target behaviours; and (d) providing an exact description of training, i.e. cueing, demonstration, information and correction. Others have pointed out the need to detail exact procedures if staff compliance is to be achieved (Powell et al., 1979). Perhaps similar specificity was responsible for Woods' (1980) success in modifying staff behaviour in classroom RO.

Thus, in addition to providing one illustration of how staff interact with patients behaviourally in 24RO, this study demonstrates the effectiveness of harnessing 24RO staff-patient interactions to bring about behaviour changes. In a second stage to the experiment it was found that large lettered and pictorial signposts, arranged to be clearly visible, had little effect on ward orientation. However, improvements were obtained when patients were trained, again through staff-patient RO interaction, to understand and pay attention to the signposts. These gains maintained. Hence the second general component of 24RO, the prosthetic environment component, was shown effective, but only in conjunction with appropriate staff-patient interaction.

Theoretical and Practical Considerations in Reality Orientation with the Elderly

The objection may be raised that the massed practice methodology of this analogue investigation into 24RO is not equivalent to the obvious spaced interactions that occur in most settings for the elderly. The low frequency of staff-patient interactions described by Hanley (1981a) is not atypical as other studies have presented similar findings (Galliard, 1978). The question could be asked whether patients with dementia can indeed learn new information or develop adaptive behaviours when the learning trials are brief and spaced as is the case in 24RO. Is mere repetition of information sufficient, or should patients be encouraged to use the information behaviourally? By examining the experimental literature on learning and memory such questions can be answered. The strategies involved in the four RO procedures of: (a) repeated information provision; (b) correction of confused behaviour; (c) prompting of positive behaviour; and (d) provision of memory aids should be made more explicit than is presently the case if misinterpretation of RO is to be avoided. Powell-Proctor and Miller (1982), for example, arrive at a number of false conclusions about RO, namely: (1) that it is not geared to the needs of the individual patient; (2) that it does not emphasise maintenance of everyday skills; and (3) that procedures such as the ward orientation training described above are not part of RO. Such misinterpretations are unfortunate and can only be avoided by clearer descriptions of the mechanics involved in applying RO in practice.

It should be noted, however, that RO was developed as a general management approach that could be applied by all staff involved with the patient. Nursing and care assistants are the backbone of the nursing team and efforts to make RO more behaviourally sophisticated must not be at the expense of making it unintelligible to staff with limited training.

Likewise RO is a 'package', a total approach to care that incorporates consideration of many important non-specific factors such as non-verbal communication, compensations for sensory loss, and staff consistency. The principle components of RO, i.e. the behavioural strategies of the staff with the patient, need to be revised, but the non-specific factors should not be altered. Others have expressed a different opinion. Carroll and Gray (1981) advocate the replacement of RO by 'memory development' - a set of principles for facilitating learning and memory. This is premature. Not only is RO already widely applied and accepted, but it is capable of incorporating the ideas of 'memory development' which are little more than some of the procedures of RO expressed in more formal scientific fashion. Approaching the matter this way 'the baby is not lost with the bath water' - the non-specific factors that are summarised in the guidelines of Table 7.1 are retained to enrich the overall RO approach.

Reality Orientation and Dementia Related Impairments

Memory and Verbal Learning

Prior to the onset of dementia even a very elderly person's learning ability is relatively intact and normal memory allows a vast amount of information to be recalled when required from the secondary memory store. It has been clearly established, however, that dementia impairs the learning of new information (Inglis, 1957, 1959). As deficits are not found in primary memory, the 'short-term' or limited capacity store, it can be assumed that the problem lies somewhere in the processes of transfer to, encoding in, or retrieval from, the secondary or 'main' memory store. The patient with dementia therefore has difficulty maintaining orientation to the present primarily because he is not learning, or cannot recall, the ongoing pieces of information that go to make up orientation to time, place and person. Functioning is further comprised by an inability to recall material from the remote and distant past - material that presumably was learned or encoded efficiently prior to the onset of illness.

Explanations for the memory and learning deficits in dementia may be grouped into those that assume a retrieval failure at the time of recall - for example, appropriate retrieval cues might not be generated at recall, or too many irrelevant items

might be retrieved in addition to the correct
response - and those that assume a defect in
establishing information and the appropriate
retrieval cues at the time of learning. The clinical
impression of relatively good distant recall, but
poor recent recall, could suggest that retrieval
mechanisms are intact and that memory disorder is due
to a failure to acquire new information. However, it
could be argued that dementia prevents the
establishment of new retrieval cues, but leaves pre-
morbid retrieval cues accessible and usable (Kenny,
1980). Using recognition procedures to test verbal
memory allows the retrieval mechanisms of free recall
to be by-passed. Employing this strategy Miller
(1978) showed some improvements for demented
patients, and concluded that recall and recognition
are impaired in dementia because of defective
retrieval processes.

Likewise, it has been argued that the
superiority of cued over free recall reflects the
inadequacy of the normal retrieval processes. Cues
are prompts that have some characteristic or
attribute of the stored material by which it is
assumed the material has been encoded. According to
Tulving and Bower (1974) the greater the
informational overlap between the memory trace and
the cue, the greater the effectiveness of the
retrieval aid.

Miller (1975) tested the ability of normals and
patients with pre-senile dementia to remember lists
of common words. For the dements, but not the
normals, presenting the initial letter of each word
at the time of recall significantly increased the
number of words recalled to near normal levels. These
results suggest that better retrieval might be
achieved given the right conditions at the time of
recall. Davis (1981), in attempting to replicate
these findings with older more demented subjects,
used semantic cues that are considered the most usual
in normal encoding. The dementia subjects did not
improve their recall as a result and Davis concluded
that a problem existed at input (failure to process
the words' semantic characteristics) in addition to
the possibility of one at output.

The general implication of these findings is
that RO techniques should be most effective if they
(1) can reduce an encoding deficit and optimise the
establishment of a strong trace; and (2) can then
provide retrieval aids to be present at recall. For
mildly demented patients, or when distant pre-morbid
memories need to be recalled in more impaired

patients, retrieval cues alone might be sufficient.

Behavioural Competence

It can be argued that in dementia the main objective is not for the patient to learn new behaviours, but rather to maintain previously acquired behaviour patterns and exercise them in the appropriate manner. The important role played by the environment in determining behavioural competence in the mentally impaired has been expressed by Lawton (1970) as the 'Environmental Docility Hypothesis', namely, that 'as individual competence decreases, the environment assumes increasing importance in determining well-being'. Both the physical and interpersonal environment are implicated. Sommer and Ross (1958) obtained a 60 per cent increase in verbal interaction by simply changing the arrangement of chairs in a psychogeriatric ward. McClannahan and Risley (1975) showed that prompting and encouragement greatly increased active use of recreational materials, whereas simply having the materials visibly available had minimal impact on their use. Similarly, Jenkins et al. (1979) demonstrated that brief announcements had limited effect on participation in indoor gardening activity while the use of direct prompting and encouragement was effective. Blackman et al. (1976) prompted attendance at a morning social activity in a home for the aged by reminding residents on awakening and by trundling a noisy serving trolley (cue) to carry refreshments to the social area. The latter presumably also acted as a reinforcement. Appropriate social activity between residents, although not specifically reinforced, increased in response to the cues naturally present in the situation and enjoyment of the interaction.

These studies illustrate that a combination of prompts from staff, encouragement and reinforcement from staff and a facilitative physical environment, can induce desirable behavioural responses in the elderly.

A Model for Reality Orientation

By repetition of basic information RO seeks to achieve new verbal learning. Encoding of new information is assisted by placing emphasis on salient cues and associations to this information which can later be used to assist recall. The purpose is not to have the patient master free recall but to enable them to achieve cued recall. RO improves memory by providing salient cues both in staff-patient interactions and in the environment. Emphasis is placed on the patient being actively involved in making successful verbal responses. Behaviourally, RO seeks to provide cues and prompts to behaviour and to retain existing functions. In some cases practice of new behaviours might be encouraged.

Carroll and Gray (1981) discuss in detail the three factors of cueing, practice and motivation that would seem to underly the procedures of RO.

Cues

Environmental cues. The memory aids component in RO needs to be carefully designed to be perceivable and perceived by those with sensory loss. Location, size, colour and surrounding light levels are all important. Sufficient cues should be available to aid memory and orientation. To increase awareness of autumn, for example, there could be calendars, autumn decorations and displays, special foods, etc.

Personal cues. These are the essence of RO. As was demonstrated by Hanley (1981b), the effectiveness of environmental cues can be enhanced if staff train the mentally impaired to attend to them and understand their meaning. As the research on mental learning and memory illustrates, staff engaged in providing information to patients can improve their responses by encouraging recognition instead of recall, e.g. 'Mrs. Smith, were you born in Glasgow or Edinburgh?', or 'Bill, did you have the pork or the chicken for dinner?' It was established by Brooke et al. (1975) that for RO to be effective, patients need to be actively involved or engaged in using the information provided in RO classes. Presumably the same applies to 24RO. The provision of information is carried out through conversation, and the guiding principle is that the effective participation of the patient is involved. This requires 'pitching' the level of demand such that the patient can succeed. The use of a recognition format is one way, the partial information (cued recall) format is another. For example, in talking abut a famous singer on record or on television, a staff member might ask the patient, 'Who's that singing? Isn't that Bing something — I think it begins with C. Yes, of course, Bing Crosby. What was that famous song of his? Remind me. Wasn't it "White" something or other ...?' The level of difficulty, i.e. the number and saliency of cues provided, can be fine-tuned to the patient's level of functioning. The value of this personal adjustment in the context of the slow progressive deterioration characteristic of dementia has already been pointed out. Drummond et al. (1979), in discussing this in relation to classroom RO, refer to it as 'leader guidance'. Providing information then involves both finding ways to repeat information to patients and also cue patients to use or recall that information.

The selection of appropriate cues can be helped if an effort is made to ensure that new information is encoded in a particular fashion. One RO therapist I knew was called Oates. In telling mentally-impaired patients her name she would say, 'My name is Mrs Oates. You know – horses.' This ensured that a ready-made cue was available (horses) when patients were being assisted to recall her name at a later date.

In a similar vein appropriate selection of cues can aid remote memory. In reminiscence therapy the methods are essentially similar to RO. Memory aids, such as old pictures, objects, and sounds from times gone by, can trigger remote memories. Likewise staff can provide verbal cues which do the same job. This requires a knowledge of the common life experiences of the cohort of older people being worked with or, when cues are being provided specifically for a particular individual, a good knowledge of that person's social history. Even a single word can be a cue that will bring a flood of memories. For example, a staff member might ask, 'What was spooning like (an old term used for dating) when you were a young girl?'

Woods (1983) found cues to be useful in eliciting correct responses from a 68-year-old patient with Korsakoff's psychosis. The extent to which cues and prompts aided learning is not clear and Woods suggests we make an effort to determine what types of cues are most effective in eliciting correct responses.

RO communication is a useful backdrop to group activities, for example, baking or sewing. Often cues present in the activity itself stimulate remote memory. The activity can be seen as providing a context for remembering, i.e. a condition similar to that under which original learning and subsequent rehearsal of behaviour occurred; retrieval, therefore, is more likely. Alternatively, this can be seen as the use of complex multiple cues which in combination stimulate memory or behaviour. For example, formal dining groups have been noted to improve eating behaviour, presumably because the multiple cues present (table cloth, place settings, etc.) stimulate previously learned and only apparently forgotten behaviours.

The final consideration in the use of cues is their application in the maintenance of appropriate behaviours. The example of the formal meal setting is primarily an alteration of the physical environment in such a way that it places greater demands on the impaired individual.

Demands must be those the individual is capable of fulfilling. Just as information and memory can be cued through personal communication so can behaviour. In this sense staff using RO act as the patient's memory. They prompt just enough for the patient to comply; for example, 'It's twelve o'clock, Bill, time for dinner' (patient goes to dining-room alone, following signposts perhaps) or 'Here's your fork Mrs Cooper. Use your fork to eat your scrambled eggs.' It has been illustrated earlier how something as simple as a prompt can increase participation in elective activities. This is not an insignificant finding when the low level of activity in many institutional settings for the mentally-impaired elderly is considered (see Chapter 6). Through careful assessment of an individual's functional impairments (see Chapter 4) staff using RO can set up strategies where these behaviours, or part of them, are prompted, time allowed for the patient to respond, and reinforcement given (staff approval and encouragement) for the patient's effort.

Throughout this discussion on cues it can be seen that the emphasis in RO is to modify the physical and interpersonal environment to compensate for the impairments of dementia. This is an essentially prosthetic approach and one that might be as potentially effective with the mentally impaired as it has been when applied to the problems of the blind, the deaf and the physically disabled. Gilleard (1980) has put the matter succinctly: 'The deficits of dementia are not located in the person but rather in the interface between the person and his environment.' Too often we place the mentally-impaired elderly in what are noxious environments lacking adequate levels of cues and sensory stimulation.

Practice and Motivation

RO not only emphasises a cueing (prosthetic approach), but also a training (rehabilitation) approach. The latter is geared to learning or relearning information and behaviours and involves practice and repetition. Woods (1983) has demonstrated that a specific learning effect occurs in personalised class RO. This was based on practice and repetition of verbal orientation items and is relatively specific to the items practised with little evidence of generalisation. Carroll and Gray (1981) point out that practice effects are enhanced through use of set routines for ADL activities, and the provision of a slow pace with only two or three items of information presented at the same time, and with no distractions - i.e. conversation should be directed at the task in hand. RO guidelines 1-4 and 7-8 (Table 7.1) reflect this concern with optimal learning conditions and practice. Perhaps by care-staff taking longer for each patient 'contact', the learning advantages of massed practice can be achieved within a spaced practice regime.

The emphasis on a set routine in RO (guideline 2) has been criticised by some as meaning a dull monotonous routine. This need not be the case. A set routine allows a schedule of activities to be learned. This is underlined by the emphasis that RO places on consistency. The responses to one event act as antecedent stimuli to prepare the person for the next event. An impaired person who lacks the ability fully to comprehend the things that are happening to him in his environment may feel more secure and demand less reassurance from staff when a schedule is followed consistently. Schedules, as Carroll and Gray (1981) point out, can provide a time perspective. Basic activities should stay the same from day to day, but a variety of interesting activities can be built in on a weekly, monthly or yearly basis, e.g. 'Monday Night Sing-along'. Planning and preparing for activities, as well as recalling them afterwards can contribute to the time perspective. Unique events, for example, the Royal Wedding, can become marker events against which lesser events can be measured and remembered. Changes in schedule can reinforce yearly happenings and current events, for example, a regular RO group replaced with a Christmas party.

When motivation to learn is considered it should be noted that RO does not advocate pressuring the mentally-impaired person. Any cause for anxiety should be minimised and pressure to perform should be avoided. Hanley <u>et al</u>. (1981) pointed out the need for meaningful material and activities to be employed, a sentiment echoed by Carroll and Gray (1981), who pointed out that these are remembered better. Meaningful, relevant learning experiences require that the patient's past interests and life history be considered - because RO emphasises the present does not mean it ignores the past!

Correcting Confused Behaviour

It is sometimes thought that RO always involves challenging or confronting the confused person with little attention paid to the consequences (Carroll and Gray, 1981). This is incorrect. The original guideline specifies 'correct residents when they ramble confusedly in speech and actions'. The other guidelines suggest that this correction be a gentle procedure, for example; 'show kindness and politeness, while being matter-of-fact'. Without attention to the correction of confused behaviour any therapeutic approach to dementia would implicitly be accepting confused behaviour as incorrectable. Care-staff would end up accepting and thereby reinforcing confused behaviour. The goal of correction is to disrupt confused speech or action sufficiently so that the more positive components of RO can be continued. Holden and Woods (1982) provide an excellent description of how to interrupt confused and rambling speech: tactfully disagree where sensitive topics are not involved, e.g. 'This is a hospital in fact, but we like to think it is as good as any hotel.' If responses to such general corrections are reasonable then discussion of more emotionally-loaded material might be attempted, e.g. bereavement, but only when the person is calm and there is time available.

Holden and Woods suggest that when time is limited or when there already is some agitation or confusion and talk is vague and incoherent, it is better not to correct confabulatory statements. Instead it is better to ignore the content of the rambling talk and use distraction. Moving the person's focus of attention onto something in the surroundings is one way.

When the patient's remarks seem to express an underlying feeling, Holden and Woods suggest that staff acknowledge the feelings expressed but ignore the content. They describe an example of an elderly lady who talked to her 'sister' in a mirror. She knew it was a mirror but had constructed a fantasy world where she was able to pass the time of day with her reflection. Holden and Woods suggest that a response such as, 'It's great to feel you have relatives near by' seems more appropriate than outright correction. The correction of confusion component of 24RO therefore relies heavily on staff sensitivity to patients' needs. The methods can vary and are not clearly related to basic principles of memory and learning.

Concluding Remarks

This chapter has attempted to point out that the goals of RO can be much broader than those usually considered. The potential effectiveness of RO procedures needs to be assessed against just such a wide range of goals. Implementation cannot be assumed and future studies should seek to demonstrate changes in staff behaviour. For those interested in applying RO this is a primary concern and work needs to be done on establishing the best staff training methods, methods that ensure staff behaviour change.

Applied consistently, RO methods should be effective if a number of techniques from memory and learning research are incorporated. The adoption of these strategies should not be at the expense of neglecting the sound common sense and simplicity of the original guidelines. Reality orientation offers the most potential of any psychologically-based procedure in the management of the dementias.

FIGURE 7.1: Schematic Graph of Self-Care Ability in Dementia Illustrating that Halting or even Slowing Down Deterioration can be Useful Aims

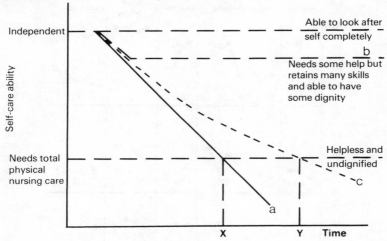

Notes:

(a)   Usual deterioration in dementia.

(b)   Stabilisation of self-care ability at an intermediate level.

(c)   A slowing-down of deterioration resulting in a higher quality of life for (c) as compared with (a) for the period of time X–Y.

From Holden and Woods (1982), reproduced with permission from Churchill-Livingstone, Edinburgh.

FIGURE 7.2: Ward Orientation Scores for Five Patients during Base Line, Ward Training and Follow-up

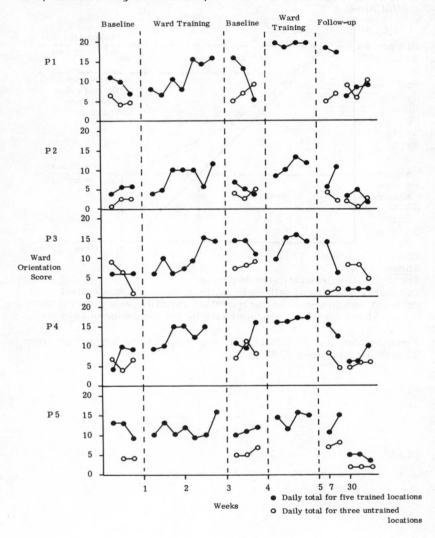

Hanley (1981b) Reproduced from J. Behav. Ther. & Exper. Psychiat, 12, 3, 241-7

TABLE 7.1: Reality Orientation Guidelines (American Hospitals Association, 1976)

Provide a calm environment.
Establish and maintain a set routine.
Give clear, simple responses to residents' questions.
Ask clear, simple questions of residents.
Speak distinctly and directly to residents.
Remind residents of time, place and person.
Correct residents when they ramble confusedly in
 speech and actions.
Explain each new procedure before asking a resident
 to do it.
Give residents plenty of time to respond.
Direct residents around by giving clear directions;
 if need be, guide them by accompanying them.
Show residents you expect them to understand and
 comply.
Show residents you expect them to care for themselves
 as much as they are truly able.
Treat residents as respected, dignified adults.
Show your interest and sincerity to residents.
Show kindness and politeness, while being matter-of-
 fact.
Do all the above consistently.

TABLE 7.2: 24-Hour RO Behaviours (as used by Hanley, 1981a)

Staff member: engages patient verbally (EPV)
                  names patient (SNP)
                  names self (SNS)
                  refers to time or place (RTP)
                  explains procedure (SEP)
                  refers to orientation aid
                  (clock, (SRP), calendar, etc.)

TABLE 7.3: Self-ratings by Staff of their Interactions with Patients vs % Observed Occurrence of These Behaviours (hospital staff $\overline{N}$ = 15)*

		Self Ratings				
	Always	Most of time	Half time	Once in a while	Never	Observed occurrence %
EPV	15	–	–	–	–	91
SNP	11	4	–	–	–	48
SNS	–	6	1	6	2	0
RTP	2	3	8	2	–	9
SEP	11	4	–	–	–	14
SRP	1	3	4	5	2	1

*From Hanley (1981a).

Note

A range of visual aids designed to enhance orientation are available from 'Orientation Aids', Dalebank, Glencaple, Dumfries, Scotland.

References

For further reading on the theory and methods of RO the reader is encouraged to read Holden and Woods (1982).

Adelson, R. et al. (1982) 'Behavioural Ratings of Health Professionals Interactions with the Geriatric Patient', The Gerontologist, 22, 3, 277-81.

American Hospitals Association (1976) This Way to Reality - A Guide for Developing a Reality Orientation Program, Chicago, Illinois.

Arie, T. (1978) 'Confusion in Old Age,' Age and Ageing, 7, Suppl., 72-6.

Blackman, D.K., Howe, M. and Pinkston, E.M. (1976) 'Increasing Participation in Social Interaction of the Institutionalized Elderly', The Gerontologist, 16, 1, 69-76.

Brooke, P., Degun, G. and Mather, M. (1975) 'Reality Orientation, a Therapy for Psychogeriatric Patients: A Controlled Study', Brit. J. Psychiat., 127, 42-5.

Carroll, K. and Gray, K. (1981) 'Memory Development: An Approach to the Mentally Impaired Elderly in the Long-Term Care Setting', Intern. J. of Ageing and Human Development, 13(1), 15-35.

Christie, A.B. (1982) 'Changing Patterns in Mental Illness in the Elderly', Brit. J. Psychiat., 140, 154-9.

Davis, P.E. and Mumford, S. (1981) 'The Nature of the Memory Impairment in Senile Dementia: a Brief Review and Experiment', paper presented at British Psychological Society, Annual Conference, Surrey.

Drummond, L., Kirchoff, L. and Scarbrough, D.R. (1978) 'A Practical Guide to Reality Orientation: a Treatment Approach for Confusion and Disorientation', The Gerontologist, 18, 6, 568-73.

Folsom, J.C. (1968) 'Reality Orientation for the Elderly Patient', J. Geriatric Psychiatry, 1, 2, 291-307.

Galliard, P. (1978) 'Difficulties Encountered in Attempting to Increase Social Interaction amongst Geriatric Psychiatric Patients: Clean and Sitting Quietly', paper presented at British Psychological Society Annual Conference, York.

Gilhooley, M.L.M. (1981) 'The Social Dimensions of Senile Dementia', paper presented at 12th International Congress of Gerontology, Hamburg.

Gilleard, C.J., Pattie, A.H. and Dearman, G. (1980) 'Behavioural Disabilities in Psychogeriatric Patients and Residents of Old People's Homes', J. of Epidemiology and Community Health, 34, 2, 142-5.

Gubrium, J. and Ksander, M. (1975) 'On Multiple Realities and Reality Orientation', The Gerontologist, 15, 142-5.

Hanley, I.G. (1980) 'Optimism or Pessimism: an Examination of RO Procedures in the Management of Dementia', paper presented

189

at British Psychological Society Annual Conference, Aberdeen.

Hanley, I.G. (1981a) 'An Evaluation of Reality Orientation Procedures with the Mentally Impaired Elderly', PhD thesis, University of Edinburgh.

Hanley, I.G. (1981b) 'The Use of Signposts and Active Training to Modify Ward Disorientation in Elderly Patients', Journal of Behaviour Therapy and Experimental Psychiatry, 12, 3, 241-7.

Hanley, I.G. and Oates, A. (1980) Class Reality Orientation, Audio-visual Services, University of Edinburgh.

Hanley, I.G., Cleary, E., Oates, A. and Walker, M. (1981) 'In Touch with Reality', Social Work Today, 12, 42, 8-10.

Holden, U.P. and Woods, R. (1982) Reality Orientation, Churchill-Livingstone, Edinburgh.

Inglis, J. (1957) 'An Experimental Study of Learning and Memory Function in Elderly Psychiatric Patients', J. Ment. Sci., 103, 796-803.

Inglis, J. (1959) 'A Paired-associate Learning Test for Use with Elderly Psychiatric Patients', J. Ment. Sci., 105, 440-8.

Kahana, E. and Coe, R.M. (1969) 'Self and Staff Perceptions of Institutionalized Aged', The Gerontologist, 9, 264-7.

Kenny, F.T. (1980) 'A Comment on Squire and Slater's Conclusion Regarding Memory Impairment in Chronic Amnesia', Neuropsychologia, 18, 367.

Kiloh, L.G. (1961) 'Pseudo-dementia', Acta Psychiat. Scand., 37: 336-351.

Kosberg, J.I. and Gorman, J.F. (1975) 'Perceptions Toward the Rehabilitation Potential of Institutionalized Elderly', The Gerontologist, 15, 398-403.

Lawton, M.P. (1970) 'Assessment, Integration and Environments for the Elderly', The Gerontologist, 10, 38-46.

Letcher, P.B., Peterson, L.P. and Scarborough, D. (1974) 'Reality Orientation - A Historical Study of Patient Progress', Hosp. Commun. Psychiat., 25, 11-13.

Lishman, W.A. (1977) 'Senile and Presenile Dementias: a Report of the MRC Sub-committee', London.

McClannahan, L.E. and Risley, T.R. (1975) 'Design of Living Environments for Nursing-Home Residents: Increasing Participation in Recreation Activities', Journal of Applied Behaviour Analysis, 8, 261-8.

Masterton, E.M., Holloway, M. and Timbury, G.C. (1979) 'The Prevalence of Organic Cerebral Impairment and Behavioural Problems within Local Authority Homes for the Elderly', Age and Ageing, 8, 226-30.

Miller, E. (1975) 'Impaired Recall and the Memory Disturbance in Presenile Dementia', Brit. J. Soc. Clin. Psychol. 14, 73-9.

Miller, E. (1978) 'Retrieval from Long-term Memory in Presenile Dementia', Brit. J. Soc. Clin. Psychol. 143-8.

Miller, E. (1977) 'The Management of Dementia: a Review of Some Possibilities', Br. J. Soc. Clin. Psychol., 16, 77-83.

Murphy, E. (1982) 'Social Origins of Depressions in Old Age', British Journal of Psychiatry, 141, 135-142.

Powell-Proctor, L. and Miller, E. (1982) 'Reality Orientation: A Critical Appraisal', Brit. J. Psychiat., 140, 457-63.

Powell, L., Felce, D., Jenkin, J. and Lunt, B. (1979) 'Increasing Engagement in a Home for the Elderly by Providing an Indoor Gardening Activity', Behav. Res. & Therapy, 17, 127-35.

Sanford, J.R.A. (1975) 'Tolerance of Debility in Elderly Dependants by Supporters at Home. Its Significance for Hospital Practice', British Medical Journal, 3, 471-3.

Smith, B.J. and Barker, H.R. (1972) 'Influence of a Reality Orientation Training Program on the Attitudes of Trainees Toward the Elderly', The Gerontologist, 12, 3, 262-4.

Sommer, R. and Ross, H. (1958) 'Social Interaction on a Geriatric Ward', Intern. J. Soc. Psychiat., 4, 128-33.

Tulving, E. and Bower, G.H. (1974) 'The Logic of Memory Representations', in Bower, G.H. (ed.) The Psychology of Learning and Motivation, Vol. 8. Academic Press, London.

Wershaw, H.J. (1977) 'Reality Orientation for Gerontologists: Some Thoughts about Senility', The Gerontologist, 17, 4, 297-301.

Woods, R.T. (1983) 'Specificity of Learning in Reality Orientatation Sessions: a Single Case Study', Journal of Behaviour Research and Therapy, 21, 173-5.

Zepelin, H., Wolfe, C.S. and Kleinplat, F. (1981) 'Evaluation of a Yearlong Reality Orientation Program'. J. of Gerontology, 36 (1), 70-7.

Chapter Eight

THE EVALUATION OF REALITY ORIENTATION

John Gerald Greene

In Chapter 7 Ian Hanley provided a critical and comprehensive account of the theory and practice of reality orientation. In this chapter we shall be concerned solely with the evaluation of this procedure. As Hanley has pointed out, RO, at least in some form, is the most widely used psychological approach to the care of the elderly confused patient, and therefore, as psychologists with our scientific tradition, we should arrive at some statement as to the objectively evaluated efficacy of such a procedure. As we shall see, however, such an exercise is not as straightforward as it appears, and much of what is written here must be viewed in the light of Hanley's comments regarding the 'conceptual dilemma' in which RO now finds itself.

One of the reasons for the popularity of RO in clinical practice must be that of the four main psychological approaches to the management of the mentally-impaired elderly patient, described by Woods and Britton (1977), it has been the most extensively reported on and investigated. Indeed, since 1974 a steady flow of controlled trials of varying quality have appeared in the literature. By controlled trials, in this context, is meant ones that have been set up prospectively (not, for example, retrospective accounts of established programmes) in which some attempt has been made to evaluate the intervention technique objectively. That is, a control procedure is used and outcome is assessed in a reasonably objective way. So far, there have been 13 published studies which fall into this category. These will now be examined with the objective of arriving at some consensus as to the efficacy of reality orientation.

Design of Trials

Details of the design of the 13 trials - all except two of which (Greene et al., 1979; 1983) have been carried out on in-patients in institutions - are summarised in chronological order in Table 8.1. As can be seen these studies vary in a number of ways.

The most common RO procedure investigated is the classroom type, and in only three studies has an attempt been made to evaluate a 24-hour RO programme, despite the fact that in the original conception the 24-hour procedure was seen as the core of the programme, and classroom RO merely as supplementary to this (see Chapter 7). This is probably for reasons of experimental rigour, as it is easier to control, maintain and monitor the more circumscribed classroom-type RO than it is the more general ward-based programme.

The length of trials vary considerably from three weeks in the study by Hogstel (1979) to 52 weeks in that by Zepelin et al. (1981). As most studies have employed 3-5 half-hour classroom sessions per week this means that the total number of hours of classroom RO being evaluated varies considerably - probably from something like $7\frac{1}{2}$ to over 100 hours.

In the majority of studies the patients receiving the active RO procedure are compared to a non-treatment control group, i.e. a group of patients who simply follow the usual ward routine. In less than half of these the control group is a matched one; that is, some attempt is made to make the treatment group and control group subjects equivalent, usually in regard to the severity of the dementia. In three studies the treatment group has acted as their own controls (Barnes, 1974; Greene et al., 1979; 1983). This procedure gives perfect matching of subjects and is appropriate where the effects of treatment dissipate rapidly, as in the case of RO.

In only three studies have attempts been made to assess the non-specific effects of the treatment procedure, that is, effects which have nothing to do with the orienting procedure. Brook et al., (1975) allowed the controls to enter the RO room and handle the material; Woods (1979) employed a social therapy group; and Greene et al. (1979) provided social stimulation for subjects during the non-RO phase.

Another source of variation has been the type of institution within which the trial has been conducted. These include psychiatric hospitals, geriatric hospitals, local authority residential homes and a day hospital. This would obviously lead to variation in the types of patient treated. Indeed, in the Harris and Ivory (1976) study the experimental group appear to have included long-stay adult psychiatric patients, as the mean age of the group was 66 years with a range of 36-81 years, and in the study by McDonald and Settin (1978), with an age range from 34-74 years, not all the subjects could be regarded as geriatric.

Finally, a variety of outcome measures have been used. Most researchers have included some measure of verbal orientation to assess outcome, which is understandable as this is the target function. In four only (Holden and Sinebruchow, 1978; Woods, 1979; Hanley et al., 1981; Greene et al., 1983) however, have additional cognitive measures been employed. Almost all researchers, (the exceptions being Johnson et al. (1981) and Hogstel (1979)) use some measure of behavioural change, usually nurses' ratings. This is not surprising since an important question in evaluating a procedure like RO is not only whether it produces an effect on the target function but, if it does, does this in turn have any implications for behaviour in general? The behavioural and mood disturbance of elderly confused patients is after all one of the most distressing aspects of their condition. (See Chapter 5 in this volume for a fuller discussion of the social implications of dementia.)

However, in only four studies (Brook et al., 1975; Woods, 1979; Greene et al., 1979, 1983) were steps taken to ensure that these behavioural measures were rated 'blind' by observers. That is, in all other cases the rater was aware which patients were receiving RO and which were not. Since, unlike orientation scales and standard cognitive tests, rating scales are largely judgemental, the possibility that such ratings are contaminated by bias exists. A further variation is that the particular rating scales used vary from trial to trial, and indeed some are purely local to the particular institution, or have been constructed in an ad hoc way for the purpose of the experiment.

These variations therefore make it difficult to conduct any detailed inter-trial comparisons. Nevertheless, certain patterns regarding the relative efficacy of RO do emerge. In discussing outcome, those studies which have been carried out with patients living in institutions will be considered separately from those in which the patients have been living in the community.

Outcome of Reality Orientation Trials With Patients in Institutions

The outcome of 11 RO studies in which patients in institutions have been the subjects will be summarised first, in terms of the three types of outcome measures - orientation, cognitive and behavioural.

Orientation
In six of the eight studies in which this was specifically assessed by means of a performance test, clear evidence of an improvement in orientation following RO was demonstrated. A convincing example of this, from the study by Citrin and Dixon (1977), is shown in Table 8.2. The exceptions to this were the studies by Barnes (1974) and Hogstel (1979). However, although Barnes found no improvement in orientation over the 6-week RO period there was a significant decline in orientation during the one-week follow up period. The possibility exists therefore that the RO procedure might, at very best, have been maintaining orientation in a deteriorating group of patients. Hogstel (1979) found no significant differences post-treatment between those receiving RO and the control group. However, in that study, subjects received a total of only 7½ hours of classroom RO, this being the shortest exposure in any of the 11 studies. The reality orientation procedure is clearly effective in producing an improvement in orientation in elderly confused persons. To what extent this effect generalises to other functions is another matter.

Cognitive Changes
In only three of the 11 studies did researchers employ objective and standardised psychometric measures of cognitive functioning in addition to those of orientation. Neither Hanley et al. (1981) nor Holden and Sinebruchow (1978) found any changes on the Koskela test or the Clifton assessment schedule following RO. Woods (1979), on the other hand, did find that improvement in orientation was paralleled by improvement on the Wechsler Memory Scale. With only one study demonstrating generalisation to other cognitive functions, as measured by standard psychometric tests, the effect of improved orientation on such functions must be open to doubt.

195

Behavioural Changes

Of the nine studies in which behaviour ratings were employed, six found no evidence of any improvement and three found some evidence. Of the six reporting no behavioural change, Barnes (1974) found no improvement in orientation, and in Holden and Sinebruchow (1978) and McDonald and Settin (1979) orientation per se was not assessed. However, in the other three studies (Woods, 1979; Hanley et al., 1979; Zepelin et al., 1981) orientation was demonstrably improved, but was not paralleled by any behavioural changes. Indeed, in the study by Woods the behaviour of all groups deteriorated significantly.

Turning to the three studies in which behaviour change was demonstrated, in those by Brook et al. (1975) and Citrin and Dixon (1977) a global rating of behaviour change was reported only, but with fairly clear results. However, where ratings of specific types of changes are reported, as in Harris and Ivory (1976) the degree of generalisation is seen to be somewhat limited and specific to certain types of behaviour. Harris and Ivory found a significant improvement in the RO group in only one of their many behavioural ratings, and no change at all on ratings of self-care. It should be noted, however, that in two of the four studies in which any sort of behavioural effects have been observed (those by Citrin and Dixon (1977) and Harris and Ivory (1976)) a 24-hour RO programme was in operation, in addition to the classroom component. This point will be returned to later. The balance of evidence, however, suggests that RO per se, and certainly the classroom type, has very limited implications for behavioural change. In brief, therefore, evaluative studies of RO with patients in institutions indicate that this procedure has a clear effect on orientation, but little effect on other cognitive functions. With regard to behavioural change, the evidence is equivocal.

Evaluating Reality Orientation with Patients in the Community

All the foregoing RO trials have been conducted with elderly persons living in institutions. It could be argued that the value of orientation to such patients is necessarily limited, living as they do in an unchanging and restricted environment. Furthermore, it is now understood that the great majority of elderly mentally-impaired persons continue to live in the community, where to be disoriented must be particularly hazardous. RO might perhaps be of greater value to such elderly people who would have greater opportunity to exercise any benefit that might accrue from the procedure.

RO has, in fact, been used with such persons, usually those attending day hospitals or local authority day centres. These are ideal settings for the use of RO since the people attending them spend most of their time living in the community, but spend some time at a place where they could obtain RO from professional staff in a consistent and systematic way, this being an essential part of any behavioural approach. There is now evidence (Greene and Timbury, 1979) that a major function of day units is to maintain elderly dementing patients in the community, and at the same time provide some relief to care-giving relatives, until such times as long-term in-patient care can be provided. Attendance at day hospitals is thus determined, in part at least, by the degree of behavioural disturbance shown by patients at home and the ability of carers to tolerate or cope with this. Generalisation effects of RO are therefore of paramount importance to such patients and their relatives and it would be of value if this could be demonstrated.

However, unlike RO with patients living in institutions little empirical evaluation has been carried out on the efficacy of RO with patients living in the community. Some beginnings have been made by the present author and his colleagues with elderly mentally-impaired patients attending a day unit in a psychiatric hospital. Details of method and outcome of two studies emerging from this work are also summarised in Table 8.1.

We began this work initially by using RO with such patients on an individual basis. This was done because we wished to personalise the information provided as much as possible. This meant including in the orientation procedure items relating to the patient's family, friends and neighbourhood, in addition to the more general time and current affairs items. This resulted in a personal orientation questionnaire being drawn up for each individual. Table 8.3 shows an example of one of these. Our primary aim at this stage was to find out the extent to which these patients could be re-oriented to their physical, familial and social network, and also to see if we could obtain generalisation effects. Single-case experimental design (Hersen and Barlow,

1976) was used for this purpose. Some of these cases are reported in Greene <u>et al</u>. (1979). To illustrate the nature and outcome of this type of experimental approach one of these cases will be described here.

An Experimental Case Study

The patient was a 72-year-old woman diagnosed as having arteriosclerotic dementia. She was regarded as being severely impaired. She had been attending the day unit for five months and was cared for at home by a married daughter with a teenage family. A quasi-experimental design of the ABAB type using repeated measurements of the personal orientation questionnaire was used. In phase A, the questions were asked and the patient told when she gave a correct answer, but not when she gave an incorrect answer. Phase B differed from Phase A in that the patient was told the answer when an incorrect one or no response was given. In both phases only correct answers were scored. Thus in both phases it was possible to assess level of orientation, but re-orientation could take place only in Phase B. The questions were administered verbally in a conversational manner and in random order on each occasion. All sessions, regardless of phase, were arranged to last for 30 minutes to control for stimulation effects across phases. The patient had two sessions per day, three days per week.

In addition to the personal orientation questionnaire, a separate list of questions was made up containing items not included in the orientation questionnaire. These included other items of orientation, items which were included in the orientation questionnaire but asked in a different form, and the recognition from photographs of persons asked about in the orientation questionnaire. These questions, referred to as generalisation items, were asked only at the end of each phase. The purpose of doing this was to see if there was any generalisation to items of information not specifically taught in the orientation sessions, and also to determine whether or not items in the orientation questionnaire were being learnt in a parrot-like fashion.

Throughout the experimental period, weekly ratings of the patient's behaviour were also made by an occupational therapist on a number of 5-point scales. These scales were arrived at in discussion with the occupational therapist who knew the patient well and what her deficits were. Items rated included such things as concentration, performance in occupational therapy (OT), response to others, and

interaction with others. Ratings were made in the
course of a group OT session which the patient
attended each day. Although the therapist knew the
patient was receiving RO she was completely unaware
of the phase procedure that was being used. Her
ratings were, therefore, 'blind'.
Figure 8.1. shows the results of this study.
Each point of the orientation score represents the
average of two daily sessions. As can be seen there
is a marked improvement in orientation during the two
orientation phases, with a decline during the second
base-line phase. Generalisation to other items of
information not taught in the orientation phases also
follows a similar pattern. However, the pattern of
the therapists's behavioural ratings depended on the
nature of the behaviour. As can be seen, only ratings
of performance in the OT groups followed the pattern
of orientation, social behaviour remaining
relatively unaffected by improvement in orientation.
This single case study demonstrates that
improved orientation can indeed generalise, but that
this is not a global effect. It follows in fact what,
in learning theory, is called 'a gradient of
generalisation' depending, it would appear, on the
degree to which this particular piece of behaviour
was dependent on orientation. Thus, there is a high
degree of generalisation to other items of
information followed by generalisation to behaviour
which has a major cognitive component, and lastly no
apparent generalisation to social behaviour. This,
once again, confirms a common finding in behavioural
research, namely the specificity of the relationship
between intervention techniques and the response
obtained. As Woods and Britton (1977) pointed out in
their review of psychological approaches to the
treatment of the elderly, improvement is apparent
only where specific targets are defined and worked
at, as in any behavioural approach. This suggests
that in those studies of RO where improvement in
several areas of behaviour has been reported (Brook
et al. 1975; Harris and Ivory, 1976; Citrin and
Dixon, 1977) improvement in some types of behaviour
may have been directly due to improved orientation,
whereas improvement in other types of behaviour, e.g.
social behaviour, may have been due to other
influences.

A Group Study
Although these results were encouraging, individual
RO is not cost-effective for everyday purposes and no
attempt had been made in these case studies to

assess behavioural change at home in any systematic way, nor the effect this might have on relatives. A group study of classroom RO was therefore begun, which focused on the implications any improvement in orientation might have for the patient and relative at home. As there were no readily available scales or measures for this purpose, it was necessary to construct two rating scales, one to obtain from the relative or chief carer an assessment of the patient's behaviour at home (behaviour and mood disturbance scale) the other to assess the degree of upset or stress being experienced by the relative (relative's stress scale) as a result of having to care for the elderly person. The construction of these scales is described in Greene <u>et al</u>. (1983).

A group ABA design with six assessment points was used in this study. The first phase consisted of a 3-week base-line period, the second a 6 week classroom RO period (six half-hour sessions per week), and the third a 6-week follow-up period. Assessments were made at three-weekly intervals, that is, before and after all phases and in the middle of the RO and follow-up phases. In addition to the relatives stress scale and the behavioural disturbance scale, all relatives were also asked to rate their mood on five symptoms, using a 10 cm visual analogue scale. The assessments also included a personal orientation questionnaire, which contained items about the patient's home situation, and the Clifton assessment schedule, to assess overall cognitive functioning of the patient.

Results of this study indicated that, as before, orientation can be markedly improved and that there was some generalisation to other cognitive functions, albeit limited. (See Greene <u>et al</u>. (1983) for a fuller account.) Figure 8.2 illustrates the findings with regard to the three rating scales completed by the relatives. A fall in score represents an improvement. Relatives had no knowledge that an RO programme was in progress, so that these ratings can be considered as 'blind'. There was some tendency for the relative to rate the patient's overall behaviour as having improved during the RO phase. Of the three components making up this scale, apathetic withdrawn behaviour, active/disturbed behaviour and mood instability, only the last showed a statistically significant improvement. There was, however, little evidence of concomitant change in self-reported stress arising from having to care for the elderly person on the part of the relative. But as can be seen in Figure

8.2 there was a clear and significant improvement in the relative's self-rating of their overall mood over the RO phase.

Once again, therefore, the generalisation effect of RO to patient's behaviour appears to be limited to certain aspects of that behaviour, in this case the emotional or affective behaviour of the patient. There is also some evidence of an improvement in the mood of the relative, although the burden of stress arising from having to care for the elderly person does not seem to be lightened.

There are two possible explanations for the improvement in the mood of relatives – it may have been that the relative was reacting to the slight improvement in the elderly persons's mood, which in turn was a consequence of improved orientation; it seems more likely, however, and this would be the most parsimonious explanation, that the relative was responding directly to the more obvious improvements in the patient's orientation. Indeed, this was borne out by the statements of a few relatives who spontaneously commented on the improvement in the mental state of the elderly person, although they were not aware that an RO procedure was taking place. Classroom RO may therefore be of some practical value to elderly confused patients in the community and their relatives, although what the mechanism of the latter is still not clear, and it would be desirable that the type of work be replicated in a different setting.

Discussion

Evidence as to the efficacy of RO from 13 evaluative studies has been reviewed in the two previous sections. We now come to the question as to what the implications of these findings are for the current status of this intervention procedure. It would seem, at the outset, that within the context of the outcome, measures used in such studies of the effects of RO are confined to an improvement in orientation with little consistent evidence that it results in any demonstrable cognitive or behavioural change. In the case of the latter, where such change has been found, it has been found to be of a highly specific and circumscribed nature.

It should come, then, as no surprise to those experienced in the use of behavioural techniques that the effects of RO should be so specific to the target, or closely related functions. As Woods and

Britton (1977) have pointed out in their review of psychological approaches to the treatment of the elderly, 'improvements were apparent only where specific targets were defined and worked at as in the behavioural approach' (p.111). The empirical literature on RO will prove to be something of a disappointment for those who have assumed that this procedure is some sort of overall package having implications for all sorts of behaviours and deficits. Clearly, specific deficits require their own specific remedies. This was aptly demonstrated in a second experiment carried out by Hanley (1981) on spatial disorientation in elderly patients. Here it was found that a programme of spatial re-orientation tailored precisely to this deficit in the setting in which it was to be utilised proved to be highly effective in comparison with verbal orientation. Despite these limitations, most researchers and reviewers generally conclude their articles on an enthusiastic note, advocating the continued use of RO as a therapeutic aide for the elderly confused person. Why should this be?

One argument put forward for retaining RO, whether of the classroom or 24-hour variety, is the view that while on its own it may not be a very effective procedure, it may act to facilitate the introduction of other more specific intervention programmes. As a brief inspection of other chapters in this volume will show, RO is only one among several therapeutic techniques that can be used with the elderly. This is a view taken by Powell-Proctor and Miller (1982) in a recent review of RO. They put it thus:

> Just because a client is over 65, or more typically 75, does not mean that radically different approaches are necessary. There is still the same need to analyse the nature of behavioural impairment and to design an inter-vention programme directed towards maximising the individual's overall adaptation and independence. If RO is used as a stepping-stone to developing more effective intervention programmes it will have served an important function.
>
> (p.462)

This brings us to a second argument that has been put forward for retaining RO, in that it raises the question of how RO would facilitate other intervention procedures. Despite the generally disappointing outcome of RO studies, most researchers, as we have said, usually end their papers on an enthusiastic note. This enthusiasm is based not on their findings but on the more subjective observations and impressions of staff members engaged in the procedure. Thus Barnes (1974) writes: 'The nursing director, the administrator and personnel unanimously reported improvements, not measured by the questionnaire, in the patients at the end of the six weeks of classes' (p.142). In a similar vein, Holden and Sinebruchow (1978) conclude 'On the basis of the information drawn from this study, plus the subjective assessment of therapists, relatives, nursing staff and paramedicals, the first objective – to provide a useful rehabilitative therapy – was achieved, but the method of assessing the changes proved unsatisfactory' (p.88). Hogstel (1979) noted that 'nurses said that several patients in the classes were more alert and happier than usual' (p.164). Finally, to underline these impressions, Hodge (1979), in an unpublished study of RO, found that of a variety of tests and ratings, in only one – a rating of the patient's cooperation by staff – was there a significant change contingent on RO. Due to these observations, and others like them, there is now a popular view among RO practitioners that the behavioural effects of RO somehow elude measurement. Notwithstanding the validity of these impressions or this viewpoint, one effect of RO is obviously to improve staff morale in an area where nihilistic attitudes have long prevailed.

It may therefore be that the real value of RO is that the existence of an active, ongoing programme may encourage care-staff to take a greater interest in their work, have a more positive attitude to their patients, run units in a less institutional way, achieve greater job satisfaction, and consequently RO leads to the creation of an atmosphere within which the use of other intervention procedures will be more easily facilitated. Future evaluative work into RO ought, therefore, to take changes in <u>staff behaviour and attitudes</u> into account as much as those of patients. Indeed, it could be argued that the utility of RO, extends well beyond its measured effect on cognitive and behavioural functioning and that <u>none</u> of the studies discussed in this chapter has <u>fully</u> evaluated RO, especially the implementation of the 24-hour variety. (See Chapter 7 in this volume on this point.)

This chapter concludes on an important technical point which may, at least in part, serve to explain the generally disappointing outcome of evaluative studies of RO. This is the distinction in use and purpose between 24-hour and classroom RO, a distinction, as Hanley et al. (1981) have pointed out, about which there has been some confusion in the literature. These authors suggest that it is no surprise that little change is evident on behavioural rating scales as a result of classroom RO because classroom RO was designed as a supplementary procedure to 24-hour RO, and it is the latter which is the means of producing behavioural as opposed to cognitive change. Thus, they argue, although the provision of orientation information is a feature of both classroom and 24-hour RO, the inference should not be made that RO assumes behavioural change to be dependent on cognitive change, 'Rather, in 24-hour RO, orientation information provided by staff serves mainly to cue behaviours which staff seek to prompt and encourage. This is done while routine activities of daily living are being performed' (p.13). What is being said here is that improved orientation per se does not lead to behavioural change, rather it acts to elicit or facilitiate new behaviours, which must be reinforced in the usual manner as dictated by behavioural principles. Or to put it another way, improved orientation does not operate in a vacuum. Opportunities must be provided for its use.

This could explain the greater effectiveness of the ward orientation programme in Hanley's study, in that locating different areas in the ward was a practical skill which the patient required to use every day and which, if successful, was presumably reinforcing. Similarly, in the single case studies by Greene et al. (1979) the orientation information was utilised by the patient in the OT groups, and only generalised to those aspects of behaviour for which it was of some direct value. Again, in the classroom RO study by Greene et al. (1983) with a day hospital group, patients were returning to their own homes and utilising the information in a natural setting. Furthermore, there was some evidence that relatives were aware of the elderly person's improved orientation and were responding to this, and possibly not only reinforcing the orientation, but also any behaviour contingent on it. In brief, any behavioural change is dependent on the opportunities available to use the orientation information. Hence the importance of a 24-hour RO programme for providing these opportunities in an institutional setting which for day patients are provided more naturally at home by relatives and friends.

The emphasis in this chapter has been on the evaluation of a particular intervention procedure. It is often thought that the main purpose of such exercises is to answer the question 'Does it work?' However, such exercises rarely come up with a simple Yes/No answer, and RO has been shown to be no exception to this. A major value of evaluative exercises is not that they provide simple answers to complex questions, but that they stimulate our thinking about treatment procedures and intervention programmes, and encourage practitioners to look more critically, and therefore more creatively, at their current practices. Procedures for use with the elderly should be no exception to this. The end result should be the improvement of such procedures, the development of others, and consequently a higher standard of care for the elderly.

FIGURE 8.1: Subject's Mean Daily Orientation Scores, Occupational Therapist's Total Weekly Ratings and Generalisation Item Scores at End of Each Phase

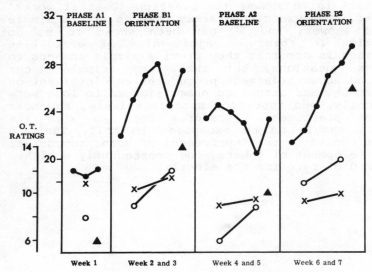

Key:
- ● Orientation score
- ○ OT performance rating
- x OT social rating
- ▲ Generalisation items

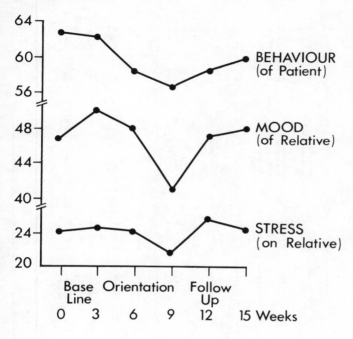

FIGURE 8.2: Group Mean Scores on Home Rating Measures at each Assessment Point

TABLE 8.1: Summary of Details of Controlled Trials of Reality Orientation

Senior author	Setting	Design	RO Procedure	RO (weeks)	group N	Control	Measures Orientation	Cognitive	Behaviour	Effects of RO on Orientation	Cognitive	Behaviour
Barnes (1974)	nursing home	Group ABA	5 classes per week	6	6	subjects own controls	23 item test	—	own scale	none, but fall-off follow-up	—	No
Brook (1975)	psychiatric hospital	matched controlled comparison	5 classes per week	16	9	entered class No RO given	—	—	modified Crichton geriatric rating scale	—	—	Yes
Harris (1976)	psychiatric hospital	matched controlled comparison	5 classes per week +24 hr RO	20	29	non-treatment	9 item test	—	own self-care and ward behaviour scales	Yes	—	no effect on self-care but some on behaviour
Citrin (1977)	geriatric hospital	controlled comparison	5 classes per week +24 hr RO	8	12	non-treatment	25 item test	—	Plutchik geriatric rating scale	Yes	—	Yes
Holden (1978)	geriatric hospital	matched controlled comparison	6 classes per week	12	16	non-treatment	—	Clifton assessment schedule	SGRA	—	—	No
McDonald (1978)	nursing home	controlled comparison	3 classes per week	5	10	non-treatment	—	—	LSI own rating scale	—	—	No
Hogstel (1979)	nursing home	controlled comparison	5 classes per week	3	20	non-treatment	18 item test	—	—	—	—	—
Greene (1979)	psychogeriatric day unit	single case	6 or 8 sessions per week	4	3	subjects own controls	POT	—	OT ratings	Yes	—	Yes on some ratings
Woods (1979)	nursing home	controlled comparison	5 classes per week	20	5	ST non-treatment	OT	WMS	CRS	Yes	Yes	No all groups deteriorated
Johnson (1981)	psychiatric hospital	controlled comparison 3 types RO	5 vs. 10 classes	4	38.21.16	non-treatment	26 item test	—	—	Yes for all 3 versions	—	—
Hanley (1981)	psychiatric hospital nursing home	matched controlled comparison	4 classes per week	12	24	non-treatment	25 item test	Koskela test	PGS	Yes	No	No
Zepelin (1981)	nursing home	controlled comparison	5 classes per week +24 hr RO	52	22	non-treatment	10 item test	—	ADL PB	Yes	—	No
Greene (1983)	psychogeriatric day unit	Group ABA	6 classes per week	6	20	subjects own controls	POT	CAS	PB RSMS	Yes	Yes	mainly relatives' mood

Key: SGRA-Stockton geriatric rating scale; LSI-life satisfaction index; POT-personal orientation test; OT-orientation test; WMS-Wechsler memory scale; CRS-Crichton rating scale; PGS-Plutchik geriatric scale; PB-patients behaviour. RSMS-relatives' stress mood scales; ADL-activities of daily living; ST-social therapy.

TABLE 8.2: Means and Standard Deviations for Reality Orientation
Information Sheet

	Pre-test		Post-test	
	M	SD	M	SD
Experimental	8.64	5.12	15.64	7.38
Control	7.77	6.65	6.89	7.42

(adapted from Citrin and Dixon, 1977)

TABLE 8.3: Example of a Personal Orientation Questionnaire

Question	Answer	Maximum Points
How old are you?	67	1
Where do you live just now?	26 Blothill Street, Yoker	3
Who do you live with?	Ann Allison, daughter	3
Is she married?	Yes	1
What is her husband's name and what does he do?	James, electrician	2
Any children?	Yes, two	1
Names of children and ages	Colin (9), Joan (6)	4
School	St Thomas	1
What was your husband's name?	William	1
What did he do?	Engineer	1
When did he die?	10 years $\pm$ 2	2
What are your children called?	Eleanor, Ann and Margaret	3
Are they married?	No, Yes, separated	3
Where does Eleanor live?	96 Byres Road, Partick	3
What does she do?	At the Clyde Cruising Board	1
Names of own siblings	Peter, Janet, Douglas	3
Any alive?	Janet	1
Where is she?	Paisley	1
What is my name?	Heather	1
What is the nurse's name?	Maisie, Sister Campbell	2
What is the name of this place?	Gartnavel Royal Hospital, Day Unit	3
How often do you come here?	3 times weekly	1
How do you get here?	Ambulance	1
Name of ambulance driver	Sandy McDougall	2
What year is it?	1978	1
What season is it?	Summer	1
What month, date, day?	-	3
Queen's name	Elizabeth	1
Husband's name	Philip	1
PM's name	Callaghan	1
Party	Labour	1
US President	Carter	1
Why do you come here?	Appropriate response	2
When were you married?	1940	1
What jobs did you have?	Auxiliary nurse, dairy, newsagents	3
What is your nearest neighbours' name?	McKenzie	1
Where are your nearest shops?	Powderhill Road	1
Names of shops (3)	Co-op, Sloan's dairy, McKay Butchers	3
Nearest bus route to home	Nos 69 and 41	2

210

References

Barnes, J. (1974) 'The Effects of Reality Orientation Classroom in Memory Loss, Confusion, and Disorientation in Geriatric Patients', The Gerontologist, 14, 138-42.

Brook, P., Degun, G. and Mather, M. (1975) 'Reality Orientation, a Therapy for Psychogeriatric Patients: A Controlled Study', British Journal of Psychiatry, 127, 42-5.

Citrin, R.S. and Dixon, D.N. (1977) 'Reality Orientation: A Milieu Therapy used in an Institution for the Aged', The Gerontologist, 17, 39-43.

Greene, J.G. and Timbury, G.C. (1979) 'A Geriatric Psychiatry Day Hospital Service: A Five Year Review', Age and Ageing, 8, 49-53.

Greene, J.G., Nichol, R. and Jamieson, H. (1979) 'Reality Orientation with Psychogeriatric Patients', Behaviour Research and Therapy, 17, 615-18.

Greene, J.G., Smith, R., Gardiner, M. and Timbury, G.C. (1982) 'Measuring Behavioural Disturbance of Elderly Demented Patients in the Community and its Effects on Relatives: A Factor Analytic Study', Age and Ageing, 11, 121-6.

Greene, J.G., Timbury, G.C., Smith, R. and Gardiner, M. (1983) 'Reality Orientation with Elderly Patients in the Community: An Empirical Evaluation', Age and Ageing, 12, (in press).

Hanley, I.G. (1981) 'The Use of Signposts and Active Training to Modify Ward Disorientation in Elderly Patients', Journal of Behaviour Therapy and Experimental Psychiatry, 12, 3, 241-7.

Hanley, I.G., McGuire, R.J. and Boyd, W.D. (1981) 'Reality Orientation and Dementia: A Controlled Trial of Two Approaches', British Journal of Psychiatry, 138, 10-14.

Harris, C.S. and Ivory, P.B. (1976) 'An Outcome Evaluation of Reality Orientation Therapy with Geriatric Patients in a State Mental Hospital', The Gerontologist, 16, 496-503.

Hersen, M. and Barlow, D.H. (1976) Single Case Experimental Designs: Strategies for Studying Behaviour Change, Pergamon Press, Oxford.

Hodge, J. (1979) Paper presented at the Annual General Conference of the British Association for Behavioural Psychotherapy, Bangor, Wales.

Hogstel, M.O. (1979) 'Use of Reality Orientation with Ageing Confused Patients', Nursing Research, 28, 161-5.

Holden, U.P. and Sinebruchow, A. (1978) 'Reality Orientation Therapy: A Study Investigating the Value of this Therapy in the Rehabilitation of Elderly People', Age and Ageing, 7, 83-90.

Johnson, C.H., McLaren, S.M. and McPherson, F.M. (1981) 'The Comparative Effectiveness of Three Versions of Classroom Reality Orientation', Age and Ageing, 10, 33-5.

McDonald, M. and Settin, J. (1978) 'Reality Orientation vs. Sheltered Workshops as Treatment for the Institutionalised Ageing', Journal of Gerontology, 33, 416-21.

Powell-Proctor, L. and Miller, E. (1982) 'Reality Orientation: A Critical Appraisal', British Journal of Psychiatry, 140, 457-63.

Woods, R.T. (1979) 'Reality Orientation and Staff Attention: A

Controlled Study', British Journal of Psychiatry, 134, 502-7.

Woods, R.T. and Britton, P.G. (1977) 'Psychological Approaches to the Treatment of the Elderly', Age and Ageing, 6, 104-12.

Zepelin, H., Wolffe, C.S. and Kleinplatz, F. (1981) 'Evaluation of a Yearlong Reality Orientation Program', Journal of Gerontology, 36, 70-7.

Chapter Nine

UNDERSTANDING AND TREATING DEPRESSION IN THE ELDERLY

Ian Hanley and Elizabeth Baikie

Incidence of Depression

Depression remains the most common psychiatric disorder in the elderly (Kay et al., 1964; Gurland, 1976; Gurland et al., 1983) and up to two-thirds of admissions to acute psychiatric units for the elderly have a primary diagnosis of depression (Church, 1983). The exact prevalence is difficult to establish as this is dependent on the precise criteria applied in diagnosis. Reliance, however, cannot be placed purely on the numbers receiving formal psychiatric treatment as depression in the elderly is one of the health problems most frequently missed by general practitioners (Williamson et al., 1964; Kline, 1976). The prevalence of diagnosed depression in the elderly is about 10 per cent, but when community surveys are conducted the incidence rises markedly. Using strict psychiatric criteria Murphy (1982) found 29 per cent of an elderly community sample to be either seriously depressed or 'borderline', while several studies of the elderly in the community have identified some degree of depression in up to 50 per cent of the samples studied. Milder degrees of depression make up most of the cases identified in the community, and whether or not these are comparable to more severe illness seen in hospital practice is still the subject of much debate. There would appear to be considerable overlap as the symptoms of identified cases in the community are very similar to those seen in patients (Wing et al., 1978). However, hospital patients are more likely to show certain symptoms, e.g. psychomotor changes and delusions, commonly associated with 'psychotic depression'.
    The debate as to what constitutes clinically significant depression in the elderly as opposed,

say, to the changes associated with the ageing process itself, is not likely to be resolved easily. With the move towards primary care and community practice the issue of whether or not depression as identified in community samples is the same as in hospital cases seems scarcely relevant. What is clear is that the percentage of elderly people showing significant signs of depression greatly exceeds the number diagnosed as suffering from a depressive illness. Depression is used in this chapter to refer to all degrees of severity and not solely to the cases that are severe enough to warrant psychiatric diagnosis on current criteria.

The Nature of Depression in the Elderly

Depression in the elderly tends to take a form which is somewhat different from that usually found in younger individuals. Alterations in sleep, appetite, drive, social and cognitive behaviour, and in physical health and vigour associated with the normal ageing process overlap with the typical depressive symptomatology listed below:

Low mood (sad, irritable, unhappy)
Loss of interest and pleasure
Sleep disturbance
*Agitation or retardation of movement
*Loss of energy, tiredness and fatigue
*Feelings of worthlessness and guilt
Thinking and concentration disturbance
*Thoughts of death or suicide
*Preoccupation with somatic complaints

* Particularly common in the elderly

It has been argued that age produces a differential pattern of response to depression questionnaires, with somatic, physiological symptoms being preferentially responded to, while emotional, 'psychological' symptoms are under-reported (Gaitz and Scott, 1972; Zemore and Eames, 1979). The tendency not to admit to feelings of depression is reflected often in situations where relatives or friends of a severely depressed elderly person who has committed or attempted suicide are found to be totally unaware of the underlying depression. Depression in the elderly is characterised often by a state of apathy with the person appearing to be disinterested in his surroundings and to lack drive.

There is a tendency in some quarters to accept such
symptoms as an unavoidable part of the ageing
process. The popularity of the disengagement theory
of ageing allows withdrawal and decreased
interaction with others to be seen as 'normal'. Levin
(1967) has argued that as younger people too tend to
become disengaged when they become depressed a
certain amount of disengagement in the elderly may be
a product of depression itself.
Depressed elderly patients often complain
excessively about their physical health. As there is
a very high rate of health problems associated with
depression in the elderly it is not uncommon for
physicians to overlook the element of depression, or
see it as a normal response, and treat only the
physical condition. Depression is also often
confounded with the symptoms of organic brain
changes. This is most likely to happen when the
elderly person shows signs of confusion. In many
depressed elderly patients minor organic changes are
often present and may contribute in part to the
development of symptoms. Depression in turn may
accentuate organic manifestations and lead to a
diagnosis of dementia. If this occurs, psychogenic
precipitating factors and the state of depression
itself may again be ignored. Such depressions,
typically severe, are often termed 'pseudo-dementia'
and their differential diagnosis from senile and
arteriosclerotic dementia is often difficult and has
attracted considerable attention from psychologists.
    This is a complex question and one that will not
concern us further here as the principle concern of
this chapter is to deal with depression in the
broadest sense of the term, and to examine ways
psychologists can approach typical depressions
presenting both in community and hospital settings.

Understanding Depression in the Elderly

Some 50 per cent of depressed elderly people suffer
their first depressive episode after age 60 and, as
we have noted, mild depression occurs in 40-50 per
cent of elderly community residents studied. Before
examining some of the theories which might help
account for the depression itself and the higher
incidence of depression in the elderly, it is worth
bearing in mind the likelihood that a complex
multifactorial model will be required, and that no
single theoretical formulation will be adequate. The
distinction between reactive and endogenous and

between psychosocial and biological factors tends to oversimplify the issue by implying that an either/or dichotomy is being sought. Aetiology is much more complex when a scientific as opposed to clinical model is employed. Figure 9.1 illustrates such a model. The futility of simplistic biology vs. environmental arguments has been clearly shown up in other areas of psychological endeavour, e.g. debates over the determinants of human intelligence. The origins of depression, the factors that either trigger the condition or make an individual vulnerable, are not understood in any detail but at least four major theoretical models of a psychological type have emerged.

Life Events, Vulnerability and Depression
External factors are well recognised in the aetiology of depression, with much attention placed on the stress concept of 'loss'. Since the ageing process usually involves progressive loss of love objects and of highly valued functions, such as sight and hearing, the link between life events and depression has attracted considerable attention. A major stimulus to this interest was the influential work of Brown and Harris (1978) who established that events with severe, long-term, threatening implications, most of which involved some major loss, played a determining role in bringing about depressive disorders, both among a general adult psychiatric population and among untreated younger women in the general population. Some 75 per cent of depressed in- and out-patients were found to have had a severe event or major difficulty in the 32 weeks before onset, and Brown and Harris estimated that 60 per cent of the conditions had been brought about by such a provoking agent.

Several other recent studies reach similar conclusions (Benjaminson, 1981; Fava et al., 1981; Vadher and Ndetei, 1981). When depressive disorders in the general population were considered by Brown and Harris they found the great majority to be preceded by provoking agents. As we have noted, the incidence of depressive symptoms in an elderly community population is high and it is interesting to speculate whether the vast majority of this group were exposed to provoking life events prior to onset. Murphy (1982) compared elderly depressed subjects and normal elderly people in the general population and found an association between severe life events, major social difficulties, poor physical health and the onset of depression. This finding is all the more significant for the fact that 13 per cent of the 'normal' community sample were diagnosed as 'borderline' depressives on the basis of the psychiatric criteria employed. These criteria included the requirements that (a) symptoms other than disturbance of mood be present; (b) symptoms occur with a high level of intensity, frequency and duration; and (c) that symptoms interfered with the individual's usual level of social functioning. Thus, of 200 community subjects sampled, 9.5 per cent had a serious depression of recent origin, 6.5 per cent had a serious depression with onset more than a year before interview, and 13 per cent were 'borderline', i.e. had a definite cluster of psychiatric symptoms of depression. Thus, some 30 per cent of Murphy's community sample were significantly depressed in the psychiatric sense, and the inclusion of some 13 per cent in the 'normal' comparison group must have acted to reduce the differences found in comparison with the depressed patient group. All the kinds of severe events that occurred to these elderly subjects as a whole, however, were more common in the depressed group as illustrated in Table 9.1.

Only 'independent' events were considered, i.e. events which could not have come about as a result of the subject's depression. The biggest difference between the groups is seen for those events that can be classed as 'severe', i.e. events such as bereavement, life-threatening illness of someone close, major personal illness, etc. The differences were highly significant with 48 per cent of the patients compared with 23 per cent of normal subjects experiencing at least one severe event. The relationship was even more significant for the community cases, with 68 per cent having had a severe event before the onset. This result is similar to that reported by Brown and Harris (1978) for younger women. The greatest difference was in the experience of severe events concerning the health of the subject. As Murphy points out, the wide range of physical conditions involved suggests that physical illness acts largely through its <u>meaning</u> for the individual rather than through a direct organic effect via biological mechanisms. This point will be returned to later when some psychological approaches to the therapy of depression are discussed.

Brown and Harris (1978) identified four vulnerability factors which increase the chances of a younger woman developing depression in the presence of a threatening life event. These were: (1) loss of mother before age 11; (2) presence at home of three or more children aged less than 14; (3) lack of an intimate confiding relationship with husband; and (4) lack of employment. In turn Murphy (1982) showed that those elderly who lack a confiding relationship appear to be most vulnerable to depression in the face of poor health and adverse life events. Undoubtedly, other predisposing factors remain to be identified. Perhaps some factors as far back as childhood and early adult experience may make some individuals vulnerable to depression in old age, and these are likely to be complex and difficult to identify accurately. Murphy (1982), for example, points out that lack of a confidant may reflect lifelong personality characteristics rather than sudden changes forced upon individuals in their later years. Again, the meaning that the individual attaches to confiding relationships would seem to be critical, as in Murphy's study those with only distant or infrequent social supports were as protected against depression as those with close and intimate confidants.

Loneliness also influences the way patients present to general medical practices with mild symptoms related to complaints of backache, tiredness, anxiety, headache, depression, irritability and dizziness (Ingham and Miller,1982). It seems as if the continuous frustration of affiliative needs or urges to divulge and exchange personal feelings, thoughts and interpersonal information, acts as a powerful mediator between stressful life events and the onset of depression. Hale (1982) found that the amount of time spent alone, the frequency of feeling lonely, and the lack of any physical contact, were all significantly related to the onset of depression in elderly women. It is disappointing to note that Murphy (1983) has shown that the availability of a confidant is ineffective prophylaxis after an individual has actually become depressed.

Although the external factors which contribute to the development of depressive reactions are often seen as examples of 'loss' they may be more accurately classified under the conceptual categories of 'loss', 'attack', 'restraint' and 'threat'. These more accurately describe the type of psychological stress involved. The concept 'loss' has been defined by Levin (1967) as 'a deficiency of those external supplies which are necessary at any particular time to satisfy the libido' p.181. A loss can vary in intensity from a minor loss, such as a brief separation from a love object, to a major loss, such as the death of a love object. Permanent loss can be of great significance and it is not uncommon for an older person to begin to slip both mentally and physically after the death of a spouse.

The concept 'attack' refers to any external force which produces discomfort, pain or injury. Attacks can vary on a physical level from mild pain to extreme physical violence, and on a psychological level from mild criticism to severe hostility. The concept 'restraint' refers to external restriction of activity that is necessary for the satisfaction of basic drives. A patient restricted to bed after a coronary for example may become depressed as a result of either this restricted activity ('restraint') or because of the coronary itself ('attack') or both. When it comes to therapy it is obviously useful to identify precisely what factor is triggering the reaction, and to uncover this information requires a differential diagnosis of 'stress' in terms of its meaning to the individual. The final concept of 'threat' refers to any event which warns of possible future 'loss', 'attack' or 'restraint'. Here again it is apparent that the threatening significance of any particular event is determined not only by the external reality but also by the individual interpretation of that reality. Some major threatening events for the elderly are those which warn of desertion, disability, suffering or death.

Physical illness, the life event most strongly linked with depression in Murphy's (1982) work, can be linked to no less than three of these four stress categories. Physical illness can threaten, restrain and attack, all at the same time which may account for the saliency of this factor in depression. Another way of looking at the impact of life events is to consider their additive impact. Data from Murphy's (1982) study suggest that as the number of events increase so does the risk of developing depression. For her community subjects the risk of developing depression was 25 per cent following one severe event, 44 per cent when a severe event occurred in the context of a marked personal health difficulty, and 50 per cent when a severe event was combined with a major social difficulty. Of those subjects with all three risk factors, 80 per cent developed depression.

Life events, then, are clearly linked with depression in the elderly and should be carefully assessed with the assistance of an instrument such as the Bedford College Life Events and Difficulties Interview (Brown and Harris, 1978).

Learned Helplessness, Attributional Style and Depression

In Seligman's model (Seligman, 1975; Maier and Seligman, 1976) learned helplessness is characterised as a syndrome that develops when an individual's apparently appropriate responses to meet his or her needs are not reinforced by the environment. This non-contingency leads to events being seen as uncontrollable and the individual becomes apathetic, lacking in response and apparently helpless. The original model, derived from experimental work with animals, was reformulated by Abramson et al. (1978) to explain helplessness in humans better. In particular, the original model did not account well for the fact that certain events are uncontrollable for only some people. Moreover, it did not explain why helplessness is sometimes general and sometimes specific, sometimes chronic and sometimes acute, i.e. it could not explain the differing manifestations of helplessness over time.

The reformulated model states that once people perceive non-contingency they attribute their helplessness to a cause. This cause can be perceived to be stable or unstable, global or specific, and internal or external. The attribution pattern adopted influences in turn the expectation of whether future helplessness will be chronic or acute, broad or narrow, and whether or not self-esteem will be lowered, i.e. the responses of persons to uncontrollability is variable and dependent on cognitive mediation through attributional style. Figure 9.2 characterises the three factors in attributional style as orthogonal.

Take the case of an elderly woman in a day hospital who has a problem in communicating her needs clearly to others. She can attribute this to (a) lack of ability (an internal-stable factor), (b) lack of effort (an internal-unstable factor), (c) factors in the situation, e.g. noise making communication difficult (an external-stable factor), or (d) lack of luck (an external-unstable factor). These attributions have strikingly different implications for how she will view her efforts on future occasions. When the third dimension of 'global-specific' is added we can predict how far the attribution will generalise. Is the failure only relevant to the particular situation involved, or does it have implications for all situations calling for communication with others? Global attributions have far-reaching implications for the individual, implying that the outcome in a variety of situations will again be independent of his responses. Helplessness deficits are hence likely to appear in a range of situations. In a parallel manner the chronicity of deficits is dependent on whether or not the individual attributes the cause to be stable or unstable. Attributing the cause of helplessness internally implies a grimmer future than attributing the cause externally since external circumstances are usually in greater flux than internal factors. Moreover internal attributions produce self-esteem deficits whereas external attributions will not.

Abramson *et al*. (1978) view depression to be made up of four classes of deficits: (a) motivational, (b) cognitive, (c) self-esteem, and (d) affective. They make a direct link between the first three deficits and uncontrollability. Retarded initiation of voluntary responses (motivational deficit) follows from the expectation of response-outcome independence. The cognitive deficit consists of difficulty in learning that responses produce predictable outcomes. The 'negative cognitive set' of depressives is displayed in their belief that their actions are doomed to failure. When lowered self-esteem is present it is accounted for by the individual seeing his helplessness as personal rather than universal, e.g. an unemployed individual who sees his situation as due to personal incompetence rather than the national economic crisis. To explain depressed affect Abramson *et al*. (1978) propose that uncontrollability per se is not a sufficient condition as there are many outcomes in life that are uncontrollable but do not sadden us. Affective changes are dependent on and vary in intensity with (a) the desirability of the unobtainable outcome, or (b) the aversiveness of the unavoidable outcome, and with (c) the strength or certainty of the expectation of uncontrollability.

The personal helplessness model of depression has a lot to say about how individuals perceive and respond to life events, the subject of the last section. The cognitive distortions predicted from the attribution of helplessness have been demonstrated in depressives. Hammen and Krantz (1976) looked at cognitive distortion in depressed and non-depressed women and found the depressed subjects selected more depressed-distorted cognitions when responding to stories with themes such as 'being alone on a Friday night'. The depressed subjects seemed to make more global and stable attributions for negative events. The implications of this for therapy will be discussed later. The next section overlaps somewhat with what has just been discussed, but deserves consideration in its own right. It too has implications for therapy which will be discussed later.

Cognitive Theory of Depression

Beck's (1967, 1976) cognitive theory of depression states that the various symptoms of the depressive syndrome can be understood in terms of a cognitive shift. The depressed individual views himself as a 'loser', over-interprets his experiences in terms of defeat or deprivation, regards himself as deficient, inadequate, unworthy, and is prone to attribute unpleasant occurrences to a deficiency in himself. In addition to the pervading negative themes relating to self, the world and the future two other areas of cognitive dysfunction have been identified. Logical systematic errors lead the patient to erroneous conclusions and attitudes, e.g. arbitrary inference, selective abstraction and over-generalisation. Idiosyncratic schemata integrate the model. They are described as relatively enduring structures (Neisser, 1976) which act as templates to screen, code, categorise and evaluate information.

Although there are obvious similarities with the reformulated learned helplessness model of depression it is clear that cognitive theory places greater emphasis on depressogenic cognitions as the central and causative dysfunction determining behavioural and affect changes which are relegated to the position of second order 'symptoms'. Although many elderly depressives do show clear evidence of cognitive distortion and reduced self-esteem, they more often present as apathetic, inert and somatically preoccupied and cognitive theory in this writer's opinion has questionable validity in explaining the development of most depressions in the elderly. Cognitive therapy (Beck et al., 1979) on the other hand, although derived from the theory, is more problem-oriented and behavioural. The effectiveness of cognitive therapy has been documented for younger depressives (Blackburn et al., 1981) but no trial has been conducted with the elderly. It may well be that the merits of cognitive therapy bear little relationship to the adequacy of the underlying theory. Such mismatch between theory and practice is not uncommon in the behavioural psychotherapies. (The reader is also referred to Williams' forthcoming book for a review of this area.)

Behavioural Theories of Depression

The specific behaviours shown by depressed patients, e.g. reduced social behaviour and personal neglect, have been interpreted within the general framework of social learning theory and schedules of reinforcement. Skinner (1953), in a functional analysis of depression, conceptualised it as a weakening of behaviour due to the interruption of established sequences of behaviour which have been positively reinforced or rewarded by the social environment. Thus depression is viewed as an extinction phenomenon.

Ferster (1965, 1966) thought that depression was characterised by retardation of psychomotor and thought processes and by a reduction or absence of previously successful behaviours. Thus the essential characteristic of a depressed person was thought to be a reduced frequency of emission of positively reinforced behaviour. He also noted that depressed people are restricted in the range of persons with whom they interact, thus making them vulnerable to change, and their activity becomes essentially passive, i.e. being reactive to the environment rather than performed spontaneously. These two latter observations appear particularly relevant to the elderly, whose social contacts may become restricted and who, through lack of power and status in society, may be passive recipients of the care offered them. Thus depression is seen as a loss or low rate of positive reinforcement. The social environment of the depressed person (e.g. his immediate family) is also seen as providing sympathy, interest and concern which strengthen and maintain depressive behaviours. As these actually become aversive, however, people around eventually avoid the depressed person, which further decreases the amount of positive reinforcement received and thus exacerbates the depression (Lewinsohn and Atwood, 1969).

Fundamental to learning theory is the observation that behaviours which are positively reinforced are maintained whereas those which are not, or which are punished, decline in frequency. In an investigation between mood and number and kind of 'pleasant activities' engaged in by depressed psychiatric and normal subjects (Lewinsohn and Libet, 1972; Lewinsohn and Graf, 1973) a significant association between mood and pleasant activities was found. In these studies the Pleasant Events Schedule (McPhillamy and Lewinsohn, 1971) and the Depression Adjective Check Lists (Lubin, 1965) were used.

Results suggested that certain kinds of activities may be more effective in alleviating depression than others. These observations are relevant for the elderly, who have less opportunity to engage in pleasant activities, e.g. social interaction and leisure pursuits, and may also explain why the adoption of an impersonal activity programme for the elderly may be ineffective.

Costello (1972) has suggested that depression results from a loss of reinforcer effectiveness rather than from a loss of reinforcments per se. Such a loss can be attributed either to endogenous, biochemical and neurological changes, or to the disruption of a chain of behaviour. This explanation appears salient when considering the elderly depressed person, who through deterioration in physical and sensory capabilities may not achieve the same rewards from activities as he/she did when these abilities were intact.

Summary
Psychological models to explain the development and maintenance of depression in the elderly place varying degrees of emphasis on the role of life events, cognitive distortion and behaviour change. In many ways these formulations are not mutually exclusive and each may have something to offer to the development of effective treatment strategies.

Psychological Therapy with the Depressed Elderly

Traditional views have emphasised the relatively good prognosis of affective disorders. However, depressive illness in old age is often characterised by frequent and prolonged relapses. Post (1972) followed up a series of 92 elderly depressed in-patients and found that three years later only 26 per cent had made a sustained recovery, 37 per cent had a recurrence with subsequent recovery, 25 per cent had recurrent attacks in the setting of chronic, mild depression and 12 per cent were continuously depressed throughout the follow-up period. Murphy (1983) among others confirmed the poor prognosis for depression in old age. In her study of 124 elderly in- and out-patients suffering a first episode of depression just over a third had made a good recovery at one year follow-up. Treatments employed with Murphy's sample included antidepressant medication, ECT and social support via day hospital and out-patient facilities. Although it may be argued that outcome studies tend to over-select the more severe cases, with mild depressions being effectively treated by general practitioners, the results are still not encouraging. They must reflect, in part at least, the degree to which traditional treatments are effective. As no substantial comparative trials of the effectiveness of psychological vs. traditional treatments have been run for depressed elderly patients it cannot be judged at this stage whether psychological techniques can do better. In any case the either/or dichotomy may not be appropriate, as a combined traditional and psychological approach has been found superior to either alone in younger depressed patients (Blackburn et al., 1981). A case can be made then for attempting to evaluate the effectiveness of psychological approaches with the depressed elderly.

The assumption that differences in therapy between elderly and younger subjects are negligible has been challenged by Church (1983). Referring to Cohen and Faulkner's (1981) work on memory for discourse, Church suggests that 'older people may be disadvantaged in recalling the meaning being "given" to them by the therapist'. As therapy becomes more verbal and interpretative in nature the elderly person will have increasing difficulty. When therapists use abstract information and techniques they may face particular problems arising from the elderly person's difficulties in changing set (Walker, 1982). Church and Bennett (1982) ran into this difficulty when applying cognitive therapy with a group of elderly patients attending a day hospital. They found a problem in applying some of the more abstract techniques, e.g. dysfunctional thought sheets (Beck et al., 1979) and found they had to focus on practical concrete events brought into the session and discussed. In the opinion of the therapists the group members had difficulty making the connection between the use of the sheets to record dysfunctional thoughts and a possible benefit to themselves. Through the discussion of real events on the other hand, group members were noticed to develop more realistic expectations which led to changes in behaviour outside the group. Garland (1982) has reported success with a practical problem-solving group for elderly patients attending a psychogeriatric day hospital. Most problems raised in the group were solved and group members developed and displayed problem-solving skills. This approach can potentially link the cognitive and behavioural approaches to depression by encouraging the patient to exercise control, take over responsibility for action and develop more realistic interpretations of events. With the emphasis on action, helplessnesses is challenged and, through discussion of events, attribution patterns and negative cognitive set may be changed. It should not be forgotten that many elderly who come into contact with health services have lost some measure of control over their own lives. From a behavioural perspective it is vital that problems are overcome and goals are reached so that reinforcement occurs for the efforts made. Therapists should be aware of reduced capabilities and pay special attention to ensuring that goals are realistic and reachable as well as valued by the elderly persons themselves. Several other factors need to be assessed before individualised treatment goals can be established. McKechnie (1974) makes a useful distinction between learning mechanisms that account for <u>reductions</u> in behaviour rates in depression and mechanisms that then play a part in <u>maintaining</u> this low rate of behaviour. The latter need to be carefully assessed in relation to the behavioural deficits displayed before treatment plans are devised.

<u>Mechanisms maintaining depressed behaviour</u>	<u>Intervention strategy</u>
1. Reinforcement of depressed behaviour	Encourage significant others not to respond to identified depressed behaviours but instead reinforce non-depressed behaviour
2. Avoidance learning	Prescribe engagement in avoided activities. Employ graded practice if necessary
3. Interference effects of anxiety	Teach anxiety management techniques, e.g. relaxation and use of imagery
4. Reduction of reinforcement value following non-reward	Identify new and more rewarding activities or examine ways in which the reinforcement value of existing activities can be increased

5. Susceptibility to   Re-establish previously
   extinction   conditioned responses
                             by ensuring that
                             they are encouraged,
                             prompted and then
                             rewarded

Mechanisms 1 and 5 require that attention be paid to how others respond to the depressed person. Relatives, friends and caregivers may need to be involved in treatment planning. In examining the social antecedents of learned helplessness in health care settings, Solomon (1982) points out that negative stereotyping and other factors can lead staff to reinforce inappropriate behaviour while failing to respond to more appropriate non-depressed behaviour. Positive efforts need to be made to ensure that all those involved with the patient reinforce the desired changes and not helplessness.

Moving back to the cognitive perspective Abramson et al. (1978) suggest that attributions can be discussed and changed in the following directions:

1. Reduce the estimated likelihood of aversive outcomes and increase estimated likelihood for desired outcomes. Environmental manipulations may assist this process. An example of this might be an elderly person who does not wish to attend a day centre expecting this to be an unrewarding experience. The therapist might encourage her to view the day centre more positively and solicit the co-operation of day centre staff to ensure that efforts are made to increase the chances of it being a positive experience, e.g. introduction to compatible others, involvement in personally meaningful activities or roles. In one day centre known to the author clients are often involved as 'helpers' rather than 'receivers', and hence a variety of roles is available.

2.

(a) Reduce the aversiveness of highly aversive outcomes, e.g. in the case of a patient who does not go shopping for fear of meeting neighbours and becoming embarrassed the aim might be to have her see this as less unpleasant than she fears. Where events are less under personal control, e.g. in the case of a valued neighbour moving away, the strategy might broaden out to encourage acceptance, resignation and establish other more realistic attainable goals.

(b) Reduce the desirability of highly desired

227

outcomes (unobtainable) through re-evaluating these outcomes and assisting their renunciation and relinquishment, e.g. where 'dependence' on one person, perhaps a family member, is the centre of the depressed person's interest the therapist might seek to have the patient relinquish this objective.

3. Change the expectation from uncontrollability to controllability

(a) When responses are not yet within the person's repertoire, but can be, train the necessary skills, e.g. where some memory impairment co-exists with depression and limits the organisation of daily activity, have the person keep a diary and write down relevant schedules and information.

(b) When responses are in the repertoire, modify the expectation that they will fail by -
(i) prompting performance of graded task assignments
(ii) changing attributions for failure from 'inadequate ability' to 'inadequate effort', e.g. a client who over-emphasises somatic complaints and uses these to justify inertia.

4. Change unrealistic attributions for failure towards external, unstable, specific; change unrealistic attributions for success towards internal, stable, global, e.g. for failure -

(a) External - 'Elderly women living alone often have difficulty finding suitable company. You are not naturally a lonely person.'

(b) Unstable - 'Everyone is unhappy when they lose someone close. You'll have opportunities to make new friends.'

(c) Specific - 'Your sister doesn't want to get too involved. She never did. You can establish greater contact with your son.'

In this way Abramson et al. (1979) see attempts to modify the depressed person's cognitive style as vital to treatment. Such attempts are quite complementary to a behavioural programme provided they are simplified to take account of cognitive deficits. One other essentially cognitive approach of as yet untested benefit in depression is life review or reminiscence (Butler, 1963; Burnside, 1981). There are suggestions that this process can benefit self-concept and life satisfaction. Lewis (1970) has demonstrated that when under social threat elderly people who reminisce tend to shift their self-concept to make present self-concept more consistent with past self-concept. This switch was interpreted as a strategy to enable reminiscents to identify with their pasts and avoid current stresses. Lewis (1970) sees reminiscence as a means of reducing cognitive dissonance between the person's self-expectations from the past and present behaviour. This may act to engender a sense of worthiness and reduce cognitive distortions in depression if past evaluations are positive. However, as depressives tend selectively to recall negative events reminiscence may be counterproductive. Further work is required to elucidate the links between current mood and morale and the outcomes of life review. Although reminiscence is a selective integrating process for each individual the outcome may have variable consequences for mood and current morale. The selective encouragement of pleasant memories, one of the techniques of Beck <u>et al</u>. (1979) may be a safer approach with depressives. As Church (1983) points out, it is necessary to establish which components of reminiscence, if any, have a beneficial effect before this technique can have more general application.

A psychological approach to therapy with elderly depressives might proceed as follows:

(a)   an analysis of recent life events;
(b)   a detailed analysis of current behaviour patterns and a retrospective analysis of behaviour before illness. The account of the patient should be compared to that of a well-informed third party;
(c)   psychometric assessment using the Beck Depression Inventory (Beck <u>et al</u>., 1961) and valid self-report measures of mood and morale such as Bigot's Life Satisfaction Index (Bigot, 1974) and Schwabb's Depression Scale (Schwabb <u>et al</u>. 1973). Gilleard <u>et al</u>., (1981) document the validity of these scales within an elderly population;
(d)   an attempt to search out the patient's view of events and understand the attributional pattern;
(e)   establish clear behavioural goals and implement these gradually and in close relationship with attempts to modify relevant attributions;
(f)   involve significant others throughout in treatment planning;
(g)   monitor progress by repeating self-report measures of mood and morale at regular intervals

and examining progress towards behavioural goals.

Obviously in many cases a psychological approach to therapy will not form the entire treatment package but may be supplemented by prescription of antidepressants. In others, e.g. depression in the context of bereavement, the specific approach adopted would need to be modified to take account of the natural grieving process and specific techniques developed to assist adjustment, e.g. guided mourning.

A psychological approach to the treatment of depression may well have most impact in the community where intervention can be earlier and where often a crisis point has not yet been reached. As general practitioners become more aware of the dangers inherent in the routine use of drugs with the elderly they are increasingly interested in using a psychological service when such is available. The psychologist interested in working effectively in the community has the challenge of working with the depressed client's actual social milieu. Some strategies for providing an effective service and achieving optimal use of available resources in this context are discussed in Chapter 11 in this volume. Community psychology with the depressed elderly may have much to offer in reducing the need for both psychiatric consultation and hospital admission.

Working with individual depressed patients along the lines suggested in this chapter is time-consuming and exhausting. There is a ring of realism in Jeffery and Saxby's comment in Chapter 11 that such an approach ultimately equates with a relatively small case-load and cannot amount to much more than a 'drop in the ocean'. Perhaps they are right in suggesting that the ultimate challenge for psychologists is to develop 'a clearly defined systematic approach to the care of the elderly which concerns itself with organisation, teams, social systems, communities and the effective use of resources'. However, it is almost certainly the case that patients will always need to be seen as individuals and their needs assessed on that basis. Perhaps the most we can hope is that the role of the psychologist with depressed elderly clients may switch from that of therapist to that of coordinator with other elements of the client's social milieu taking over greater responsibility for the provision of 'treatment'. It may well be that the most effective way to reach Jeffery and Saxby's objective is for the psychologist working in his own 'patch' to <u>demonstrate</u> through his case management the effectiveness of a psychological/social treatment approach and in doing so link resources in such a way as to benefit future referrals.

FIGURE 9.1: A Scientific Model of the Aetiology of Depression

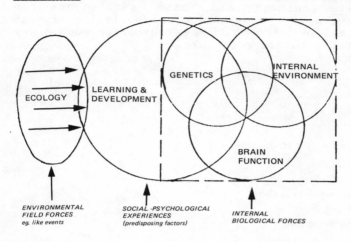

ENVIRONMENTAL
FIELD FORCES
eg. like events

SOCIAL -PSYCHOLOGICAL
EXPERIENCES
(predisposing factors)

INTERNAL
BIOLOGICAL FORCES

FIGURE 9.2: Factors in Attributional Style

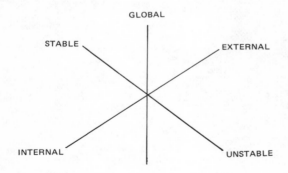

TABLE 9.1: Type of Severe Event: Rates per 100 Subjects in the Year Before Interview (from Murphy 1981)

	Normal (n = 168)	Patients and community onset cases (n = 119)
Separations/deaths	13	18
(Death of spouse or child)	(3)	(9)
Major negative revelation about someone close	0	3
Life-threatening illness to someone close	5	13
Financial/material loss	0	5
Physical illness of subject	6	28
Enforced change of residence	1	3

References

Abramson, L.Y., Seligman, M.E.P. and Teasdale, J.D. (1978) 'Learned Helplessness in Humans: Critique and Reformulation', Journal of Abnormal Psychology, 87, 49-74.

Beck, A.T., Ward, C.H., Mendelson, M., Mock, J.E. and Erbaugh, J.K. (1961) 'An Inventory for Measuring Depression', Archives of General Psychiatry, 4, 556-71.

Beck, A.T. (1967) Depression: Clinical, Experimental and Theoretical Aspects, Hoeber, New York.

Beck, A.T. (1976) Cognitive Therapy and the Emotional Disorders, International Universities Press, New York.

Beck, A.T., Rush, A.J., Shaw, B.F. and Emery, G. (1979) Cognitive Therapy of Depression, Guilford Press, New York.

Benjaminson, S. (1981) 'Stressful Life Events Preceding the Onset of Neurotic Depression', Psychological Medicine, 11, 369-78.

Bigot, A. (1974) 'The Relevance of American Life Satisfaction Indices for Research on British Subjects before and after Retirement', Age and Ageing, 3, 113-21.

Blackburn, I.M., Bishop, S., Glen, A.J.M., Whalley, L.J. and Christie, J.E. (1981) 'The Efficacy of Cognitive Therapy in Depression', British Journal of Psychiatry, 139, 181-9.

Brown, G.W. and Harris, T.O. (1978) Social Origins of Depression, Tavistock, London.

Burnside, I.M. (1981) 'Reminiscing as Therapy: An Overview', Nursing and the Aged, 98-113.

Butler, R.N. (1963) 'The Life Review: An Interpretation of Reminiscence in the Aged', Psychiatry, 26(1), 65-76.

Church, M. (1983) 'Psychological Therapy with Elderly People', Bulletin of the British Psychological Society, 36, 110-12.

Church, M.A. and Bennett, A. (1982) 'Group Cognitive Therapy with Elderly Patients Recovering from Depression', paper presented at the Annual Conference of the British Society of Gerontology, Exeter.

Cohen, G. and Faulkner, D. (1981) 'Memory for Discourse in Old Age', Discourse Processes, 4, 253-65.

Costello, C.G. (1972) 'Depression: Loss of Reinforcers or Loss of Reinforcer Effectiveness', Behaviour Therapy, 3, 240-7.

Fava, G.A., Munari, F., Pavan, L. and Kellner, R. (1981) 'Life Events and Depression - a Replication', J. Affective Disorders, 3, 159-65.

Ferster, C.B. (1965) 'Classification of Behavioural Pathology', in L. Krasner and L.P. Ullman (eds.), Research in Behaviour Modification, Holt, Rinehart & Winston, New York.

Ferster, C.B. (1966) 'Animal Behaviour and Mental Illness', Psychological Record, 16, 345-56.

Gaitz, C., and Scott, J. (1972) 'Age and the Measurement of Mental Health', Journal of Health and Social Behaviour, 13, 55-67.

Garland, B.J. (1982) 'A Problem-Solving Group in a Psychogeriatric Day Centre', paper presented at the Annual Conference of the Psychologist Special Interest Group in the Elderly, London.

Gilliard, C.J., Willmott, M. and Vaddadi, K.S. (1981) 'Self-report

Measures of Mood and Morale in Elderly Depressives', British Journal of Psychiatry, 138, 230-5.

Gurland, B.J. (1976) 'The Comparative Frequency of Depression in Various Adult Age Groups', Journal of Gerontology, 31, 283, 82.

Gurland, B.J., Copeland, J., Kuriansky, J., Kelleher, M., Sharpe, L. and Dean, L.L. (1983) The Mind and Mood of Ageing: Mental Health Problems of the Community Elderly in New York and London, Croom Helm, London, Haworth, New York, pp.44-60.

Hale, W.D. (1982) 'Correlates of Depression in the Elderly: Sex Differences and Similarities', Journal of Clinical Psychology, 38, 253-7.

Hammen, C.L. and Krantz, S. (1976) 'Effect of Success and Failure on Depressive Cognitions', Journal of Clinical Psychology, 38, 253-7.

Ingham, J. and Miller, P. (1982) 'Consulting with Mild Symptoms in General Practice', Social Psychiatry, 17, 77-88.

Kay, D.W.K., Beamish, P. and Roth, M. (1964) 'Old Age Disorders in Newcastle upon Tyne', British Journal of Psychiatry, 110, 146-58.

Kline, N. (1976) 'Incidence and Prevalence and Recognition of Depressive Illness', Dis. Nerv. Syst., 37, 10.

Levin, S. (1967) 'Depression in the Aged: The Importance of External Factors', in S. Levin and R.J. Kahanna, Psychodynamic Studies on Ageing, Creativity, Reminiscing and Dying, International University Press, New York.

Lewinsohn, P.M. and Atwood, G.E. (1969) 'Depression: A Clinical Research Approach', Psychotherapy: Research and Practice, 6, 166-71.

Lewinsohn, P.M. and Graf, M. (1973) 'Pleasant Activities and Depression', Journal of Consulting and Clinical Psychology, 41, 261-8.

Lewinsohn, P.M. and Libet, J. (1972) 'Pleasant Events, Activity Schedules and Depression', Journal of Abnormal Psychology, 79, 291-5.

Lewis, C. (1970) 'Reminiscence and Self-concept in Old Age', Doctoral dissertation, University of Boston.

Maier, S.F. and Seligman, M.E.P. (1976) 'Learned Helplessness: Theory and Evidence', Journal of Experimental Psychology, 105, 3-46.

Murphy, E. (1982) 'Social Origins of Depression in Old Age', British Journal of Psychiatry, 141, 135-42.

Murphy, E. (1983) 'The Prognosis of Depression in Old Age', British Journal of Psychiatry, 142, 111-19.

McKechnie, R. (1974) 'A Dual Process Model of Depression', paper presented at the Annual Meeting of the British Psychological Society, Scottish Division.

Neisser, U. (1976) Cognition and Reality: Principles and Implications of Cognitive Psychology, Freeman, San Francisco.

Post, F. (1972) 'The Management and Nature of Depressive Illnesses in Late Life: A Follow-through Study', British Journal of Psychiatry, 121, 393-404.

Schwab, J.J., Holzer, C.E. and Warheit, G.J. (1973) 'Depressive

Symptomatology and Age', Psychosomatics, 14, 135-41.

Seligman, M.E.P. (1975) Helplessness: On Depression, Development and Death, Freeman, San Francisco.

Skinner, B.F. (1953) Science and Human Behaviour, Macmillan, London.

Solomon, K. (1982) 'Social Antecedents of Learned Helplessness in the Health Care Setting', The Gerontologist, 33, 282-7.

Vadher, A. and Ndetei, D. (1981) 'Life Events and Depression in a Kenyan Setting', British Journal of Psychiatry, 139, 134-7.

Walker, S. (1982) 'An Investigation of the Communication of Elderly Subjects', MPhil thesis, University of Sheffield.

Williams, J.M.G. (1984) The Psychological Treatment of Depression, Croom Helm, London.

Williamson, J., Stokoe, I.H., Gray, S., Fisher, M., Smith, A., McGhee, A. and Stephenson, E. (1964) 'Old People at Home: Their Unreported Needs', Lancet, 1, 1117-20.

Wing, J.K, Mann, S.A., Leff, J.P., and Nixon, J.M. (1978) 'The Concept of a Case in Psychiatric Population Surveys', Psychological Medicine, 8, 203-17.

Zemore, R. and Eames, N. (1979) 'Psychic and Somatic Symptoms of Depression among Young Adults, Institutionalized Aged and Non-Institutionalized Aged', Journal of Gerontology, 34, 716-22.

Chapter Ten

SEXUALITY AND THE ELDERLY

Elizabeth Baikie

Introduction

Since Masters and Johnson (1970) initiated the
development of treatment for sexual dysfunction,
there has been an increase in the demand for
psychosexual counselling and in the availability of
treatment. Since then other writers have expanded on
and devised their own individual approaches in sex
therapy (e.g. Kaplan, 1974). Treatment tends to be
behaviourally oriented, rather than concentrating on
intra-psychic processes. Emphasis is also placed on
treating the couple, through focusing on behavioural
change, improving communication and modifying
attitudes which might impede behavioural change.
Where necessary the individual is helped to accept
and feel comfortable with his or her own sexuality.
The basic principles of such an application of
behavioural psychotherapy can be summarised as
follows (Bancroft, in press):

1.   Clearly defined and appropriate behavioural
goals are set and the patient asked to attempt them
before the next session.
2.   Those attempts and any difficulties encountered
are examined in detail.
3.   The attitudes, feelings, 'resistances' that
make those behavioural goals difficult are
identified.
4.   Those attitudes, etc. are modified so that the
behavioural goals become possible.
5.   The next behavioural goals are set, and so on.

Psychosexual counselling is now widely available in
many settings, such as hospital out-patient clinics,
family planning clinics, and marriage guidance
centres. This is carried out by various professional

237

groups, e.g. doctors, nurses, clinical psychologists, social workers and marriage guidance counsellors. Treatment of the couple is carried out by either one therapist or a co-therapy team. Where a regular partner is unavailable or unwilling to be involved in psychosexual counselling, individual clients may be seen by the therapist if it is thought that appropriate therapy can be offered and realistic treatment objectives worked towards, without the participation of a partner. Positive change, however, may thus be limited.

With respect to the elderly, society is now manifesting an interest not only in survival <u>per se</u> but in the quality of life. Service provision has focused on basic needs of the elderly, such as health maintenance, income continuance, job availability and housing (Pfeiffer, 1975). Research into the physiology, psychology and sociology of old age has also been flourishing and this has helped to dispel some of the myths of the ageing process, e.g. intellectual and cognitive functioning in the elderly. Sexuality and the elderly, however, has not received enough attention and there is a paucity of information available on the range and scope of sexual expression for the elderly and those who care for them.

But what constitutes 'old age'? We may be referring to at least a span of 30 years and what possibly characterises the elderly most is their variability. Each person ages with a unique pattern of learning experiences, social support, health status and personality characteristics. Our knowledge of sexuality in the elderly is still not comparable to that of adolescents and adults. Even in our enlightened society there still exists a taboo against sex in old age, particularly reinforced by those who, through religious beiefs or for other reasons, see sex as primarily for procreation rather than pleasure. Furthermore, adult children may experience difficulty in accepting their elderly parents' sexual needs. Young staff may feel uncomfortable about asking their elderly clients (as well as younger ones) about sexual topics and in some restrictive institutions overt expression of sexuality may be labelled 'disinhibited behaviour' and treated with medication.

In the absence of objective data many stereotypes of sexual behaviour in old age exist (Pfeiffer, 1975):

1.   Sexual desire and activity ceases to exist with onset of old age.
2.   Sexual desire and activity should cease to exist with the onset of old age.
3.   Those who say they are still active are morally perverse or lying.
4.   Overt expression of affection or sexual interest is often ridiculed or met with disapproval.

As a result the elderly may come to respond accordingly to society's labelling of them, and institutional staff, through lack of acceptance of their residents' sexual needs or their own embarrassment, may further undermine their residents self-esteem and acceptance of their sexuality. An increasing awareness of the sexual needs of other groups has been developing recently, e.g. with the mentally handicapped and physically disabled. Psychosexual counselling is now available for those who through spinal injury, surgical disfigurement or cardiac disease have become unable to have a fully satisfying sex life. In the United Kingdom SPOD, (1) the Association for the Sexual and Personal Relationships of the Disabled, have made a valuable contribution through their advisory leaflets for the handicapped. A satisfying expression of sexuality should be seen as a right not just a privilege. Tending to an individual's physical needs is not sufficient.

How important is sexual activity to the elderly? Masters and Johnson (1981) see sex as a natural function akin to the bodily functions of respiration and digestion and therefore equally important to well-being. Sexuality in the elderly thus merits attention. Thomas (1982) interprets this as the 'essential vitamin model of aging sexuality' and thus sexual deprivation is seen as harmful. He proposes the 'popcorn theory' of sexuality as an alternative, i.e. he emphasises the sensual pleasures of sexuality and the element of choice in this aspect of behaviour. Thus sex in old age is not essential but can determine the quality of life. He also warns us of the danger of projecting our own younger values and patterns of behaviour on to the elderly.

It is with some regret, however, that in my clinical experience as a psychosexual counsellor, I have observed that referrals mainly consist of those under 55 years of age. Various explanations may account for this. The younger adult group have benefited from the so-called 'sexual liberation' and now desire as satisfactory a sex life as possible.

The elderly may have been subject to a more restrictive attitude towards sex and may not see sexual fulfilment as appropriate for them. They may be victims of society's negative attitudes towards sex in old age and may also have less opportunity to discuss sexual problems. We may see a change, however, when the present generation, thought to be relatively liberated sexually, enter their sixth or seventh decade. Attendance at ante-natal, post-natal and family planning clinics may facilitate discussion of sexual concerns for younger women but there is less opportunity for women who are no longer of childbearing years to discuss such fears. This has been seen by Bancroft (1983) as one explanation for the finding, in a large survey of general practice, that women using oral contraceptives are approximately four times as likely to complain of sexual difficulties than those using other methods. Another factor affecting referral rates may be the professional's attitude towards sex in later years, for example, if the general practitioner is not sensitive to the sexual needs of his/her elderly patients, he/she may miss relevant behavioural cues. Even if these are acknowledged, he/she may not think that sexual fulfilment is justifiable and may thus not refer an elderly couple or individual for psychosexual counselling. Furthermore he/she may be unaware of psychosexual counselling services available.

Studies on Sexuality and the Elderly

Kinsey's studies on sexual behaviour (1948, 1953) provided some data on sexual behaviour in the aged. The sample consisted of 14,084 males and 5,940 females. This included 106 men and 56 women over 60 years of age and thus the aged are under-represented in these studies. On the basis of the sexual histories of 87 of these males, he concluded that at age 60 only one in five men was no longer capable of sexual intercourse, but at age 80 this had risen to three in four. He also concluded, however, that the rate of decline in absolute frequencey of sexual outlets (sexual intercourse, masturbation and nocturnal emissions) on average did not decline any more rapidly in old age than between the ages 30 to 60. Married men at all ages had a higher frequency of sexual outlet, single and post-marital males had frequencies only slightly below those who were married. In a smaller sample of women over 60 years of age he extrapolated that there was a gradual decline in frequency of sexual intercourse between age 20 and 60, which was attributed to the ageing process in the male. Secondly, there was no evidence of any ageing in the sexual capacities of the female until later in life. Although drawing his conclusions primarily from women under 60, he noted that single and post-marital females had much lower rates of sexual activity than of those who were married. These two conclusions may exemplify two salient points: this sample may represent a less emancipated group of women who may still view themselves as being the sexually passive partner and also, owing to the tendency for women to marry older men and to outlive their husbands, may no longer have a sexual partner in their later years of life.

Newman and Nichols (1960) previously reported a positive correlation betwen strong sexual feelings in youth and continued sexual interest in old age. With respect to women, Masters and Johnson concluded, as did Kinsey, that the post-menopausal sex drive was to a large extent related directly to the sexual habits established during the child-bearing years. The use of fantasy, thought to be the most important single determinant of sexual arousal, is said to decline in both sexes with age (Cameron and Biber, 1973).

The longitudinal studies on community volunteers at Duke University, the first one starting in 1954, and a subsequent one in 1969, demonstrated that sex continues to play an important role in the lives of many elderly persons. Verwoerdt, Pfeiffer and Wang (1969) reported that in both older males and females the incidence of high and moderate sexual interest exceeds the incidence of sexual activity.

In a study of the institutionalised aged, White (1982) found that attitudes, knowledge regarding sexuality, and sexual interest were significantly related to sexual activity. As demonstrated in other studies with the non-institutionalised aged, previous high activity appears to lead to high current activity in institutions. Of sexually inactive residents, 17 per cent indicated a desire to be sexually active. There was a very low positive correlation between attitudes and knowledge, suggesting the absence of opportunity to learn about sexuality. This may reflect society's attitudes towards sex at the turn of the century when those in this sample were in their youth. Absence of privacy and availability of willing and desired partners was also found to be obstacles to sexual behaviour. Kaas

(1978) in a comparison of the difficulties between elderly nursing home residents and nursing home staff in attitudes towards sexual expression of the elderly, demonstrated that both groups were accepting of sexual expression. The staff did not therefore appear to have restrictive attitudes, although their actual behaviour may have conflicted with their attitudes. Although indicating they would allow sexual expression amongst the residents, they believed all such behaviour should be reported. With regard to masturbation, both residents and staff denied that this was an acceptable form of expressing sexuality, although in the staff's case this response was less strong. This has been shown to be related to education and religion. Katchadourian and Lunde (1972) reported that the better educated and less devout are more accepting of masturbating. The majority of residents in Kaas' study indicated that they did not feel sexually attractive and would not enjoy sexual activity if they had a willing partner. As noted by White (1982) this study also demonstrated that lack of privacy was seen by both staff and residents as a deterrant to sexual expression.

About 25 per cent of men over 60 who are still having sexual intercourse engage in regular masturbation (Kinsey et al., 1948; Rubin, 1963). Similarly 25 per cent of women between the ages of 60 and 70 with a sexual partner masturbate, as do 39 per cent of widows (Christenson and Gagnon, 1965). Catania and White (1982) investigated the cognitive determinants of masturbation, for it does not appear to be only the availability of a partner which is a determining factor. In a study of a group of elderly living in the community, they found that frequencey of masturbation was most strongly related to internal as opposed to external locus of control. Internal locus of control refers to the extent to which an individual perceives events and rewards as related to his/her own behaviour, whereas an individual who perceives his/her locus of control as external sees these outcomes as being determined by chance, fate or other powerful individuals.

How does this relate to sexuality? Catania and White see masturbation as indicative of sexual regulation in those who view their locus of control as internal. In addition, their study demonstrated that those without sexual partners tended to masturbate more frequently than those who had partners. Those with a high degree of sexual knowledge also showed a high frequency of masturbation and the authors interpreted this as those with internal locus of control tending to seek more sexual information. They also viewed masturbation as a means of maintaining sexual identity, that is, a proof of continuing sexuality, when faced with society's negative views towards sexual activity in old age.

An overview of existing literature on sexuality and ageing has been summarised by White (1982). The conclusions are as follows:

1. Sexual attitudes and behaviour patterns in old age are a continuation of lifelong patterns.
2. Research on the cohorts studied to date suggests that males are more sexually active than females, with perhaps the exception of the very oldest age groups where males and females do not differ significantly.
3. When sexual interest or activity ceases or declines in the ageing female, it is largely due to declining interest or illness in the male partner. Females show no sexual decline that is not best explained by the male pattern and its effect on the availability of a willing partner.
4. Males evince a gradual decline in sexual activity with advancing age, though this may be a cohort difference as some males actually evince an increase in activity with advanced age. It remains for extensive longitudinal data to resolve that question.
5. Physiological changes in the sexual organs with advanced age, though presenting some difficulties to some individuals, are not enough to explain decreased or non-existent sexual activity in either sex. The effects of such changes are largely based upon the individual's attitudes toward these changes and appropriate medical-psychological intervention and support.
6. Aged males are more frequently studied than aged females. Such is particularly surprising in light of the increasingly greater proportion of females in increasingly older age groups (for example, in 1970 there were 72.1 males for every 100 females over the age of 65).
7. It is difficult to find research on ageing and sexuality that does not suffer from extreme sample bias and that includes attempts to validate self-report data. This is likely to be as much a function of poor research strategy as the difficulty in getting the aged to talk candidly about their sexuality.

Two key factors may determine sexual expression in
later life, cultural beliefs and psychological
changes.

Cultural Factors
Masters and Johnson (1981) see the elderly as
'victims of ageism', which discourages sexual
activity in old age. At the other end of the age
spectrum, in infancy, we see similar negative
attitudes, but in this case towards infantile
sexuality, as exemplified by parents' discouragement
of their children's interest in their genitalia. The
observation that young children do show sexual
responsiveness has been well documented by Freud in
his writings on infantile sexuality.

The significance of a culture's attitude
towards sex and the ageing process in determining
sexual expression is illustrated in Winn and Newton's
(1982) cross-cultural study of sexuality in ageing.
They observed variability in sexual behaviour
depending on the culture. In 70 per cent of the
societies studied, continued sexual activity was
noted. Expectations of continued activity for older
men were recorded, which was viewed as a reflection
of minimal, if any, loss of sexual potency until very
late in life. With respect to women, continued sexual
interest and activity were reported by 84 per cent.
In half of these cases this was related to a change
in the female's childbearing role. Different
patterns of sexual relationships were noted; a
tendency for older men to marry younger women and
conversely older women forming sexual relationships
with younger men were observed. Older women were
often used as sexual initiators and instructors for
younger men. This may also relate to availability of
older men as sexual partners. A parallel situation is
evident in western society, where the tendency for
women to outlive men results in a disproportionate
number of women without sexual partners.

The relationship between one's sexual identity
and fertility is significant. For many in our society
it is seen as a loss and a significant life crisis.
In Winn and Newton's study half of the reports of a
reduction in sexual activity correlated with the
decreased self-value as a wife as a result of no
longer being fertile. In other societies, however,
the menopause was not seen as a distressing event
linked to sexual or physical decline. In these
instances sexual activity tended to continue after
the menopause.

Biological Factors

Before discussing the nature of sexual dysfunction it is appropriate to consider normal sexual response. Sexual response can be the result of various factors, such as touching, kissing, caressing, coitus, masturbation, sexual fantasies and sensory stimulation, including sight and sound. The body's physiological responses in both men and women can be categorised in three main phases: arousal, orgasm and resolution. Arousal in the man is manifest by various changes, including erection of the penis, increased respiration and subjective feelings of excitement. In the female, increased vaginal lubrication and swelling of the outer lips of the vagina are apparent. The upper two-thirds of the vagina elongate and 'balloon', the uterus increases in size and rises in the pelvis and the clitoris erects and retracts. These changes in both sexes result from localised vasocongestion. With increased arousal the man ejaculates. The woman, if she reaches orgasm, experiences rhythmic contractions of the vaginal wall and uterine contractions may also occur. In the resolution phase the body gradually returns to the non-aroused state and a subjective feeling of calm takes place. In the male the refractory period follows orgasm and during this period he is unresponsive to further sexual stimulation for a period of time. This refractory period lengthens with increasing age.

Sexual difficulties can occur at various stages of the sexual response cycle, that is, there may be disturbance of libido, arousal or climax, or a combination. Sexual difficulties can be classified as shown in Table 10.1.

Loss of libido and dyspareunia (painful intercourse) can occur in both sexes. These sexual difficulties are classified as problems, when they occur persistently during sexual activity. The various sexual dysfunctions can also be further divided into primary and secondary types, i.e. present from the first attempt at intercourse, or having developed after a period of good sexual functioning. Furthermore, they may also be global or situational in that the difficulties may only occur in certain situations, e.g. a woman may have difficulty reaching orgasm with her partner but not during masturbation, and a man may suffer from erectile failure with one particular partner but not another.

Causes of Sexual Problems in the Elderly

As in the younger age group any of these sexual difficulties can occur in the older adult. Psychological factors such as performance anxiety and poor communication may exacerbate the difficulties. The physiological changes accompanying ageing and how the individual/couple interpret these will also be significant factors. Masters and Johnson (1981) discuss the major changes in sexual physiology and ageing in the over 55s (Table 10.2). In addition to these physiological changes which may accompany ageing, sexual activity in the elderly may be affected by certain factors which will have determined earlier sexuality. These include early coital experience, social and economic background, the availability of an interested partner, and presence or absence of sexual problems in younger adulthood.

Causes of Sexual Problems

Many of the reasons for sexual problems in young adults will also be pertinent to the elderly. Common causes for sexual difficulties have been summarised by Greenwood and Bancroft (1976). These include:

1. misunderstanding or lack of information about sex;
2. bad feelings about sex or its consequences;
3. problems in the relationship;
4. bad feelings about oneself;
5. unsuitable circumstances;
6. alcohol, drugs, medicaments;
7. being in generally poor condition.

Once these difficulties start they are usually maintained by performance anxiety and a tendency to be a 'spectator' of one's own sexual behaviour. Poor communication within the relationship will reinforce these difficulties.

Certain causal factors may be more prevalent in the older age range, some of which have been noted by Duddle (1982). Stiff, painful and paralysed limbs or having a catheter or stoma may cause mechanical problems. The effects of illness, such as anxiety in the hypertensive patient, post-coronary patient, or patient who has suffered a stroke, may lead to concern about becoming sexually aroused. Spouses may also be concerned about engaging in sexual activity for fear of precipitating symptoms in their partners. Various illnesses may also exert direct effects on sexual functioning. Impotence or retrograde ejaculation may occur after prostatectomy. In a minority of women who have had hysterectomies, uterine contractions during orgasm may cause problems. Oestrogen deficiency may result in vaginal dryness. The ageing process may have a negative effect on a person's perceived body image, e.g. thinning hair and loss of skin elasticity may lead to a loss of perceived attractiveness. Changes in body image after mastectomy, or having a catheter or stoma, may also adversely effect one's confidence. Loss of sensory capacities, e.g. in vision, hearing and touch, may reduce sensory input and thus reduce the ability to become sexually aroused. Depression, which is common in old age and may reflect the many losses which can occur, such as loss of status, loss of spouse or loss of friends, may be associated with loss of libido. It has been shown that the availability of a confidant seems to have a protective value against depression in old age.

Treatment of Sexual Problems

Provision of basic information on the physiological changes and their effects on sexual performance of both partners is the first thing to consider. This may be particularly salient as the elderly may not have benefited from the advantages of sex education, and changes in attitudes towards sex, which have been present in the formative years for those who are currently young adults. This basic education may prevent undue development of performance anxiety for the older man, who finds that it takes longer to develop an erection, for example. In the absence of this understanding, subsequent impotence may develop and his partner may misinterpret his lack of response as the result of her loss of sexual attractiveness, loss of interest in her by her partner, or the misbelief that he has another sexual partner. Understanding, good communication and practical help in the form of her providing tactile penile stimulation may help. Instruction on non-genital caressing and sufficient time spent on foreplay may help to reduce pressure to perform, as well as helping the couple to discover fully sexual aspects of love play. This is particularly important when full intercourse is difficult or painful. For the female sufficient foreplay may help to encourage the development of vaginal lubrication and other aspects of arousal and thus prevent painful intercourse and vaginismus in anticipation of pain. Where vaginismus is a problem, instruction in vaginal muscle training may help. At a practical level treatment with oestrogen may help vaginal dryness and painful uterine spasms. Lack of vaginal lubrication can also be helped by a lubricating jelly. Adequate counselling may also circumvent the development of the widow's syndrome and widower's syndrome. This has been observed in those of mid-to late 50s after a period of sexual abstinence, usually about one year. In the male this may manifest itself as an episode of impotence and in the female as a loss of vaginal response to sexual stimulation.

Furthermore, the elderly may benefit from discussing their problems with their peers to discover that their sexual needs are important and merit fulfilment. This may help them to ventilate their anxieties and needs, which they may otherwise feel they lack the social permission to express, owing to the taboos which were discussed at the beginning of this chapter.

As discussed already, psychogenic impotence may be alleviated by counselling and anxiety reduction, but when due to organic factors, practical advice may also be appropriate. Sexual aids, such as a Blakoe ring, or a stiffening sheath which fits over the penis, may facilitate penetration. Surgical implant of pieces of silicone into the penis have also been tried in order to produce a semi-permanent erection sufficient to allow penetration. What may be more acceptable, however, is counselling as to alternative ways of achieving sexual satisfaction apart from intercourse. Couples may be helped by advice on different positions for lovemaking and the use of manual and oral stimulation. Younger disabled couples who are unable to achieve full intercourse have benefited from an open discussion of such alternative forms of lovemaking. A vibrator may help a woman reach orgasm when her partner finds manual caressing difficult, and may also help males who have problems in achieving ejaculation. Whatever the advice offered, due awareness should be paid to the personal goals, needs and attitudes of the couple or individual, especially as the younger counsellor's sexual values may differ. Such alternatives and sexual aids, however, may be unacceptable to the older person with a more 'sheltered' sexual history.

Sexuality in the Institution

Within the institution lack of privacy or lack of availability of a sexual partner may create sexual difficulties. Wasow and Loeb (1975) reported that although the nursing staff they interviewed indicated that the elderly should be allowed to have freedom of sexual expression, they gave little support for this among the residents in their nursing home. Kaas (1978) indicated that both staff and residents in his study denied that masturbation is an acceptable expression of sexuality, but it may serve as a relief of sexual tension, a pleasurable experience, and a way of maintaining sexual function, particularly where a partner is unavailable. Staff may need to air their own fears about masturbation, however, as they may reject it for themselves as an acceptable form of sexual behaviour, as well as fearing the reaction of the institution. When planning institutions or in the day-to-day running of them, full cognisance should be paid to the individual's needs for privacy. Finally, as noted by Kaas (1978), as many of those resident in institutions do not see themselves as being sexually attractive, staff can play an important role in boosting morale by emphasising the importance of caring for one's physical appearance. Sexuality at any age has many facets. It does not only mean sexual intercourse, but the ability to perceive oneself as a sexual being, who is still attractive to the opposite sex. Achieving sexual satisfaction by means other than coitus, as well as essential pleasure derived from touch and the confirmation of one's sexual attractiveness through dressing attractively and social interaction, such as dancing, are also important. In the institution, staff should give due attention to these more general, non-genital aspects of sexual behaviour and encourage their expression in the residents with whom they work.

In conclusion, it is unfortunate that there still exists a paucity of literature on sexuality and ageing. Those of us who have not yet reached late adulthood to old age should be sensitive to the sexual needs of the elderly, whether they are resident in the community or in institutions, whether they have a sexual partner or not, and we should try to facilitate their sexual fulfilment through the provision of information and appropriate counselling. Above all, we should be aware of any negative values and misconceptions about sexuality and ageing, which we may hold. If we can avoid the trap

of perpetrating 'ageism', we may help the elderly to
lead a full life as sexual beings.

<u>TABLE 10.1</u>: Sexual Difficulties

		Definition
Male	erectile failure	inability to achieve an erection of sufficient strength and duration to allow penetration and coitus
	premature ejaculation	occurrence or orgasm and ejaculation before or immediately after entering the female during coitus
	ejaculatory failure	inability to experience orgasm or to ejaculate in the presence of normal erection and sexual desire
Female	vaginismus	involuntary spasm of the muscles surrounding the vaginal entrance, which occurs when attempt is made to introduce anything into the vagina, e.g. penis, finger, tampon, gynaecological instrument. Often associated with dyspareunia
	orgasmic dysfunction	persistent inability to experience orgasm
	general sexual dysfunction/ female unresponsiveness	inability to become aroused, enjoy lovemaking and reach orgasm

TABLE 10.2: Changes in Sexual Physiology and Ageing in the
Over 55s

Male   slower erectile response, requiring more tactile
            stimulation
          decrease in expulsive pressure of seminal fluid ejaculated
          reduction in volume of ejaculate
          reduction in subjective ejaculatory demand (urge
            to ejaculate)

Female   slowing in rate of production of lubricating fluid
          loss in elasticity of the walls of the vagina
          reduction in ease of involuntary lengthening of the
            vaginal barrel and increasing of transcervical diameter
            in response to sexual stimulation
          increased probability of creation of small fissures in
            timing of vaginal barrel in response to penile penetration
            or prolonged thrusting
          increase in length of time to reach orgasm
          decrease in duration and intensity of orgasm
          development of painful spasms of uterine musculature
            during orgasm
          vaginismus

Notes

1.   SPOD, The Diorama, 14 Petro Place, London NW1 4DT.

References

Bancroft, J. (in press) 'The Treatment of Sexual Problems' in R. Kendall and A. Zealley (eds.), Compendium of Psychological Studies, Church Livingstone, Edinburgh.
Cameron, P. and Biber, H. (1973) 'Sexual Thought Throughout the Lifespan', Gerontologist, 13, 144-7.
Catania, J.A. and White, C.B. (1982) 'Sexuality in an Aged Sample: Cognitive Determinants of Masturbation', Arch. Sex. Behav., 11, 237-45.
Christenson, C.V. and Gagnon, J.H. (1965) 'Sexual Behaviour in a Group of Older Women', J. Gerontol., 20, 351-6.
Comfort, A. (1980) 'Sexuality in Later Life', in Birren, J.E. and Sloane, R.L. Handbook of Mental Health and Aging, Prentice-Hall, Englewood Cliffs, N.J.
Duddle, C.M. (1982) 'Sexual Problems of the Elderly - Some Practical Solutions', Geriatric Medicine, February.
Greenwood, J. and Bancroft, J. (1976) 'Counselling for Sexual Problems', in J. Bancroft (1983) Human Sexuality and Its Problems, Churchill Livingstone, Edinburgh.
Kaas, M.J. (1978) 'Sexual Expression of the Elderly in Nursing Homes', The Gerontologist, 18(4).
Kaplan, H.S. (1974) The New Sex Therapy, Brunner/Mazel, New York.
Katchadourian, H. and Lunde, D. (1972) Fundamentals of Human Sexuality, Holt, Rinehart & Winston, Chicago.
Kinsey, A.C., Pomeroy, W.B. and Martin, C.R. (1948) Sexual Behaviour in the Human Male, W.B. Saunders, Philadelphia.
Kinsey, A.C., Pomeroy, W.B., Martin, C.E. and Gebhard, P.H. (1953) Sexual Behaviour in the Human Female, Saunders, C. Philadelphia.
Masters, W.H. and Johnson, V.E. (1966) Human Sexual Response, Little, Brown, Boston.
Masters, W.H. and Johnson, V.E. (1970) Human Sexual Inadequacy, Little, Brown, Boston.
Masters, W.H. and Johnson, V.E. (1981) 'Sex and the Ageing Process', J. Amer. Ger. Soc., 29, 9, 385-90.
Newman, G. and Nichols, C.R. (1960) 'Sexual Activities and Attitudes in Older Persons' J. Amer. Med. Assoc., 1973, 33-5.
Pfeiffer, E. (1975) 'Sexual Behaviour in Modern Perspectives' in Howells, J.G. (ed.), The Psychiatry of Old Age, Churchill Livingstone, Edinburgh/London.
Rubin, I. (1963) 'Sex over 65', in Geigel, L. (ed.), Advances in Sex Research, Harper, New York.
Thomas, E.L. (1982) 'Sexuality and Aging: Essential Vitamins or Popcorn?', The Gerontologist, 22, No. 3, 240-3.
Verwoerdt, A., Pfeiffer, E. and Wang, H. (1969) 'Sexual Behaviour in Senescence', Geriatrics, 24, 137-54.

Wasow, M. and Loeb, M. (1975) 'Sexuality in Nursing Homes', in I. Burnside <u>Sexuality and Aging</u>, Univ. Southern California Press, Los Angeles.

White, C.B. (1982) 'Sexual Interest, Attitudes, Knowledge and Sexual History in Relation to Sexual Behaviour in the Institutionalized Aged', <u>Arch. Sex. Behav.</u>, <u>11</u>, 11-21.

Winn, R.L. and Newton, N. (1982) 'Sexuality in Aging. A Study of 106 Cultures', <u>Arch. Sex. Behav.</u> <u>11</u>, 283-98.

Chapter Eleven

EFFECTIVE PSYCHOLOGICAL CARE FOR THE ELDERLY

David Jeffery and Peter Saxby

Concern has been expressed from many quarters that the increasing numbers of elderly people in the population are placing a growing burden upon the health and social services and, especially, that the strain upon the in-patient and residential aspects of care is becoming overwhelming. Various solutions have been proposed and an emphasis is being placed upon care in the community. Of particular concern is the rise in the numbers of the elderly who are, or will be, suffering from dementia. It has been estimated that one in five people over the age of 80 suffers from dementia and that the proportion of the over 80s in the population will continue to rise into the year 2000 (Health Advisory Service, 1983). This increase in the number of demented elderly has been dubbed the 'silent epidemic'. Psychologists who have become interested in the care of the elderly have responded to these concerns by applying their skills of assessment, therapy and evaluation to the problems of the elderly in general and dementia in particular (Woods and Britton, 1977; Mumford and Carpenter, 1979; Church, 1983).

This book bears witness to the dramatic progress that psychology has made in the relatively short period that psychologists have been interested in the care of the elderly. However, these developments pose a number of problems for those who wish to establish an effective psychological service. These problems arise because the majority of recent writings have been within a mainstream academic clinical psychology model which embodies a limited role for the psychologist providing a service. Recent attempts have been made to define an alternative role model, both with the elderly and in other specialist areas (Gottesman, 1977; Hawks, 1981). In this chapter we shall detail the problems and limitations of present developments and elaborate on an alternative model for the provision of an effective service.

Current Trends

We have seen major developments in the psychological care of the elderly in four broad areas: assessment, therapy for memory and orientation difficulties, adaptations for older people of behavioural and cognitive therapy, and behavioural programmes for problems of the institutionalised elderly. The assessment of the elderly has become far more sophisticated. Less than 20 years ago it was necessary to adapt assessment techniques developed for other populations (Oberleder, 1967), but now we have specialist assessment for the evaluation of behavioural and cognitive impairment, neuro-psychological examination, and criteria referenced tests of diagnosis (Kendrick et al., 1979; Albert, 1981). The development and evaluation of therapeutic approaches for elderly people with memory and orientation difficulties, and their attendant behavioural problems, has been a major growth area. Memory training, remotivation, reminiscence and reality orientation therapies have all received considerable attention and such developments have put psychology in the forefront of the fight against therapeutic nihilism (Holden and Woods, 1982; Zarit et al., 1982). Efforts have been made to adapt psychological therapies that were first developed for younger client groups, particularly behavioural and cognitive therapies with anxious, depressed and bereaved elderly people (Emery, 1981). Finally, we have seen progress in the application of behavioural principles to the problems of the institutionalised elderly such as incontinence, lack of engagement in social and recreation activities, reduced mobility and poor self-care (Hood, 1981; Sanavio, 1981).

We shall explore the problems that these developments pose for the establishment of an effective service for the elderly by asking three questions: Who are the clients? What is the underlying philosophy? Is the level of intervention appropriate?

Who are the Clients?
It is important to consider who may be benefiting from our actions toward the elderly. The majority of psychological help is directed towards solving

problems that elderly people pose <u>for others</u>. The 'identified patient' is very often resident in an institution, and the real clients are the carers who are reporting 'problems'. In community settings it may be just as likely that we shall be acting as agents for others - relatives, neighbours, GPs - rather than as agents for the elderly themselves. Clearly, there may be a conflict of interests between those concerned, and attempts should be made to resolve this, before embarking upon an intervention designed to make management easier.

Our aim is to meet the psychological needs of the elderly themselves, and it is, of course, not only the institutionalised and confused elderly who experience difficulties. It is well established that old age brings not only problems particular to that time, but that problems found in earlier stages of adult life become more severe.

The elderly are especially likely to face losses. Bereavement brings loss of economic and social status as well as loss of emotional attachment. Social isolation is often increased by the death or disability of friends, siblings and other cohort members, and the relocation of offspring and other family members. Physical disability and poor health lead to loss of mobility and independence, while the loss of social roles and status result from stereotyped expectations of the limited ability of older people and age-demanded retirement from employment. These losses mean that the elderly frequently face multiple difficulties of a chronic or acute nature at a time when their resources for dealing with such problems may be reduced (Goodstein, 1981).

We can, therefore, expect that psychological problems of adult life such as depression, anxiety and stress-related disorders, marital and sexual problems, will be at least as common in old adults as in younger people, and this is supported by various community surveys (Zarit, 1980). Murphy (1982, 1983), for example, has shown that depression in the elderly is closely related to the incidence of stressful life events and that there is a rather poor prognosis. At a one-year follow-up of 124 elderly depressed patients only one-third had a good outcome, poor outcome being due to continuing life stress. Wenz (1980) has demonstrated that the higher suicide rate amongst elderly people is a result of a maturation effect in that the increased stresses of old age - widowhood, isolation and loneliness - aggravate or accelerate any already established

257

tendency to self-destruction.

However, despite the prevalence of problems of adult life in the elderly, as a group they are much less likely to receive psychological help than younger adults, and more likely to be prescribed psychotropic medication (Kucharski et al., 1979; Ford and Sbordone, 1980). Resistance on the part of therapists to psychotherapeutic involvement with the elderly is well documented (Lewis and Johansen, 1982), and we may speculate that psychologists have become more involved with the dependent elderly and their carers because they pose less of a threat to self-esteem. Whatever the case, it will not be possible for psychologists to meet the needs of the elderly for psychotherapy and counselling through individual or group contact. As with other age groups, the population is too large (Hawks, 1981). Psychologists must find other ways of making available pscyhological help. Community-based approaches such as self-help groups and voluntary counselling may be most appropriate, coupled with strong preventive efforts.

What is the Underlying Philosophy?

The second question raised by the transfer of mainstream clinical psychological thinking concerns the appropriateness of this model. What theories currently guide the action of psychologists working with the elderly, and are these appropriate? Psychological intervention with older adults has been based predominantly upon a behavioural model, reflecting a focus upon problems occurring in institutional care. The issues that have largely occupied clinical psychologists have been concerns about helping older people learn or relearn the skills of daily living and orientation information, and about the effects of institutional environmental contingencies upon the behaviour of the dependent elderly, such as engagement in activities and incontinence.

Psychologists have attempted to tackle directly the problem of the confused elderly through the use of reality orientation (Holden and Woods, 1982) and memory training strategies (Zarit et al., 1982). These applications of behavioural ideas have been very influential in filling a therapeutic vacuum and thereby giving professional carers and support staff a sense of hope and purpose. However, despite the widespread and enthusiastic support for these approaches, the results of controlled trials are disappointing, in so far as they show only minimal and short-lasting improvement in cognitive functioning and very poor generalisation to behaviour (Powell-Proctor and Miller, 1982). Since these therapies are time-consuming, repetitive and demanding, the very limited transient changes seen in clients are only too likely to lead to exhaustion and disillusionment in therapists and carers carrying out the work. We need to take a fresh look at the purpose and underlying rationale of these well-intentioned procedures.

In much clinical work, and even in some research studies, the term 'confusion' is not clearly defined and there is often a failure to consider the multiple facets both of the causation of confusion and its presentations. A person who is labelled confused may show a combination of cognitive, emotional and behavioural disturbances, and these may be transient or long-lasting, situation-specific or generalised. Retraining programmes typically do not take into account specific difficulties, nor do they have clear goals for each individual.

The underlying model of confusion embodied in reality orientation and memory training approaches may well over-simplify matters, laying too much emphasis on biological processes, so that confusion is explained by neurological and physical changes in the individual which are considered to be the result of disease or advanced chronological age. However, in trying to influence confusion and other aspects of disordered functioning, it is necessary to take into account physical and socio-cultural aspects of the environment. In many ways, whilst it is more difficult for the individual psychologist to focus upon the nature of the environment-person interaction, we may be much more successful in achieving our goals by bringing about changes in these areas. For example, simple rearrangement of living areas and timetables can lead to increases in social behaviour in the institutionalised elderly. Inducing those involved with the elderly to view behaviour regarded as problematic differently may be an efficient solution to a crisis (Herr and Weakland, 1979).

We must also consider whether restoring cognitive functioning in older adults so that it resembles that of young adults is necessarily an appropriate goal. Life-span developmental psychologists are questioning the appropriateness of regarding some of the changes of ageing as undesirable or pathological (Labouvie-Vief, 1982). Tentative steps are being taken to expand Piagetian cognitive developmental psychology into later adulthood and so view those cognitive changes, often called rigidity, slowing and conservatism, as a cognitive developmental stage beyond the early adult formal operational stage, rather than a deterioration.

Is the Level of Intervention Appropriate?

The third question we are faced with in the search for effective psychological care for the elderly is that of the appropriate level of application of psychological intervention. The elderly account for some 15 per cent of the population and, whilst the proportion of elderly in the population is expected to stay much the same in the next 20 years, the proportion of those over 75 is expected to continue to increase (HMSO, 1983). Since it is these 'old old' people who suffer from the highest incidence of physical illness and psychological difficulty, and who have the fewest physical, social and economic resources, it is expected that the elderly will present an increasing need for social, medical and psychological care in the next two decades. A recent National Health Service report (Health Advisory Service, 1983) with the expressive title 'The Rising Tide', outlined the problem that all sectors of the community - health and social service, voluntary and private agencies, families and individuals - are facing in providing care for the elderly, and emphasised the importance of the coordinated planning and development of a comprehensive service. The range of service required covers everything from community education, advice on management, care at home, family support, response in crisis, assessment, treatment, rehabilitation and after-care to continuing care in hospital. Faced with this great and increasing need, the work of psychologists with individual elderly clients is no more than a drop in the ocean. Trying to meet the psychological needs of a sizeable proportion of the elderly by maintaining the role embodied in the techniques psychologists have been developing, is likely to lead to unappealing outcomes. The psychologist will either toil away with individual clients making no appreciable impact on the overall problem, or will eventually retreat exhausted from a series of 'hit-and-run' troubleshooting forays into care systems. In either case psychologists are only dabbling around the fringes of the wider context of provision of care for the elderly, and they risk generating the perception that psychology is peripheral to the care

for the elderly, and psychologists no more than
dabblers or players of intellectual games of no real
substance.

An Alternative

Current patterns and trends in the development of
psychological care for the elderly have resulted in
efforts being misdirected. Models for interventions
are inappropriate and inadequate and are peripheral
to the provision of care for the vast majority of the
elderly since they lead psychologists to work at the
wrong levels of care provision. This is the essence
of our criticism of recent developments. We believe
there is an alternative approach for practitioners
which addresses the problem of the effective
provision of care rather than the development of
schemes for the evaluation and remediation of unusual
problems or problems for carers at an individual or
small-group level. Having demonstrated that
therapeutic nihilism is unjustified, our first
priority must be to influence systems so that
effective psychological care may be provided for the
elderly as a population. What is required to fulfil
this role is a thorough grasp of relevant
psychological theory and a clearly-defined
systematic approach to the care of the elderly which
concerns itself with organisation, teams, social
systems, communities and the effective use of
resources.

Psychological Theory

Psychological theories and models which may be
relevant to the effective provision of psychological
care are those which are concerned with the mutual
interaction of the individual and the environment.
Such theories may be found within the areas of
social, developmental and environmental psychology.
Life-span developmental psychology, for example,
provides a heuristic framework for understanding the
changes of later life by placing these changes within
a dialectical framework of the mutual interaction of
individual and environment (Windley and Scheidt,
1980; Labouvie-Vief, 1982). This may be the most
useful tool for countering the still prevalent
biological decrement model of old age development.
Another paradigm from life-span developmental
psychology which may serve as a valuable corrective
to the propensity of younger people to view all the
elderly as the same, has resulted from the

progressive development of theories of activity preference and adaptation to the change in the elderly. Continuity theory (Covey, 1982; Ryff, 1982) has replaced earlier theories of activity or disengagement as the optimal outcome of successful ageing. The continuity of experience, skills and preferences throughout the life-span are emphasised, and the complex nature of the interrelationships between biological, psychological and social influences that lead to stability or change in each individual are elucidated. It follows from this approach that it is important to pay close attention to each person's life-course when considering their care, and it is not appropriate to prescribe from theory how they may best arrange their lives. It is not the case that all elderly people are best adjusted when disengaged from society or that they necessarily need to replace lost roles.

Environmental psychology places a clear emphasis upon the importance of the physical and social environment. Lindsley (1964) first suggested that 'prosthetic' environments should be developed in which compensation could be made for disabilities of the elderly. Aspects of the physical environment from the arrangement of chairs (e.g. Sommer and Ross, 1958) to the design of residential homes (e.g. Harris et al., 1977) have been considered. The social environment is equally important, especially for the very dependent elderly whose interaction with the physical environment is largely guided and mediated by others. The influence of the behaviour of care staff on the elderly is receiving detailed study (e.g. Barton et al., 1980) and theories from social psychology, such as learned helplessness and reactance theory, are being applied to the behaviour of hospital patients and staff (e.g. Raps, 1982; Solomon, 1982).

Other theories from social psychology may be helpful in understanding the behaviour of care staff and relatives. For example, much of what may be said about the needs and care of the elderly can be regarded as 'common sense'. Such propositions as 'the elderly are individuals and should be treated as such', and 'older people should be afforded dignity and respect', appear self-evident and yet it is manifestly clear that many genuinely caring people do not put these commonsense ideas into practice in their work with the elderly. The three factor theory of attitudes, which allows for a loose linkage between the emotional, cognitive and behavioural aspects of an attitude (Eiser, 1980), and attribution theory (Shaver, 1978) may help us to understand such phenomena and guide the development of approaches to assist care staff to act according to their beliefs. Applications of social systems theories can guide our behaviour in interactions with elderly people and their social networks and also in our understanding of the effects of institutions. Herr and Weakland (1979) and Keller and Hughston (1981) have developed approaches to therapy with elderly people and their families which are based upon a systematic understanding of the interactions which lead to or perpetuate problems. The 'natural' social supports of the elderly in the community, the interactions between the family and the institution caring for an elderly person and the influence of institutional structures on the care of the elderly have all been studied within this framework (e.g. Cohen and Sokolovsky, 1981; Kayser-Jones, 1982; Montgomery, 1982). We have outlined some of the psychological theories and models which have been demonstrated to be useful in guiding the applied clinical psychologist in the provision of effective psychological care. There are undoubtedly others. Our point is that mainstream clinical psychology needs to be supplemented with such theories to provide a sufficient resource.

The Provision of Care

How can these theories and ideas guide us in the provision of effective psychological care for the elderly? What we must do is disseminate skills and knowledge as widely as possible and so influence the behaviour and attitudes of the caregivers and service-providers. Because of their larger numbers, greater contact and potential to control environments, they are much more influential with individual elderly people in need of care than scarce and expensive psychologists can be(Hawks, 1981). We shall go on to discuss various ways in which psychologists can work, including: (i) facilitating service functioning; (ii) evaluation of care provision; (iii) applied research; (iv) education and training; and (v) influencing the community.

Facilitating Service Functioning
At the most direct level psychologists offer assessment and therapy for individuals. This direct contact role may well enhance psychologists' sensitivity and awareness of clients' and carers'

needs, and may improve credibility and acceptability to other staff. However, this should only be part of a psychologist's work, and in most settings is usually best offered as part of a multidisciplinary team service. Within a team the psychologist may be able to fulfil another function, that of consultant to the staff group itself. This may mean providing resources of a material or informational kind, such as devising assessment procedures, undertaking literature searches, or organising informal teaching sessions. Street (1981) considers ways of developing a further role for psychological therapists through the application of a systems approach to the work group. This may be a loosely organised team like a community psychogeriatric service, or a more formally constituted group such as the staff of a residential home. He reviews the literature on family therapy approaches as applied to other social groups and finds little of substance in applications outside the family, but goes on to describe his experiences as a clinical psychologist consultant to children's homes in which there is a 'family group' orientation. His understanding of staff interactions and the processes that enhance or impede task resolution, and his advice on the development of an effective consultancy role can be applied very helpfully to other settings. As a consultant, his aims are to clarify the team's choices through the definition of alternative strategies, and to facilitate decision-making and action based on expertise rather than formal or length-of-service authority. He lays considerable stress on the importance of avoiding direct case involvement when working as a consultant to the staff group. The emphasis should be on 'the total environment rather than the particular person presenting with difficulties'. Tizard et al. (1975) have pointed out how even opposing models of care generally have an underlying inappropriate assumption that staff organisation, buildings and the like have little bearing on the nature of care provided. Focusing on the staff as a 'family' begins to redress this imbalance by moving away from over-concentration on inner psychological events towards physical and social environments.

We need to attend to the social network in which clients are functioning, and to make practical use of information acquired. For example, the assessment of clients in the community should include an inventory of the supportive resources that are potentially available. Major objectives of intervention might then be to 'free up' and nurture these resources

(Cohen and Sokolovsky, 1981). Herr and Weakland (1979) have described an approach to intervening in social systems based upon the brief therapy model in family therapy (Watzlawick et al., 1974). The basis of this approach is that the problems an elderly person presents are often caused by ineffective or inappropriate attempts at solving difficulties by themselves, their family and supporters. The many resources available (such as friends and neighbours, relatives, home-help, meals-on-wheels, day care, social work and medical services) thus become blocked or work against each other. An example would be of a middle-aged married couple who insist that the wife's elderly mother has become incapable of looking after herself since her husband's death and should be taken into a residential home, whilst the elderly woman, her neighbour and home-help are equally adamant that all is fine. The difference of opinion has escalated into something approaching open conflict with everyone feeling anxious, exhausted and frustrated. A brief systems intervention would be for the therapist to convene a meeting of everyone concerned in order to hear from each person their opinion, identify the solutions that they have attempted, and then move to finding a way of helping the network solve its problem. The therapist takes care to validate the concerns and efforts of all members of the network and sometimes this is sufficient to reduce anxiety and 'free up' the system. On other occasions specific suggestions or actions may be needed. In our example it was revealed that the daughter was anxious for the safety of her mother and concerned that she was lonely. The frequent but uncoordinated visits of the daughter, neighbour and home-help made the elderly woman more disorganised than necessary, and a rescheduling of visits and an agreement about the rights and duties of each member of the network was sufficient to resolve the problem.

Evaluation of Care Provision

The way that provision of care by agencies is evaluated often seems to be over-simplistic and concerned with cost-effectiveness, for example, 'head counting' of rates of admission and discharge, or estimation of unit costs per client seen. There may be a reluctance to examine the quality of a service rather than its amount and range. This is a sensitive area and the naive researcher may be entering a minefield if others feel threatened. Resistance may come from individual practitioners who fear that their competence is being challenged, or at the organisational level of an agency providing services. Butcher and McPherson (1983) remind us that whilst some goals of organisations are formal and concerned with primary tasks that are ostensibly open to examination, for example, day hospitals treat patients, there are likely to be other less formal 'operative' goals which have limiting effects, for example, 'administrators will aim to prevent mistakes and inefficiency becoming public knowledge'.

Smith (1982) holds that new services often do not develop rationally and statements about outcomes are retrospectively related to goals with an 'ideological gloss rather than an accurate description'. He points out that objectives and goals are altering constantly and should themselves be topics for research investigation. Evaluation has to take account of the different interpretations of problems and solutions by various groups. Consider, for example, how the functions of a psychogeriatric day hospital might be seen in very different ways by doctors, social workers, relatives and the patients themselves. Tinker (1981) considers the needs of the elderly from several different perspectives. Evaluative studies often examine <u>normative</u> needs, those defined by experts, and do not consider <u>felt</u> or <u>expressed</u> needs of clients themselves.

We are arguing for a broad framework in evaluation that does not uncritically accept a particular set of objectives for care, definition of needs or level of outcome. Progress has been made by psychologists and others in developing assessment tools and undertaking evaluative exercises that look at the broad issue of the quality of care provided, and offer alternative recommendations. Evans <u>et al.</u>, (1981) have shown that a detailed and critical examination of care institutions is possible, given considerable time and goodwill. They examine many aspects of residential care of the elderly through observation and interviews with staff and residents. Another article by two of these researchers relates their findings to contemporary research and theory, as well as to prevailing social views about care for the aged (Hughes and Wilkins, 1980).

A number of studies in the United States have examined quality of care in institutional settings. Some have looked at objectively verifiable characteristics as indicators of quality of care. Moos and associates, for example, have developed an assessment procedure for characterising the social and physical environment of sheltered care settings

(Moos and Lemke, 1979; Moos *et al.*, 1979), called the Multiphasic Environmental Assessment Procedure (MEAP). It consists of five instruments that together assess physical and architectural resources, policy resources, resident and staff resources and the social climate. Whilst it can be used simply to describe care environments at any point in time, the MEAP is also suitable for evaluating environmental change and the impact of the environment on individuals, and has potential as a tool for giving feedback and facilitating change in the institution.

Other studies have used ratings of quality of care by the staff in the settings (for example, Winn and McCaffree, 1976). Harel (1981) contends that the most useful approach to quality of care is to use a conceptual scheme that incorporates characteristics of the environment with resident needs or preferences, and investigates their relationship to resident satisfaction and well-being (Kahana, 1974). Such studies suggest that more account should be taken of individual requirements which can be met only through flexibility in care provision.

Applied Research

Studies examining aspects of care of the elderly are extensively reviewed elsewhere, for example, Birren and Schaie (eds.) (1977), Patterson and Jackson (1980), Turner (1980), Holden and Woods (1982), Powell-Proctor and Miller (1982) and Denham (1983). The emphasis has been on individual and intra-personal factors, and it is to be hoped that research in the future will concentrate on examining the effects of both the physical and social environment. A paper by Snyder *et al.* (1978) gives an excellent sample of a study that combines direct observation with the creation of a taxonomy of behaviour and interpretation in terms of a psychosocial model, together with prescriptive advice for management. They investigated the problem of wandering by elderly residents in institutions, and hypothesised that this may reflect several needs, including security, stress reduction, exercise and industrious activity, as well as apparently non-goal-directed behaviour. Care strategies that were recommended included rehabilitation, adaptations of the physical environment, and provision of alternative activi-ties. Successful management was seen as being dependent upon full assessment of individuals and a coordinated plan of care by staff and families. Finally, the authors discussed philosophical issues of care and the ethical questions that may be raised.

One of the most interesting approaches to care to emerge in recent years is the 'action research' approach. This is well illustrated by Towell and Harries (1979), who are concerned primarily with developing innovations in care within formal health service settings, but the framework has wider application. Since change is required in the care staff, they themselves are given the main responsibility for devising and carrying out research projects which involve the investigation of care problems and the initiation of alternative approaches. Where managers are involved, their central task is to facilitate and regulate the system within whch the care workers operate. Savage et al. (1979) demonstrate the effectiveness of this approach with psychogeriatric care. A self-generated work study by psychiatric nurses showed that the majority of their time was spent on activities related to meeting physical needs of patients, or on administrative tasks. When staffing levels were high, more time was spent on these activities rather than being directed towards other goals, such as meeting the psychological and social needs of the patients. A gradual process of change was initiated and evaluated at each stage, which resulted in very satisfactory outcomes such as increased autonomy for patients, more time for staff to communicate with patients, improved staff morale and attitudes, increased contact with community agencies, and so on.

The role of 'experts' such as clinical psychologists in action research projects is to offer advice, join project committees concerned with forward planning and maintenance of change programmes, attempt to influence the climate of support and to help disseminate research findings. They must resist taking over projects, since a basic tenet of this approach is to give autonomy and control to the key workers. Such time-limited, systematic projects will strengthen the view that provision of care should be continually adapting to the needs of clients and carers and that evaluation is a responsibility of the whole care group, whether they be employed staff, volunteers or family.

Education and Training

Psychologists are often seen by other professionals as having an educative role. It is worth noting that psychologists may need to do more than provide teaching on request. In the absence of awareness by others of the importance of an educational input, psychologists may have to initiate programmes, and to take some responsibility for evaluating their impact.

People providing care for the elderly fall into one of three groups. First, staff employed by statutory or voluntary care agencies include a very wide range of occupations whose training may have been extensive and highly specialised, or limited and rudimentary. Second, voluntary workers, whilst often coming from diverse backgrounds, are not usually trained for their work with the elderly. And third, the informal carers, who provide the bulk of care for the elderly in the community - relatives, friends and neighbours - are not only untrained but may have no support of any kind. Without doubt, all three groups, employed, volunteer and informal carers, are ill-prepared, and education and training would reduce the stresses and difficulties inherent in their tasks.

The underlying philosophy of care should be one that emphasises meeting the individual needs of those cared for, whilst encouraging them to retain as much independence as possible. All educational programmes should begin by developing an understanding of what is normal for elderly people, and this may well mean challenging inappropriate beliefs, stereotyped attitudes and misinformation about the aged (Winn et al., 1978). Carers need to be stimulated to examine their attitudes towards ageing and to look critically at how they behave with those for whom they care. Solomon (1982) proposes that apathetic and overdependent behaviour in some elderly people can be explained by 'learned helplessness' (Seligman, 1975). Social factors leading to its development include negative stereotyping by carers, and their demand that those for whom they are caring fulfil a 'sick role'. In addition, the effects of an unequal interpersonal exchange may lead carers to believe that the benefits of providing other than basic care are outweighed by the costs to themselves, so that needs other than immediate physical ones are ignored or go unrecognised. Whilst such outcomes are most likely to occur in institutional settings where those cared for are the most dependent and least in control, the model that Solomon proposes also has applicability in community settings, since interactions between, say, husbands and wives may become just as distorted as those between nursing assistants and patients.

The focus of training should be on promoting coping behaviours and well-being in individuals, rather than over-concern with real or imagined pathology and deficiencies. At the same time, any educational programme should emphasise the central importance of the environment in determining behaviour. Winn <u>et al</u>. (1978), in discussing nursing homes, conclude that training should be directed as much towards what we should expect from our institutions as what we should expect from patients within such institutions. In general, we need to ensure that carers recognise that where an individual cannot function adequately in a particular setting, there may be a responsibility to adapt the environment, rather than trying to change the competence of the individual, or (perhaps worst of all) simply accepting the <u>status quo</u> (Windley and Scheidt, 1980).

Knowledge about ageing and appropriate attitudes towards the elderly are essential for all carers, but effective training and education must aim for more than this. What we require from our carers is that they <u>behave</u> so as to facilitate the maximum potential and well-being of those cared for. There is very often a considerable disparity between what we know and believe and how we act. In formal care settings a common difficulty is that staff have knowledge about helpful approaches to care, and are well motivated, but are prevented from acting effectively. In a recent study we surveyed six residential homes (Saxby and Jeffery, 1983) and showed that all grades of staff were well informed about appropriate ways to help confused residents and that attitudes towards the elderly were generally positive. All of the homes we visited had identified a need for more training. We concluded that what was required was a limited amount of specific skills training in certain areas, and that managers needed to facilitate appropriate staff behaviour, through good organisation, availability of resources, encouragement and monitoring of the staff's work. Evans <u>et al</u>. (1981) recommended that a prerequisite to the development of good practice was the training of supervisory staff in residential homes. By comparing a number of homes they showed that resident-oriented care (as contrasted with institution-oriented) was not wholly dependent upon the degree of disability amongst the residents. Two crucial factors that determined organisational practice were the 'commitment and style of leadership' of the officers-in-charge and the levels of communication and consensus between members of staff.

The tendency to offer training in formal settings to the more junior staff should, therefore, be resisted unless supported by the cooperation and participation of more senior supervisors and managers. One essential task of trainers is to identify the key personnel who can support and maintain (or sabotage) the changes that training aims to bring about. We must be careful not to misdirect our efforts in response to requests for training. What may be needed are changes in organisational policy and procedure. These may be beyond our direct influence - for example, increasing staffing levels - but we may be able to act in a counselling or facilitative way (Street, 1981) to bring about desirable outcomes, such as 'giving permission' to care assistants for increased social involvement with patients or residents.

There is some evidence, summarised by Solomon (1982), that with professional workers a combination of didactic presentation and opportunity for small group discussion is helpful in changing attitudes towards and increasing knowledge about the elderly. Campbell and Chenoweth (1981) report the successful use of a similar approach with volunteer and informal carers. Where skills training for care staff is also required, group approaches that include modelling and role-playing have been of benefit (Lopez and Silber, 1981).

There have been recent reports of the introduction of skills training for the families of dependent elderly people living in the community. Haley (1983) illustrates the value of instructing families in the use behavioural methods to modify specific problems of their elderly relatives. However, he includes some cautionary notes. Behavioural approaches should be used in conjunction with other supportive psycho-social services, and the limitations set by the levels of competence of both clients and carers must be recognised. The latter point is made by Zarit et al. (1982) who have completed several studies investigating memory retraining classes for confused clients and their relatives. Not only were the effects of training on the impaired individuals small in magnitude and short-lived, but the relatives reported feeling more depressed after the course. Zarit et al. (1982) subsequently organised groups which provided counselling and support for relatives and focused directly on relieving caregivers' feelings. They concluded that these, combined with practical problem-solving advice, were more helpful in reducing strain on the carers than were the memory classes.

The importance of providing psychological support for carers in the community will be discussed below. The implications for training are that aims and objectives must be not only of practical utility, but should not increase unreasonably the burden on carers. They should not be misdirected from other essential tasks, or misled into over-optimistic expectations about what is achievable. The use of prolonged rehabilitation and retraining programmes that will produce little worthwhile change in those cared for may prevent carers from making necessary preparations and adjustments for the future. We should be wary of proposals like that made by Stirling (1980), who suggested that a training package might be developed for relatives along the lines of the Portgage Guide, a home teaching system for parents of handicapped children.

Even when specific objectives can be shown to have been met at the end of training, it can be hard to evaluate whether these lead to worthwhile and lasting changes. For example, responses to questionnaires may show that attitudes have been modified, but will this lead to changes in care-givers' activities? We may demonstrate that people have improved their levels of skill in communicating or leading groups, but will they use and maintain these in practice? One way of trying to ensure that effective training has occurred is to set specific observable objectives directly related to the care situation. These may be targets for behavioural change in the client, or in the activities of the carer, or the environment for which carers have responsibility. One of the authors (P.J. Saxby) is developing a training programme for care staff in residential homes that aims to describe in general terms the psychological needs of the elderly and ways of meeting them, and then to encourage staff to attain specific objectives which are consistent with these needs. Some examples are given below.

Needs	Ways of meeting needs	Possible objectives
Control	Making decisions and influencing policies	1. Setting up a residents' committee
		2. Allowing a choice of room and/or room mate

Group identity	Encouraging inter-actions with others	1. Arranging a weekly game of Bingo 2. Developing a friendship between two residents
Privacy	Giving opportunity to get away from others	1. Providing a secluded space for entertaining visitors

Carers can best learn about a particular psychological model or therapy through relating it to their own experiences. For example, we have achieved some success with the introduction of behavioural methods in hospital and residential home settings by giving staff the opportunity to re-analyse problem situations in behavioural terms following a minimum of didactic teaching. Participants are encouraged to find their own solutions, often through the medium of small group discussion. What is important is not just the specific model and skills, but also the chance for staff to 'step back' from the usual pressure of their work settings and have the opportunity to review their roles and extend their perceptions of what they are capable of achieving.

Influencing the Community
Tinker (1981) describes the current provision of community care for the elderly in Great Britain, and reviews the development of formal and voluntary services, as well as the roles of family and friends. She brings out the importance of various aspects of the concept of community care, including social policy, psychology and sociology. The difficulty in defining community care is noted, there being two extremes of meaning: the provision of agency-managed domiciliary services (which are an alternative to institutional care) and, on the other hand, an 'ill-defined cosy picture of a group of local people "caring" for their neighbours'. It is clear that informal community care by relatives and friends is not always sufficient, and that adequate care for the elderly has to be provided through a combination of formal and informal, institutional and community resources. Close family relatives, especially daughters, play a vital role in supporting incapacitated old people in their own homes (Shanas, 1979; Stoller and Earl, 1983). Assessments should be made of carers' needs which may include psychological support (Bergmann, 1979; Wheatley, 1980), medical and nursing help, domiciliary services, suitable

housing, provision of extra finance (e.g. Attendance Allowance, payable in Great Britain), and so on. Whilst there are sound psychological and social reasons to encourage the maintenance of the elderly in the community for as long as possible, it should be remembered that even with outside support, the burden on those living with the handicapped elderly can be very considerable. One advantage of the family therapy approach described earlier (Herr and Weakland, 1979) is that the needs of all concerned can be identified more clearly.

Analysis of care needs is a complex task and not the province of one specialisation alone like clinical psychology or the closely related fields of community psychology and psychiatry. However, we can outline a number of useful roles for psychologists. At a broad level, we can develop theories and models for understanding why and how psychological care is provided. Caplan and Killilea (eds.) (1976) offer a good example in their systems theory analysis of self-help and mutual support groups. At a service level, psychologists may be involved with assessing and meeting needs in the community. The elderly have frequently to face major life changes for which brief counselling or continuing support may be very valuable in reducing stress and unhappiness. This may be best provided through voluntary and self-help organisations. The potentially damaging consequences of retirement may be ameliorated by educational preparation, for example, evening classes, or through membership of a mutual aid group such as the Pre-Retirement Association in the UK. Adjusting to the consequences of bereavement and working through grief may require professional support (Herriott and Kiyak, 1981), but sufficient help may be provided from voluntary and fraternal organisations such as widows' groups, church meetings, and so on. Psychologists should be aware of the local resources that are available, and, if necessary, offer their professional support to them.

The elderly themselves consider physical illness to be their most pressing problem (Tinker, 1981). We need to examine the contribution that psychology can offer to educational and clinical programmes designed to prevent illness, improve health and reduce excess deficits (Campbell and Chenoweth, 1981). Psychologists should also consider the importance of influencing the policies of local and national government care agencies. One way of doing this is through presentation of empirical data about the efficacy of particular kinds of care. Hard evidence may affect priority decisions about allocation of resources, and influence planning. However, examination of rational evidence about the effectiveness of care is not the only way in which decisions are made about its provision. This is also dependent on prevailing social views about how deserving of support particular groups are and, to some extent, on their perceived political strength. The elderly are often seen as having little contribution to make in society generally, and so are denied satisfactory 'exchange relationships' with others, being placed in the position of receivers rather than givers. The effect on individuals is to lead to a lack of activity and sense of purpose in life, which is likely to be accentuated by retirement and consequent economic restrictions. Psychologists should, therefore, be concerned to change social attitudes. One way that this may be brought about is by the facilitation of useful roles for the elderly, which may range from family support by the elderly (e.g. baby sitting), through visiting neighbours, to participating in voluntary care work, such as Hospital Car Services or peer group counselling, (Campbell and Chenoweth, 1981). Laufer and Laufer (1982), for example, report a programme in which foreign language students were taught conversation and literature by German-speaking residents of a nursing home. This study shows how imaginative thinking can create opportunities for the elderly to use the skills they retain, despite physical frailty and handicap.

In England, Age Concern have encouraged local 'Link Schemes' through which the elderly exchange help on a time rather than financial basis, so that a professional task may be offered in return for a manual one. Sager (1983) has recently outlined proposals for a mutual exchange system which would mobilise voluntary support. Time that is available from more able old people such as the newly-retired (and other groups such as the young unemployed) would be given to help the elderly in need. A 'token' system, underwritten by local or national government, would ensure that the carers could themselves subsequently receive help.

Psychologists could contribute to the initiation, maintenance and evaluation of projects designed to extend the contribution that the elderly make to society, and should be active in increasing public awareness of their value for all concerned.

Finally, perhaps, psychologists should be more aware of the potentially powerful effects of the media. We should try to present our theories and empirical findings in a popular format. There are several ways in which this can be done. Specific advice about care provision can be given in handbooks (see, for example, Hooker, 1976; Keddie, 1978) or through local radio phone-ins. Newspapers and magazines can be used to publicise projects, or as a forum for debating contentious issues. Two popular books about the elderly which received wide interest and acclaim were those of Blythe (1979) and Comfort (1977). Both authors stress the potential for achievement and fulfilment in old age, and the essential continuity and integrity of most individuals' personalities and competence throughout their lives. We should take steps to ensure that such popular material has a sound psychological basis.

Conclusions

We have discussed the role of psychologists in influencing the context of care for the elderly in directions indicated by a thorough knowledge of the psychology and sociology of ageing. In conclusion we shall draw together a number of principles for effective intervention.

It is essential to direct our attention towards wider areas than individual clinical consultancy. Such activity develops competence and enhances credibility, but the practitioner should be aiming to link into a network of professional relationships so that work can be initiated that will have wider and more lasting impact - the service facilitation and evaluation, training, project research and community care aspects described earlier.

Psychologists should be concerned not only with tactical aims of assessment and therapy, but much more with strategic objectives of influencing attitudes and policies in care agencies and more generally in society. There is a danger that this may be little more than a rather grandiose hope, and in practice we must begin with what is possible. Some guidelines to techniques of extending power and influence are available from organisational psychology. Useful summaries are those of Butcher and McPherson (1983) and Georgiades and Phillimore (1975). Perhaps a good starting-point for psychologists is to observe and describe both good and bad psychological care practices in local settings. This may give opportunities for collaboration with other care providers in introducing innovations and reducing inappropriate activities. Such an approach will quickly identify how resources are controlled and allocated within systems and should lead psychologists to consider ways of contributing to higher management and policy making. Much of the time this may be achieved through recognised channels, advisory or executive committees and the like. However, when the chips are down, psychologists may feel it necessary to move beyond their usual professional role and take political action, either individually or through a pressure-group.

Finally, psychologists should look closely at their own training and intra-professional relationships. If we are to function in the ways described above, then training should include not only adequate coverage of academic and practical aspects of ageing and caring for the elderly, but also place a much greater emphasis on the skills needed to be an effective trainer, manager, political operator, and so on. Consideration should be given to providing more multidisciplinary training which may promote understanding and respect and facilitate team-building. We need to break down barriers of professional compartmentalisation so that, for example, within the field of clinical psychology we should be encouraging the contributions of other specialists such as social, environmental and organisational psychologists, and trying to increase the probability that research into ageing undertaken by academic institutions will have practical applications.

References

Albert, M. (1981) 'Geriatric Neuropsychology', Journal of Consulting and Clinical Psychology, 49, 835-50.

Anderson, N.N. (1974) 'Approaches to Improving the Quality of Long-term Care for Older Persons', The Gerontologist, 14, 519-24.

Avorn, J. and Langer, E. (1982) 'Induced Disability in Nursing Home Patients - A Controlled Trial', Journal of the American Geriatric Society, 30, 397-401.

Barton, E., Battes, M. and Orzech, M. (1980) 'Etiology of Dependence in Older Nursing Home Residents During Morning Care: The Role of Staff Behaviour', Journal of Personality and Social Psychology, 38, 423-31.

Bergmann, K. (1979) 'How to Keep the Family Supportive', Geriatric Medicine, August, 53-7.

Barren, J.E. and Schaie, K.W. (eds.) (1977) Handbook of the Psychology of Ageing, Van Nostrand, New York.

Blythe, R. (1979) The View in Winter, Allen Lane, London.

Branch, L.G. and Jette, A.M. (1983) 'Elders' use of Informal Long-term Care Assistance', The Gerontologist, 23, 51-6.

Butcher, D. and McPherson, I. (1983) 'The Organisational Context of Clinical Practice', Bulletin of the British Psychological Society, 36, 45-8.

Campbell, R. and Chenoweth, B. (1981) 'Health Education as a Basis for Social Support', The Gerontologist, 21, 619-27.

Caplan, G. and Killilea, M. (eds.) (1976) Support Systems and Mutual Help Multidisciplinary Explorations, Gruen & Stratton, New York.

Church, M. (1983) 'Psychological Therapy with Elderly People', Bulletin of the British Psychological Society, 3b, 110-12.

Cohen, C. and Sokolovsky, J. (1981) 'Social Networks and the Elderly: Clinical Techniques', International Journal of Family Therapy, 3, 281-94.

Comfort, A. (1977) A Good Age, Mitchell Beazley, London.

Covey, H. (1982) 'A Reconceptualisation of Continuity Therapy: Some Preliminary Thoughts', The Gerontologist, 21, 628-33.

Denham, M.J. (ed.) (1983) Care of the Long-stay Elderly Patient, Croom Helm, London.

Eiser, J. (1980) Cognitive Social Psychology, McGraw-Hill, Maidenhead.

Emery, G. (1981) 'Cognitive Therapy with the Elderly', in G. Emery, S.D. Hollon, and R.C. Bedrosian (eds.) New Directions in Cognitive Therapy, Guildford Press, New York.

Evans, G., Hughes, B., Wilkin, D. and Jolly, D. (1981) The Management of Mental and Physical Impairment in Non-specialist Residential Homes for the Elderly, Research Report No. 4, Research Section, Psychogeriatric Unit, University Hospital of South Manchester.

Ford, C.V. and Sbordone, R.J. (1980) 'Attitudes of Psychiatrists Toward Elderly Patients', American Journal of Psychiatry, 137 (5), 571-5.

Georgiades, N.G. and Phillimore, L. (1975) 'The Myth of the Hero-innovator and Alternative Strategies for Organisational Change', in Kiernon, C.C. and Woodford, F.P. (eds.) Behaviour Modification
278

<u>with the Severely Retarded</u>, Associated Scientific Publishers, Amsterdam.

Goodstein, R. (1981) 'Inextricable Interaction: Social, Psychological and Biologic Stresses Facing the Elderly', <u>American Journal of Orthopsychiatry</u>, 51, 219-29.

Gottesman, L.E. (1977) 'Clinical Psychology and Ageing: A Role Model', in W.D. Gentry (ed.) <u>Geropsychology: a Model of Training and Clinical Service</u>, Ballinger, New York.

Haley, W.E. (1983) 'A Family-behavioural Approach to the Treatment of the Cognitively-impaired Elderly', <u>The Gerontologist</u>, 23, 18-20.

Harel, Z. (1981) 'Quality of Care, Congruence and Well-being among Institutionalised Aged', <u>The Gerontologist</u>, 21, 523-31.

Harris, H., Lipman, A. and Slater, R. (1977) 'Architectural Design: The Spatial Location and Interactions of Old People', <u>Journal of Gerontology</u>, 23, 390-400.

Hawks, D. (1981) 'The Dilemma of Clinical Practice - Surviving as a Clinical Psychologist', in McPherson, I. and Sutton, A. (eds.) <u>Reconstructing Psychological Practice</u>, Croom Helm, London.

Health Advisory Service (1983) <u>The Rising Tide: Developing Services for Mental Illness in Old Age</u>, NHS Health Advisory Service, Surrey.

Herr, J.J. and Weakland, J.H. (1979) <u>Counselling Elders and their Families</u>, Springer, New York.

Herriott, M. and Kiyak, H. (1981) 'Bereavement in Old Age: Implications for Research and Therapy', <u>J. Gerontological Social Work</u>, 3, 15-43.

Hildebrand, H.P. (1982) 'Psychotherapy with Older Patients', <u>British Journal Medical Psychology</u>, 55 (1), 19-28.

HMSO (1983) <u>Social Trends</u>, 13, Government Statistical Service, London.

Holden, U.P. and Woods, R.I. (1982) <u>Reality Orientation Psychological Approaches to the 'Confused' Elderly</u>, Churchill Livingstone, London.

Hood, J. (1981) 'Behaviour Modification for the Aged', <u>Psychology</u>, 18, 43-5.

Hooker, S. (1976) <u>Caring for Elderly People: Understanding and Practical Help</u>, Routledge & Kegan Paul, London.

Hughes, B. and Wilkin, D. (1980) <u>Residential Care of the Elderly: A Review of the Literature</u>, Research Report No. 21, Research Section, Psychogeriatric Unit, University Hospital of South Manchester.

Kahana, E. (1974) 'Matching Environments to the Needs of the Aged: A Conceptual Scheme', in J. Gubrium (ed.) <u>Late Life: Recent Developments in the Sociology of Ageing</u>, C.C. Thomas, Springfield.

Kayser-Jones, J. (1982) 'Institutional Structures - Catalysts of or Barriers to Quality Care for the Institutionalized Elderly?', <u>Social Science and Medicine</u>, 16, 935-45.

Keddie, K.M. (1978) <u>Action with the Elderly: A Handbook for Relatives and Friends</u>, Pergamon Press, Oxford.

Keller, J. and Hughston, G. (1981) <u>Counselling the Elderly: A Systems Approach</u>, Harper & Row, New York.

Kendrick, D., Gibson, A. and Moyes, I. (1979) 'The Revised Kendrick Battery: Clinical Studies', <u>British Journal of Social and Clinical</u>

Psychology, 18, 329-40.

Kucharski, L.T., White, R.M. and Schratz, M. (1979) 'Age Bias and Referral for Psychological Assistance and the Private Physician', Journal of Gerontology, 34, 423-8.

Labourie-Vief, A. (1982) 'Growth and Ageing in Life-span Perspective', Human Development, 25 (1), 65-78.

Laufer, E.A. and Laufer, W.S. (1982) 'From Geriatric Resident to Language Professor: A New Programme Using the Talents of the Elderly in a Skilled Nursing Facility', The Gerontologist, 22, 548-50.

Lewis, J. and Johansen, K. (1982) 'Resistances to Psychotherapy with the Elderly', American Journal of Psychotherapy, 36, 497-504.

Lindsley, O. (1964) 'Geriatric Behavioural Prosthetics', in R. Kastenbaum (ed.) New Thoughts on Old Age, Springer, New York.

Lopez, M.A. and Silber, S.L. (1981) 'Counselling the Elderly: A Training Programme for Professionals', Educational Gerontology, 7, 363-74.

Montgomery, R. (1982) 'The Impact of Institutional Care Policies on Family Integration', The Gerontologist, 22, 54-8.

Moos, R.H. and Lemke, S. (1979) Multiphasic Environmental Assessment Procedure: Preliminary Manual, Social Ecology Laboratory, VA Medical Center, Palo Alto, California, USA.

Moos, R.H., Gauvain, M., Lemke, S. and Mehren, B. (1979) 'Assessing the Social Envionments of Sheltered Care Settings', The Gerontologist, 19 (1), 73-82.

Mumford, S. and Carpenter, G. (1979) 'Psychological Services and the Elderly', Bulletin of the British Psychological Society, 32, 286-8.

Murphy, E. (1982) 'Social Origins of Depression in Old Age', British Journal of Psychiatry, 141, 135-42.

Murphy, E. (1983) 'The Prognosis of Depression in Old Age', British Journal of Psychiatry, 14, 111-19.

Oberleder, M. (1967) 'Adapting Current Psychological Techniques for Use in Testing the Ageing', The Gerontologist, 7, 188-91.

Parsons, H. (1981) 'Residential Design for the Ageing (for example the bedroom)', Human Factors, 23, 39-58.

Patterson, R.L. and Jackson, G.M. (1980) 'Behaviour Modification with the Elderly', in R.M. Weisler and P.M. Miller (eds.) Progress in Behaviour Modification, Vol. 9, Academic Press, New York.

Powell-Proctor, L. and Miller, E. (1982) 'Reality Orientation: A Critical Appraisal', Brit. J. Psychiat. 140, 451-63.

Raps, C. (1982) 'Patient Behaviour in Hospitals: Helplessness, Reactance or Both?', Journal of Personality and Social Psychology, 40, 1036-41.

Ryff, C. (1982) 'Successful Ageing: A Developmental Approach', The Gerontologist, 21, 209-14.

Sager, A. (1983) 'A Proposal for Promoting More Adequate Long-term Care for the Elderly', The Gerontologist, 23, 13-17.

Sanavio, E. (1961) 'Toilet Retraining Psychogeriatric Residents', Behaviour Modification, 5, 417-27.

Savage, B., Widdowson, T. and Wright, T. (1979) 'Improving the Care of the Elderly', in D. Towell and D. Harries, (eds.) Innovation in Patient Care, Croom Helm, London.

Saxby, P.J. and Jeffery, D. (1983) 'Working with Confused People in Residential Homes for the Elderly: A Survey of Staff Opinions', Social Work Today, (in press).

Seligman, M.E.P. (1975) Helplessness, W.H. Freeman, San Francisco.

Shanas, E. (1979) 'The Family as a Social Support System in Old Age', The Gerontologist, 19, 169-74.

Shaver, K. (1978) 'Attributional Error and Attitudes Towards Ageing', International Journal of Ageing and Human Development, 9, 101-13.

Smith, G. (1982) 'Some Problems in the Evaluation of a New Psychogeriatric Day Hospital', in R. Taylor and A. Gilmore (eds.) Current Trends in British Gerontology, Gower, Aldershot.

Synder, L., Ruppercht, P., Pyrek, J., Brekhus, S. and Moss, I. (1978) 'Wandering', The Gerontologist, 3, 272-80.

Solomon, K. (1982) 'Social Antecedents of Learned Helplessness in the Health Care Setting', The Gerontologist, 22, 282-7.

Sommer, R. and Ross, H. (1958) 'Social Interaction on a Geriatric Ward', International Journal of Social Psychiatry, 4, 128-33.

Stirling, E. (1980) 'Support of the Elderly in a General Practice', paper presented at the British Psychological Society Conference, London, December.

Stoller, E.P. and Earl, L.L. (1983) 'Help with Activities of Everyday Life: Sources of Support for the Non-institutionalised Elderly', The Gerontologist, 23, 64-70.

Street, E. (1981) 'The Family Therapist and Staff-group Consultancy', Journal of Family Therapy, 3, 187-99.

Tinker, A. (1981) The Elderly in Modern Society, Longman, London.

Tizard, J., Sinclair, J. and Clarke, R.V.G. (1975) Varieties of Residential Experience, Routledge & Kegan Paul, London.

Towell, D. and Harries, C. (eds.) (1979) Innovation in Patient Care, Croom Helm, London.

Turner, R.K. (1980) 'Behavioural Approaches to the Management of Incontinence in the Elderly' in D. Mandelstam (ed.) Incontinence and its Management, Croom Helm, London.

Watzlawick, P., Weakland, J. and Fisch, R. (1974), Change, Norton, New York.

Wenz, F. (1980) 'Ageing and Suicide: Maturation or Cohort Effect?', International Journal of Ageing and Human Development, 11, 297-303.

Wheatley, V. (1980) 'Relative Stress', Community Care, 28 August, 22-3.

Windley, P.G. and Scheidt (1980) 'Person-environment Dialectics: Implications for Competent Functioning in Old Age', in L.W. Poon (ed.) Ageing in the 1980's: Psychological Issues, American Psychological Association, Washington, DC.

Winn, F.J., Elias, J.W. and McComb, G.S. (1978) 'Staff Attitudes Towards the Aged in Nursing Homes: A Review and Suggestions for an Alternate Approach to Training', Educational Gerontology, 3, 231-40.

Winn, S. and McCaffree, K.M. (1976) 'Characteristics of Nursing

Homes Perceived to be Effective and Efficient', The Gerontologist, 16, 415-19.

Woods, R.T. and Britton, P.G. (1977) 'Psychological Approaches to the Treatment of the Elderly', Age and Ageing, 6, 104-12.

Yesavage, J. and Karoon, T. (1982) 'Psychotherapy with Elderly Patients', American J. Psychotherapy, 36 (1), 41-55.

Zarit, S. (1980) Ageing and Mental Disorders, The Free Press, New York.

Zarit, S.H., Zarit, J.M. and Reever, K.E. (1982) 'Memory Training for Severe Memory Loss: Effects on Senile Dementia Patients and their Families', The Gerontologist, 22 (4), 373-7.

INDEX

Abbreviated Mental Test
    (AMT) 14
Action Research Approach 268
Activities of Daily Living
    Assessment (ADL)
    22-39, 42, 46-8;
    reliability 23;
    validity 23, 48
admission 41
ageing:
    activity theory of 137;
    developmental theory of
    136,147
ageism 147, 238-9
aggression 75, 78, 80, 130
agitation 73, 75, 78, 169
agnosia 70, 77, 78, 80-1
alcohol 68
Alzheimer's Disease 4, 88-9,
    93, 98, 131, 166
Amnesic Syndrome 64-5
apathy 45, 50, 101, 115, 214
apraxia 30, 70, 75, 78, 81;
    constructional 78;
    dressing 78

Babcock Tests 3
Barthel Index 23-4, 25
Behaviour Analysis 50-1,
    61-83, 139-40
behaviour modification 61-2,
    128, 199, 225-8, 237,
    256, 259
behavioural observation 50
behavioural rating 10, 43-55;
    and senile plaque counts 2

content analysis 54;
    factor analysis 44, 53;
    limitations 49-52;
    surveys 42
Bender Gestalt Test 5
Benton Visual Retention
    Test 5
bereavement 91, 148, 230, 256
biofeedback 80
Block Tapping Test (Corsi) 5
brain damage:
    measures 3-6

caregiver see supporters
Clifton Assessment Procedures
    for the Elderly 15, 195
Clifton Assessment Schedule
    (CAS) 6, 10, 14
clinical assessment 2;
    reliability 2
cognitive assessment 1;
    diagnostic accuracy 13;
    mental state screening
    instruments 7-12, 14;
    physical disability 29;
    predictive accuracy 13;
    psychometric test
    battery 3, 6-7;
    validity 6
Cognitive Difficulties Questionnaire
    30
cognitive impairment 1-16
cognitive retraining 75
cognitive therapy 227-8
Coloured Progressive Matrices 6
communication 130;

SOCIAL SCIENCE LIBRARY

Manor Road Building
Manor Road
Oxford OX1 3UQ
Tel: (2)71093 (enquiries and renewals)
http://www.ssl.ox.ac.uk

This is a NORMAL LOAN item.

We will email you a reminder before this item is due.

Please see http://www.ssl.ox.ac.uk/lending.html
for details on:

- loan policies; these are also displayed on the notice boards and in our library guide.

- how to check when your books are due back.

- how to renew your books, including information on the maximum number of renewals. Items may be renewed if not reserved by another reader. Items must be renewed before the library closes on the due date.

- level of fines; fines are charged on overdue books.

Please note that this item may be recalled during Term.

**This book is to be returned on or before
the last date stamped below.**

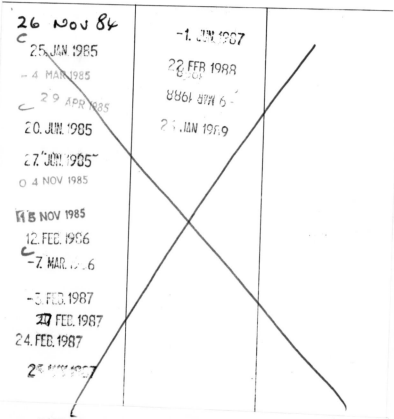

26 NOV 84

25 JAN 1985

- 4 MAR 1985

29 APR 1985

20. JUN. 1985

27. JUN. 1985

0 4 NOV 1985

15 NOV 1985

12. FEB. 1986

-7. MAR. 1986

-3. FEB. 1987

27 FEB. 1987

24. FEB. 1987

-1. JUN. 1987

28 FEB. 1988

-9 MAR 1988

2 JAN 1989

HANLEY, Ian and HODGE, John (eds) IL 94

Psychological Approaches to the
Care of the Elderly